Moveable Feasts

what to eat and how to cook it
in the great outdoors

About the Authors

In the working week Amy-Jane Beer is a biologist and a freelance writer and editor, with several books on natural history to her name. At other times she can usually be found in the kitchen or the great outdoors. She is a keen kayaker, hill walker and runner, and has recently taken up mountain biking, but keeps falling off.

Roy Halpin is a teacher of geography and geographical information systems (GIS). He has been involved in outdoor education for 20 years and is a qualified coach in several disciplines. He is never happier than when out exploring hills, rivers and dales with his friends – on foot, by kayak or on two knobbly tyres.

Roy and Amy were married in 2006 and spent their wedding night, where else but in their tent. For more information about Roy and Amy visit **www.wildstory.co.uk**.

Moveable Feasts

what to eat and how to cook it
in the great outdoors

by
Amy-Jane Beer and Roy Halpin

CICERONE

2 POLICE SQUARE, MILNTHORPE, CUMBRIA, LA7 7PY
www.cicerone.co.uk

First edition 2008

ISBN-13 978 185284 534 6

Photographs are reproduced with kind permission of Jon Allars (p12) Ian Jones (p31, p75, p76, p82), Orna O'Toole (p175 (top), p227), Paul Sterry (pp156–159), ASI (p18) and Rob Howard at Sleepmonsters (p165). All other photographs are by the authors.

A catalogue record for this book is available from the British Library.

Dedication

This book is dedicated to the memory of Martin Beer

Acknowledgements

We owe an enormous debt to the people who kindled and encouraged our love of all things outdoors. For Amy, these people were her parents, Martin and Sally Beer, and four wonderful Duke of Edinburgh's Award Scheme leaders – Graham Prickett, Liz Doherty, Roger Street and Nick Stephens. Roy would like to thank his Mum, Wendy Spicer, whose unstinting hard work gave him opportunities to learn and the freedom to explore. Thanks also to his Scout leaders, particularly Peter Honeycomb and Peter Brooks and to two inspirational teachers, John Rigglesworth and Clive Atkins.

Several people have helped in the writing of this book, as proofreaders and consultants, or providing ideas, inspiration and expertise. Our sincere thanks to: Ady Barker, UK Training Manager of the Duke of Edinburgh's Award Scheme, our nutrition and medical advisors Dr Moni Campbell and Dr Elinor Hayes, Dave Carter, Paul 'Driller' Jones, Nic Hayes, Ben Hayes, Sally Beer, Kate Stainsby, Daz Clarkson, Camilla and Richard Bennett and Michelle Wallace.

Thank you to our guest recipe contributors: Sue Robertson, Sugoto Roy, Matt Tidy, Charlotte Webb, Simon Willis and Simon Yates. We've benefitted from your experience, enjoyed your ideas and really appreciate you giving us permission to publish them here.

Many thanks to our gang of tasters, testers and photographic models: Jon and Sarah Allars, Sam and Geoff Ayers, Jo Bartliff, Paul Bartliff, Sally Beer, Christian and Hélène Bouet, Barbara Bray, Ruth Cantrell, Tim Clarke, Ed Cooper, Alice Courvoisier, Jack Duncanson, Zack Halpin, Ben, Nic, Izzy and Milly Hayes, Emily Hill, Rachel Hindle, Ian 'Indian' Jones, Jo Kilner, Paul Kilner, Rik Lawson, Niki and Bill Norman, Orna O'Toole, Karl Palin, Clare Parkin, Nic Pearce, Adam Pears, James Penso, Ted Piper, Ian Puckrin, Sally Radford, Steve Rough, Craig Scott, Roger 'Badger' Shicluna, Paul Simpson, Kate Stainsby, James 'Gladys' Stott, Nigel Summersgill, Pete Thistle, Lewis Tickle, Helen Wigmore, Vic Wright. You're all just smashing.

Special thanks to Gareth and Helen Davies at Lane Foot Farm in Thornthwaite, our favourite little campsite in the Lake District. We love the fact that you don't have a bar or a shop, and especially that you didn't bat an eyelid when we turned up late one night and asked if we could pitch our tent before you even had a campsite! We look forward to many more visits.

We're grateful to Ralph White and Andy Babbage at Rosker, Paul Cornthwaite at Lyon UK, Brenda Horton at Hydro-Photon Inc, Bengt Jonsson at Trangia, Mike 'the Stove' at Basecamp, Mike Parsons and Jen Longbottom at the Original Mountain Marathon and Ian Williams at Expedition Foods, all of whom were generous with information and kit.

It's important to say that relatively few of the ideas we've accumulated over the years have come out of thin air. In most cases, the advice and information we're passing on in this book has come from other people – friends, teachers, instructors, fellow campers, other authors and a few random strangers. At the back of the book is a list of reading material we've found useful. We've tried to give credit as best we can, but if you are one of the people who have helped us and you've not been mentioned by name, please accept our apologies. We hope you are happy for us to be passing on your ideas in the spirit you gave them to us. Thank you all.

CONTENTS

WHY THIS BOOK?

This book is aimed at people who, for whatever reason, spend lots of their leisure time in the outdoors – people like ourselves and our friends, who generally eat well, without being obsessive about it. We're a fairly fit bunch, but few would describe themselves as 'serious' athletes. We're just your average outdoorsy types who enjoy a good day out followed by a good feed. We enjoy a variety of sports, such as running, kayaking, walking, climbing, mountain biking and so on, but also spend a lot of time just hanging out, in campsites and in pubs. We don't imagine this is anything unusual. There are thousands of folk like us who enjoy a spectrum of outdoor activities. So the focus of this book is very broad.

A large part of the inspiration for this book came from Amy's sister, Nicola Hayes. It was Nic's idea to write a recipe book that would inspire campers, in particular youngsters, to try something other than noodles and other just-add-water menus. The scope of the book has grown since then to become our take on how to eat and live well, outside.

If you're a novice camper, we hope we can help you avoid some common mistakes and enjoy your first experiences enough to want to keep doing it! If you already have a bit of experience, you'll probably know that there is always something new to learn about the outdoors, and there should be plenty here for you too. You might be planning a trip, or thinking of entering a competitive event or outdoor challenge such as walking a long distance footpath, taking part in an adventure race or doing a Duke of Edinburgh's Award expedition. Or you might just fancy a family holiday without the restrictions of package deals or guest house rules. Whatever your reason for camping we hope you find it as fun and fulfilling as we do.

There's no need for anyone to read this book from cover to cover – although you're welcome to do so! The structure of the book should make it easy to dip in and out for whatever bits are useful to you. You'll find that what you need to know changes over time, as the way most people enjoy the outdoors evolves over the years, incorporating different sporting activities and styles of camping.

Amy and Roy

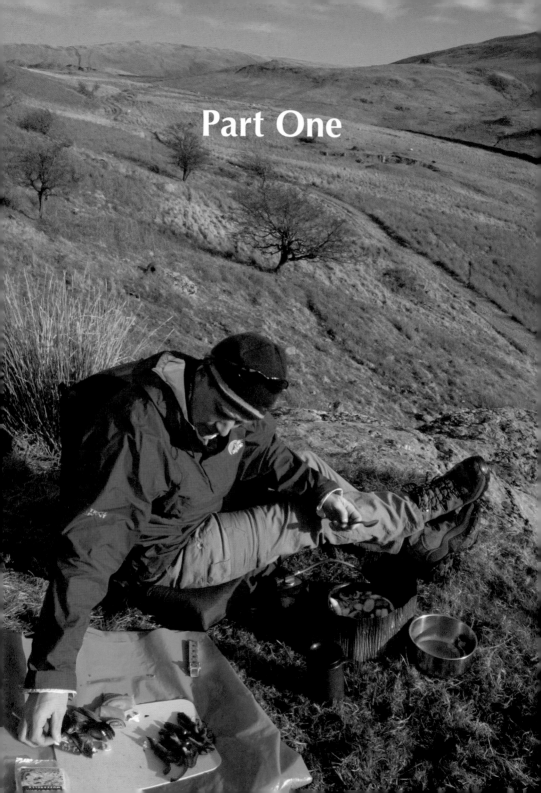

Part One

CHAPTER 1
Food and the Great Outdoors

Food and the outdoors are two of the great pleasures in life. Enjoyed together they can be the making of seriously special experiences. Picture your favourite wild landscape early in the evening. You're pleasantly weary from the day's exertions, whatever they may be. You've pitched your tent, a snug bed awaits, and you're with your favourite companions. Now imagine you can smell something delicious cooking... not just a rehydrated ready meal, but real food – tasty, hot, with fresh local ingredients, and nutritionally balanced to help your body recover overnight and fuel you well into tomorrow's adventures. You eat while watching the sun go down. Life really doesn't get much better.

Of course it's not always like this, but if you spend enough time in the outdoors with the right knowledge and a bit of application, there are certainly times like this ahead – lots of them.

CAMPING IN THE UK

The way many of us camp in the UK is rather different to overseas. We live on a relatively small island in which there are few large expanses of true wilderness. As the countryside is crisscrossed by roads, we are often able to pitch camp directly from the boot of the car if we want. This is very liberating for the camp chef – with few restrictions on weight and volume, your menu need be limited only by your imagination.

Unlike many other countries, the national parks of the UK are sprinkled with settlements, including fair-sized towns with supermarkets, cafés, shopping centres and markets, so even when not using a car, you rarely need to carry more than a couple of days worth of supplies. This has quite a significant effect on the kind of food taken when backpacking. In Asia or North America, trekkers or hikers might carry large quantities of staple ingredients, such as lentils, flour or oatmeal, with which to make a variety of simple meals. In the UK, we're more likely to carry small packets of specific ingredients bought with particular menus in mind, and re-stock regularly.

The relative accessibility of the British outdoors can also mean we're potential suckers for gadgets that might not work very well. This is because those who are used to making long, self-supporting trips tend to use simple, bombproof equipment that is easy to maintain and whose design has stood the test of time – they know their lives may depend on each piece of kit doing its job with complete reliability, and are thus unlikely to buy on a whim. The 'weekend warrior' of the UK, on the other hand, loves innovation, and outdoor shops and websites carry an overwhelming array of shiny camping gizmos that claim to be lighter, or perform their allotted task faster or more efficiently, than the others.

The appetite for such things is a powerful driving force in innovation, and has undoubtedly influenced the development of some really brilliant kit. However, it also means that there is a huge amount of over-engineered gimmickry out there, so beware the disease we call 'shinything-itis' – it tends to afflict visitors to places such as Ambleside, Keswick, Betws-y-Coed and Fort William, with the most severe outbreaks occurring on wet bank holiday weekends!

The booming outdoor kit business is fuelled by an equally healthy outdoor publishing industry, with dozens of magazines and websites offering advice on everything from where to take your next trip to choosing the right ultra-light, antibacterial, breathable, glow-in-the-dark, performance potholing underpants. In writing this book, we're very aware that we're making ourselves part of all that. All we can say is that while we hope our ideas are useful, they are only ideas, and there are lots of alternatives. Whether or not you buy something is entirely up to you, but we suggest that if you don't need it, don't buy it. Chapter 3, *Equipment*, should help you decide which kit you really need and what you can do without.

A breakfast rich in slow-release carbohydrates is a sensible way to start the day.

This book does not deal specifically with the kind of camping where you have an indoor kitchen at your disposal, such as staying in huts, cabins, caravans, camper vans, motor homes or RVs. That said, if you're trekking between huts, much of what goes for backpacking still applies, and while Chapter 7, *The Camp Kitchen*, won't really apply to the caravan and camper-van fraternity, some of the advice on packing and planning will still be useful.

If you've already done some camping, the chances are you've had plenty of evenings where the menu comprises an instant-soup starter followed by cheesy pasta from a packet, with a slab of cake or chocolate for dessert. Of course there's nothing wrong with this – it's a hot meal, it's easy, and it keeps everyone fuelled until morning. But you probably wouldn't want to eat it every night, and why should you stick to the same old thing when there's not much worth eating that can't be cooked outdoors? It seems a shame that for many people, the camp-food experience never seems to progress any further than a rather bland functionality.

Cooking in camp should be not just about fuelling your body, it should be about food! We can't see any point in having an immaculate camp, and the shiniest all-singing, all-dancing stove and equipment, if all you're going to cook is ration packs or dehydrated ready meals. We've eaten some fantastic meals prepared in camps around the UK and overseas, and even brought the ideas back to the home kitchen. Part of the magic often comes from using local foods – you'll find more on this in Chapter 8, *Wild, Local and Seasonal Food*.

Wonderful organisations such as the Duke of Edinburgh's Award Scheme, the Scout Association, Outward Bound, the Boys' and Girls' Brigades, not to mention countless switched-on schools and local and national outdoor activity centres, are responsible for introducing thousands of people to the joys of the outdoors. The main focus of the experiences offered by these groups varies – participants might be encouraged to challenge themselves physically, to learn new skills such as navigation, or just to take time to appreciate the natural world. This is all great, but there is often surprisingly little emphasis on food. This is odd, because in other contexts we spend a massive amount of time thinking about nutrition and cooking. Teaching kitchen skills in the outdoors is a brilliant way of imparting knowledge that can be useful in other situations.

On a long evening in camp, preparing a meal can be part of the entertainment. This is equally true whether you're camping solo or as part of a group. If you're alone, cooking is something to do to amuse yourself. In a group, it can be a great way of engaging everyone in an activity where each person has a vested interest in the outcome.

Nutrition plays an important part in the performance and enjoyment of any outdoor sport.

FOOD AND PERFORMANCE

We reckon that most people who love the outdoors have a great deal in common, even though their achievements and aspirations may differ. High on the list is the simple love of being self-sufficient in a wild landscape. And it doesn't matter if your preferred discipline is walking, running, climbing, paddling or biking – food is a part of the experience, and a significant factor in performance and enjoyment.

Many people are now beginning to think more carefully about what they eat, and if you've spent any time involved in energetic sports, such as running, mountain biking or hill walking, you'll probably already be aware of the impact food can have. At best, a bad meal can put the dampeners on a great day out; in a race or other challenge, even the perception that one has not eaten well might impact on performance. At worst, poor nutrition can leave you vulnerable to dangerous conditions such as exhaustion and

hypothermia. A good meal, on the other hand, can restore poor spirits and raise morale like almost nothing else. It's part physiology, part psychology, but mostly common sense.

◀ *Nutritional state is important in maintaining the positive attitude required for adventure sports.*

KEEPING CAMPERS HAPPY

Outdoor activity makes you hungry, and at the end of a long day few things boost morale more effectively than a good meal. Despite this, people often say they're simply too hungry to be bothered to cook something special when they're camping. That slightly frantic 'Just feed me now, I don't care what it is' feeling will be familiar to many readers, and while there's much to be said for the pleasure of tucking into a meal you're really ready for, trying to pitch camp, set up a cooking area and prepare a meal with low blood sugar isn't fun. This is often crunch time, when happy hikers or bikers become unhappy, fractious campers, and whinges, grumbles and petty irritations rise to the fore. The temptation to just lie on the grass or crawl into your sleeping bag is enormous, and the tougher the day has been, the harder it is to be motivated.

The trick to avoiding this kind of slump is to eat regularly during the day. Snacks on the move are at least as important as the evening meal. If, in the course of an otherwise enjoyable day, you're suddenly feeling a bit grouchy and out of sorts, the chances are that low blood sugar is a factor, so forget about not eating between meals and grab some nosh! If you keep up a steady intake of energy during the day, you should arrive at camp in reasonable spirits, and with enough energy left over to do what's needed. You'll find more detailed information on energy requirements and how to meet them in Chapter 2, *Essentials of Nutrition*.

A good strategy is to divide up the camp chores – talk about who will do what before you arrive, so that things start happening as soon as you get there. Pitching the tent is one job, fetching water and getting a brew on the go is another. If everyone has a task, things happen more quickly, and no one feels either put upon or left out – having no job can be just as frustrating as feeling you're expected to do everything.

If there are people in a group who aren't confident or experienced enough to just get on with something, they tend to end up hanging about, getting cold and getting in the way. If there are spare bodies in your team, make them part of things by giving them a job, such as unpacking sleeping bags so they loft up nicely before bedtime, fetching water, or making tea. Or make them feel better about doing nothing by reassuring them that all is in hand and suggesting they just relax for a while.

Within 10 minutes, everyone can be sitting in comfort with a well-earned cuppa and a snack – something that will keep the hunger pangs at bay for as long as it takes to prepare a proper meal. With everyone comfortable, the preparation of the evening meal can become a leisurely and enjoyable process – almost as good as eating it.

CHAPTER 2
Essentials of Nutrition –
What Your Body Does with Food

For the serious athlete, diet is as much a part of the everyday routine as training sessions. If you want an engine to run at peak performance, you must give it the best possible fuel, but of course there's more to it than that. Scientists recognise that diet not only affects our physical performance, but also influences us mentally and emotionally. By eating the right food at the right time, the human body can achieve phenomenal feats requiring not only strength and endurance, but also quick thinking, prolonged concentration and mental toughness. Most people who enjoy the outdoors don't consider themselves elite athletes, but even the most casual of outdoor pursuits enthusiasts will notice the difference made by good food to how they feel when out and about.

The adage that you are what you eat is true up to a point, but unless you're young enough to still be growing, most of the food you ingest on a daily basis is not converted to flesh and bone, but to raw energy. Eating a balanced diet is important, but your body is an adaptable machine, and shortfalls one day can usually be made up the next. Assuming you have no pre-existing deficiencies, your body won't run out of essential vitamins and minerals, proteins or amino acids on, say, a one- or two-day trek. You can, however, seriously deplete your carbohydrate reserves if you're working hard and not refuelling properly, so for most outdoor challenges, it's chiefly **energy-giving carbohydrates** we need to concentrate on.

Your body expends energy in many ways, even while you're resting. Your cells use energy day and night – to churn out the structural compounds from which you are built, antibodies to help you fight infection, signalling chemicals such as hormones and neurotransmitters, and catalysing proteins called enzymes, without which the zillions of chemical reactions needed to keep you alive simply won't happen. All this goes on before you do anything that feels remotely like physical exercise.

A lot of muscle action is largely unconscious too. You can generally rely on your heart to beat, your lungs to expand, empty and expand again, your eyelids to blink, your food to be pushed and squeezed through your gut and, happily, a series of sphincters to prevent continuous unregulated evacuation of your bladder and bowels. Skeletal musculature ensures that on a good day at least, we can rouse ourselves from a slump and go about our daily business without feeling any real strain. This subconscious activity is called the **basal** (or resting) **metabolism**, and depending on age, size and level of fitness, it will burn anything between **1000 and 2000 kilocalories a day**.

Energy expenditure is measured by the output of heat from the body. The unit of heat energy is the joule or calorie. A **calorie** is the amount of heat energy required to raise the temperature of 1g water from 15°C to 16°C. A **kilocalorie** is 1000 calories,

and it's kilocalories (kcals) we're interested in (when people talk about 'food calories' they actually mean kilocalories, hence the kcals referred to on food labels). In this book we sometimes refer to calories in general terms, but all specific references are in kilocalories.

The amount of energy bound up in food is pretty astounding. A piece of sliced white bread the size of a first-class stamp contains approximately 1kcal, enough to boil 1g icy water 10 times. Two full slices would boil a kettleful. Weight for weight, table sugar contains about four times the energy of dynamite – there's enough in a small chocolate bar to blast you over a kilometre into the air, if it can be harnessed efficiently enough. Fortunately the only way to do this is to eat the chocolate then walk up a mountain or climb lots of stairs. Your body is the most extraordinarily efficient combustion engine you can imagine.

The fuel that is actually 'burned' in your cells is a chemical called **adenosine triphosphate** (ATP). You don't eat ATP, at least not directly. ATP is made using **glucose**, which is obtained by breaking down food or stored reserves. Glucose can also be consumed directly, for the fastest possible conversion into raw energy. The process of ATP production also uses up a lot of oxygen, which is why you have to breathe faster and more deeply when you start working hard. When your cells burn ATP, the energy released can be used to generate movement (for example the transport of molecules through cell membranes or the ratcheting of the tiny fibres that makes muscles contract) or to build new compounds.

Chocolate – more energy than dynamite.

FOOD GROUPS

Carbohydrates

Carbohydrates (or carbs) contain the easily freed chemical energy on which your body runs routinely. If you don't eat carbs, your body has to obtain them from other sources, such as reserves of glycogen, fat or protein. In extreme cases it gets them by breaking down muscle tissue. All these are less efficient methods of getting fuel to your cells, and they make you feel lousy. Trendy low-carb diets mess with your internal chemistry. If you're going to do anything remotely active, you need carbohydrates in your diet.

Carbs come in different forms, which are broadly classified as either simple or complex. Simple carbs are sugars. Complex carbs are things like starch and glycogen – larger molecules that can be broken down into simple carbs.

Types of Carbohydrate

Glucose
Whatever type of carbohydrate you ingest, there is only one form that the body actually makes use of, and that is the simple sugar glucose. All other useable forms of carbohydrate are first converted into glucose before being used to fuel your essential body processes.

Other Simple Sugars
Like glucose, fructose (also known as fruit sugar) and galactose (brain sugar) are **monosaccharides** – single sugar molecules. Both are useful sources of energy, but because they have to be converted to glucose first, they don't 'burn' as fast. Table sugar (granulated or caster sugar) is sucrose – a double sugar (or **disaccharide**) made up of glucose and fructose. Likewise lactose (milk sugar) is a disaccharide comprising glucose and galactose.

Glycogen
Glycogen is a complex carbohydrate and it's good stuff. Your body makes lots of it and stores it in your muscles and liver, so when you start working hard, there's a ready source of fuel right there. Glycogen converts quickly into glucose and thence to ATP.

An average 70kg man has about 1700kcal of fuel stored as glycogen in his body before beginning exercise. Of this, about 82% is in his muscles, 15% is in his liver and 3% circulates in his blood. It can be mobilised quite easily once the muscles start working, and will allow him to perform steady exercise, such as running, biking or walking uphill, for about 90 minutes. To find out what happens when glycogen runs out, read *Hitting the Wall*, below.

Some sports drinks contain 'glucose polymers'. These are linked-up glucose molecules that pack a big punch in terms of energy, but are less sweet and thus easier to take when exercising.

Starch
Starch is a complex carbohydrate produced by plants for long-term storage. Green plants use energy from the sun to make simple sugars, which can be used right away, or converted into starch and stored in roots and tubers for the following season. Hence carrots, turnips and potatoes all contain starch, and your body can convert it to glucose.

Cellulose
Cellulose is a tough complex carbohydrate formed in plants to give rigidity to leaves and stems. We can't digest cellulose, which is one reason we don't eat grass, and why some of the plant matter we do consume passes right through us as 'roughage' or 'fibre'.

Hitting the Wall and 'Bonking'
Even a fit individual engaged in strenuous exercise will find themselves flagging after about 90 minutes, which is the time it takes for reserves of

glycogen stored in the muscles to begin running out. These reserves can't be replaced until the athlete either rests or takes on additional carbs, and if neither of these things happens, the muscles have to utilise another source of fuel such as muscle protein or reserves of fat.

In a normal individual protein and fat will be enough to keep things ticking over, but because they can't be mobilised as quickly as glycogen, performance will be reduced. If the athlete continues to push hard without taking on more carbs, he or she will soon reach the point where the demand for fuel simply cannot be met. At this point, the athlete 'hits the wall'. This phenomenon came to mainstream public attention with the rise of mass participation in endurance events such as the London Marathon in the early to mid 1980s. The distressing sight of jelly-legged athletes collapsing two or three hours into the event became familiar to participants and spectators alike. Twenty years on, such collapses are much less common. The other aches and pains are undimin-

Thanks to better understanding of the way the body uses fuel, tens of thousands of moderately fit individuals now manage to cross the magic 26.2 mile mark with what appears to be relative ease.

ished – legs feel as heavy as lead, backs ache, toes bruise, feet blister and burn, but with the aid of energy drinks and gels, sweets, bananas and plenty of water, it's possible to just keep going. This is something that someone who has truly hit the wall simply cannot do.

'Bonking' is a similar condition, familiar to many of those who have attempted endurance sports. It's a feeling of dizziness and overall weakness – perhaps blurred vision or faintness – that happens when **insufficient glucose is delivered to the brain**. Normally sure-footed, clear-thinking individuals can become fuddled and clumsy, and if this happens during a tricky descent on a mountain bike or while trying to navigate in adverse mountain weather, it can be dangerous. Fortunately it's easily avoided and simple to fix with proper fuelling. By continually topping up blood-sugar levels, you can stay sharp and avoid ever having to rely on your glycogen stores. As long as these reserves stay intact, you will never bonk or hit the wall. Of course, refuelling isn't a cure for exhaustion – even the finest athletes have their limits. Nor is it a substitute for training – but it helps.

Glycaemic Index

The glycaemic index (GI) is a system that ranks foods according to the effect they have on levels of glucose in the blood (blood sugar). It was originally developed to enable diabetics to control fluctuations in their blood-sugar levels, and adapted by sports scientists to help athletes maintain a steady delivery of fuel to hard-working muscles. Before long, GI was also picked up by the mainstream diet industry, but unlike many other diet trends, this one is based in solid science, and most nutritionists subscribe to it as an important part of healthy eating. Many food manufacturers now provide GI information on packaging.

A GI rating is not simply a reflection of how much glucose or sugar a food contains. Rather, it indicates the accessibility of the sugar, and this can be affected by all sorts of factors, including fat and fibre content and method of preparation. The higher the GI number, the faster and bigger the sugar hit. Pure glucose has a GI of 100.

Cold saps an enormous amount of energy, and all winter adventure sports should be regarded as endurance activities. Energy levels can be topped up with carb-rich snacks and drinks.

High GI foods include sports drinks, sweets such as Jelly Babies, and sweet biscuits, as well as some more surprising foods. For example, gram for gram, a baked potato will give you a more abrupt sugar rush than the same weight of honey. Rice cakes, crackers, most bread and couscous all score higher than table sugar. High GI foods are great if you want a quick boost that will take effect right away, but not so great if you want the surge to last. Glucose never stays in the bloodstream long because cells that need it extract it right away and burn it off immediately. Any excess is taken in by the liver and muscles (and to a lesser extent by some other organs) and converted to glycogen for storage. Either way, a high GI 'hit' is over almost as quickly as it began, often leaving you feeling worse than before, as the sudden rush will confuse your body into suspending the mobilisation of stored reserves of glycogen and fat. **You can use high GI foods to top up your blood sugar during exercise, and to restore energy reserves afterwards, but little and often is the key to avoiding big highs and huge crashes.**

Medium to high GI foods, with scores in the 60s and 70s, are things like oatmeal, Mars Bars, couscous and raisins. These start releasing sugars quickly, but the

It's important to eat soon after stopping prolonged exercise, so make your early evening meal something you can prepare quickly and easily.

'high' is longer than for the very high GI foods. This makes them great for refuelling on the go.

Medium to low GI foods include baked beans, white rice and pasta, and the super-low category includes things like pulses, low-fat yoghurt, skimmed milk and barley, as well as some surprisingly sugary things like apples, bananas, apricots and various sports bars. These foods won't give you much of a lift during heavy exercise, but eaten in advance – for example for breakfast – and grazed on during the day, they'll keep you supplied with a steady flow of energy.

Carb-loading

Carb-loading is a technique used by endurance athletes to **maximise the amount of stored glycogen** in their muscles before an event. This allows them to work hard for longer before hitting the wall. The improvement isn't spectacular – increasing glycogen levels in muscles by half can improve performance by 2–3% at best. This might not sound much, but over a long endurance event, a 2% margin might make an enormous difference.

The process of carb-loading is not as simple as cramming yourself with pasta the night before an event. When the process was originally developed, it was a week-long programme that began with a gruelling four-day 'depletion process'. During this phase, the athlete would train hard on a low-carb diet, to the point where their reserves of glycogen were reduced to a minimum. This, it was thought, would create the physiological conditions most conducive to rapid accumulation of glycogen stores. During phase two, the athlete would rest and consume a high-carb diet. These days, most athletes skip the depletion phase. They still train hard, but eat normally. Then, three or four days before the event they begin to 'taper'. They ease off training, doing less each day, and usually nothing on the last two days, while eating a high-carb, low-fat diet.

Good foods for carb-loading include syrupy tinned fruit, honey, jam and sugary drinks. High-volume complex carbs like pasta, bread and rice are not enough on their own – their high fibre content makes it difficult to eat them in sufficient quantity. The Australian Institute of Sport recommends their athletes consume 7–12g carbohydrate per kilogram of body weight per day when carb-loading. For a lean 65kg runner, this means the equivalent of half to three-quarters of a 1kg bag of sugar.

It should be obvious, but it needs saying all the same, that carb-loading is not an excuse for pigging out. If you do the loading and fail to do the exercise afterwards, guess what? You'll put on weight, and fast. And even if you do go out and burn off every last calorie, loading isn't a process that can be repeated week after week. Because effective loading requires two to four days rest, if you did it repeatedly you'd lose fitness through the frequent disruptions to your training. **It's only worth doing for an occasional big event for which you've been training consistently.**

The average fell runner burns between 600 and 1000 calories per hour.

Trained muscles carb-load much more effectively than untrained flab. Muscles that haven't worked properly in years lose their capacity to store glycogen. Weight for weight, the muscles of a well-trained athlete can store three times as much glycogen as those of a true couch potato. So if you're not already fit, carb-loading is a pretty meaningless exercise.

How much carbohydrate?
So carbohydrate is essential, but how much you actually need depends on what you intend doing. **For an average, moderately active person, carbs should be a little over half (approximately 55%) the daily energy intake.** On a day that

includes an hour or so of formal strenuous exercise (such as cycling, running, aerobics or footy practice), carbohydrate intake should be in the region of **5–6g per kilogram of body weight**. Taken as complex carbs, this is a lot of food – the 350g needed by a 70kg man like Roy equates to six-and-a-half cups of rice, or a dozen large bananas, or about 30 Weetabix, or 26 slices of white bread! But once you start replacing some of the bulky carbs with concentrated ones, like jam or sugary drinks, the volume required diminishes rapidly.

This quantity of carbs also needs to be balanced against other food types, because energy also comes from fats and proteins – too much extra there and the surplus won't be burned off. For very highly trained athletes, especially lean, muscular ones whose body weight (unlike ours!) doesn't include a few chubby bits, the requirement is higher – up to 7g per kilogram of body weight.

A carb-rich evening meal helps replenish glycogen reserves so you can go and do it all again next day.

Under certain conditions, carbohydrate requirements can increase dramatically. These include days of strenuous activity, such as hill walking with a pack, fell running, mountain biking, or any outdoor activity in

which the cold is a factor. On such days, carb intake should increase to between 7g and 10g per kilogram of body weight for a moderately fit individual. Of this, a proportion should be taken before, during and after the activity concerned. During an endurance activity lasting several hours – for example a long mountain bike ride or a marathon – you should aim to get down 60g carbs per hour or 1g a minute.

Just in case there's any doubt here, this information is not designed to help you lose weight – it's about taking in energy in a form appropriate to various levels of activity. It assumes you're at a healthy weight, which you intend to maintain. If you wish to lose weight, you should do it by eating sensibly and exercising, and if need be under consultation with your GP. This isn't a diet book, but see *Special Diets* below for more information.

CARBOHYDRATE CONTENT, CALORIFIC VALUE AND GI OF SOME COMMON FOODS (APPROXIMATE VALUES)

Some of these are surprising – check out the jacket potato for GI, and the carb/calorie hit from a smear of jam! Obviously these figures are generalised – there can be enormous variation between and even within brands, depending on the exact source and nature of ingredients. Check product packaging if you want precise information.

Food	Carbs (g)	Kcals	GI (average)
100g glucose	100	400	100
250g bowl of porridge (including milk)	c. 30	c. 165	58
30g bowl of cornflakes	c. 26	c. 170	81
Weetabix biscuit	19	65	70
Thick slice white bread	c. 20	c. 110	70
Thick slice wholegrain bread	c. 17.5	c. 100	52
Muesli bar (33g)	c. 19	c. 125	55–70
Mars Bar (62g)	44	284	65
Two-finger Twix (58g)	38	284	44
Tinned peaches in syrup (120g)	c. 18	c. 72	50–70
Mixed fruit salad (100g)	c. 9.5	c. 42	55
Large banana (120g peeled)	c. 24	c. 105	50–55
Dried apricots (60g)	c. 35	c. 152	31
Large jacket potato (250g)	c. 50	c. 200	75–95
Mashed potato (180g)	c. 20	c. 107	85
Small tin baked beans (200g)	c. 18	c. 120	56
Pasta serving (100g uncooked)	c. 73	c. 355	45
White rice serving (100g uncooked)	c. 77	c. 355	60 70
500ml full-fat milk	c. 24	c. 324	25 30
Serving strawberry jam (30g)	c. 20	c. 85	40–60
1 Jelly Baby	5	20	80
250ml fruit juice	c. 27	c.117	40–60
330ml sports drink (Original Lucozade)	21	92	95
Energy bar (65g SIS Go bar)	43	200	n/a*
Energy gel (41g Power Bar gel)	26	105	n/a*

* The context in which these bars are eaten can influence their GI value and so the manufacturers cannot give a figure.

Fats

Oh, the F word. As a society we seem to be obsessed with it, mainly because most of us carry at least a bit too much. A certain amount of fat is essential, however. Every one of the umpteen billion cells in your body is wrapped in a super-fine double membrane made of fat, or lipid as biologists prefer to call it. Your nerves and brain are sheathed in an essential insulating layer of fat and the steroid hormones are lipid-based too.

Seeds are rich in unsaturated fats including essential fatty acids.

Many women agonise over 'flabby' thighs or bum size, while men can be equally despondent over a bit of belly bulge. These are the places we tend to store spare fat, and a few reserves are normal and not unhealthy. Fat deposits (adipose tissue) cushion our delicate internal organs and help us conserve body heat. Women typically store more fat than men (on average about 25% of body weight compared to 15%). This isn't because women are less fit or healthy; it's because of the biologically inescapable truth that women, not men, have babies. With the help of pregnancy hormones, the extra reserves can be mobilised to nourish a developing foetus or to provide milk for a newborn, but it can be virtually impossible to shift them under any other circumstance. Even skinny lasses should have a few wobbly bits.

In addition to being an essential component of healthy body tissue, fat is a great source of energy – if you're really going to be pushing yourself over an extended period (days or weeks, not hours) some fatty food, like hard cheese or chocolate, will help you pack in the calories you need.

Weight for weight, fat contains twice as many calories as carbs, so under very extreme circumstances a **high-fat regime** can be the only way to incorporate sufficient energy into the diet. During their epic unsupported trek across Antarctica, Ranulph Fiennes and Mike Stroud each burned 8000–11,000kcal a day. Since they had to pull all their food on sledges, food weight was a major logistical factor, and they were forced to adopt a diet comprising almost 60% fat. Even so, they found it impossible to balance their energy expenditure, and both men lost over 20kg body weight in the endeavour. The South African explorer Mike Horn reputedly prepares for polar expeditions by drinking olive oil by the pint in order to prepare his body for the quantity of fat he needs to consume to meet the 12,000kcal a day fuel bill he says he faces on his treks.

This is all quite fascinating but for the average person such extreme diets are well beyond the realms of necessity. The point is that fat, even the saturated animal fat that dieticians warn you off, isn't all bad, and some is essential.

Types of Fats

Fats come in two forms: those that are solid at room temperature (mainly animal fats), and those that are liquid (mainly plant and fish oils). All types contain a blend of constituent molecules known as triglycerides. A triglyceride is made up of one molecule of glycerol and three fatty acids. The fatty acids come in three kinds – **saturated**, **monounsaturated** and **polyunsaturated**. In plant oils the fatty acids tend to be unsaturated (apart from coconut, which has one of the highest saturated fat contents of all plant foods), while animal fats contain a high proportion of saturated fats. (The 'saturated' bit refers to hydrogen atoms. In saturated fatty acids there are hydrogen atoms attached to all the available bonds in the molecular structure; unsaturated fats have one or more vacancies for hydrogen atoms.)

From a culinary point of view, solid animal fats are important because they taste great, imparting both flavour and texture. However, they are not an essential part of the diet and it's wise to limit your intake. Fish oils, on the other hand, have all sorts of health benefits. They include a high percentage of unsaturated fatty acids, including omega-3 (see below), and are a great source of certain fat-soluble vitamins, including A and D. Runners and other athletes often take fish oil supplements to improve joint condition.

You've probably heard diet experts and nutritionists talk about **trans fatty acids**, or trans fats. These are unsaturated fats that have been saturated artificially by a process of hydrogenation (the addition of hydrogen atoms). Usually this is done to convert fats that would normally be liquid at room temperature into a more solid state – for example in the production of margarine from vegetable oil. Trans fats are increasingly linked to elevated blood cholesterol levels, and thus to the incidence of cardiovascular disease. This is enough to persuade many people to revert to butter instead of margarine for everyday use, although saturated animal fats are no better for us than they ever were, and it's still important to moderate your intake.

Some fatty acids required by the body can't be manufactured there – the only way to get them is through the diet, hence they are known as **essential fatty acids** (EFAs). There are two groups of EFAs, namely omega-3 and omega-6. The reason we hear lots about omega-3s and less about omega-6s is that the latter are much easier to come by, and most of us get plenty in our routine consumption of plant products. The omega-3 group, of which there are several members, is less abundant. The most beneficial types are the long-chain varieties found in fish oils. Shorter-chain omega-3 fats are found in certain seeds, soya and milk, especially organic varieties. They can be converted to long chains by the body.

Vegetable oils are sometimes blended with solid animal fats to make spreads that are soft at fridge temperature.

Cholesterol is an essential component of all your cells – it's present in the membranes and involved in the manufacture of vital molecules, including steroid hormones, bile and vitamin D. Most of the cholesterol in your body is made there. It's also made in the bodies of other animals, so most people take in a fair amount with the animal fat in their food. The more cholesterol you consume, the less your body manufactures. Where there is excess to be mopped up, it is collected and bound up with molecules called lipoproteins, of which there are two main types: **high-density lipoproteins** (HDLs) and **low-density ones** (LDLs).

HDLs are sometimes called 'good cholesterol' because they carry excess cholesterol from the body tissue to the liver, where it is broken down or repackaged ready to be excreted, principally as bile. LDLs are 'bad cholesterol'. They carry cholesterol from the liver to other cells that need it, but at high levels, they accumulate in blood vessels, appearing to contribute to the hardening and blockages associated with heart disease, strokes and other circulatory problems.

This is a drastic oversimplification of a complex issue, but it gives you the general picture. Some people have high cholesterol because they eat too much of it, while others have a propensity to produce more LDLs than HDLs, and are thus naturally more at risk. In short, cholesterol isn't inherently bad, but your body produces plenty without you needing to add much to it, and some of us are better at getting rid of excess than others. Foods containing higher levels of cholesterol include anything with animal fat, but especially eggs, meat (particularly offal) and shellfish. It's common sense to enjoy these in moderation.

Proteins

Proteins are the building blocks of body tissues – the materials we need to repair cells and grow new ones. Dietary proteins help to mend tissues you might have damaged as a result of your exertions, so it's important to take some on board every day. Some proteins are structural, for example the keratin that makes up hair and nails, the collagen that gives your skin elasticity, and the actin and myosin that make up muscle fibres. Other proteins serve as hormones and neurotransmitters, contribute to antibody production, help transport other vital compounds around the body, and regulate and facilitate virtually every aspect of body chemistry.

Proteins are made up of smaller compounds called amino acids. There are 20 different amino acids associated with the human body, and they can be strung together in different combinations to make particular proteins – similar to the way letters of the alphabet make words. You might hear some of these molecules referred to as peptides – a peptide is essentially just a small protein, a short chain of amino acids.

The process of digestion breaks down proteins into **amino acids**, and your cells have the ability to re-string them to make whatever new proteins are needed at the time. When you eat you are recycling the amino acids from proteins assembled by another organism and using them to build new proteins of your own. Some amino acids can be manufactured in the body, while others can only be obtained in the diet. Good sources of protein include meat, fish, dairy products, eggs, nuts, seeds, pulses and wheat grains.

You need to eat protein every day, as any excess will be converted to carbohydrate or fat rather than stored.
Proteins can contribute indirectly to your energy requirement, but the process is less efficient than that which releases energy from carbs, so there's no point eating more protein in a day than you need.

Fifteen-minute soya curry, p219

Micronutrients

In addition to carbs, fats and protein, a balanced diet includes a wide range of other compounds – mainly **vitamins** and **minerals** – that have important functions. For example B vitamins help to regulate energy metabolism and play a key role in releasing energy from food. If your body's micronutrient stores are depleted, it could affect the way you process other constituents of your diet. For the most part, you won't need to worry about micronutrients on short camping trips. If you're getting a good variety of food types you're probably getting adequate micronutrients too, but if you're going to be relying on pack food for more than a couple of days it's more important to get the mix right.

Vitamins can be subdivided into those that are **fat soluble** (A,D,E and K) and those that are **water soluble** (B group and C). Fat-soluble vitamins are stored in the liver, so it's virtually impossible to become deficient in the short term, unless you are chronically malnourished or have a medical condition that prevents you from absorbing fat properly. Body reserves of most water-soluble vitamins, on the other hand, are relatively low, and so deficiencies can begin to manifest themselves after relatively short periods of deprivation.

Vitamin C is the most unstable of the vitamins, and is easily destroyed by the storage or cooking of food. Humans are unable to produce a key enzyme that allows most other animals to make vitamin C from glucose. We share this quirk with other primates, bats, guinea pigs and some birds, and like them we have to obtain vitamin C from our diet. The best source is fresh food, especially fruit. Dried fruits contain a bit less vitamin C than fresh, though they are still a good source of other vitamins. On a trip lasting four days or more, vitamin C supplements are an easy way to top up. Around 10mg a day is enough to prevent scurvy. Mega-dosing vitamin C won't do you any good, because any that isn't used will be excreted into the urine. It won't do you any harm either, for the same reason.

The minerals you need regularly include iron, iodine, zinc, sodium, potassium and calcium. A balanced diet that includes grains, fruit, vegetables and meat will usually give you plenty of each. Under normal circumstances **supplements are a less effective way of delivering necessary minerals to your cells than natural sources**, but you might consider taking them on a trip if you're going more than three or fours days without access to fresh ingredients.

Salt

Nutritionally it's not usually necessary to add salt to food, but many of us do so in order to enhance flavour. Too much sodium in the diet can lead to heart problems, while too little will lead to a deficiency known as **hyponatremia**, of which one symptom is painful and debilitating muscle cramps. Sodium is used by the body to help keep blood and other fluids at the proper dilution.

Sweat contains about 3g salt per litre, so if you're sweating copiously for long periods, through exercise, heat, or both, you should make sure you take in a little extra salt to make up for what you're losing. In the recovery period after exercise, you can't rehydrate fully until sodium losses have been replaced. Taking an isotonic sodium-containing drink before exercise

A BALANCED DIET

A balanced diet conforms to a sort of pyramid, with a broad base of starchy foods, a middle tier of fruit, vegetables and protein, and a narrow pinnacle of fats.

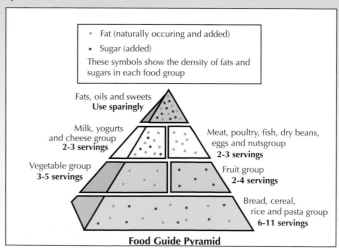

- Fat (naturally occuring and added)
- Sugar (added)

These symbols show the density of fats and sugars in each food group

Fats, oils and sweets
Use sparingly

Milk, yogurts and cheese group
2-3 servings

Meat, poultry, fish, dry beans, eggs and nutsgroup
2-3 servings

Vegetable group
3-5 servings

Fruit group
2-4 servings

Bread, cereal, rice and pasta group
6-11 servings

Food Guide Pyramid

can help to increase blood volume, which leads to improved endurance. We use a pinch of salt in our recipes for hydration drinks (see p281) and keep a few salt sachets in the first aid kit.

You can buy hydration spoons cheaply from TALC, an organisation dedicated to providing low-cost healthcare to the developing world (info@talcuk.org).

Striking a proper balance is tricky – too much sodium taken on its own can cause dehydration, so be careful. Use only **very small amounts** and always take it with plenty of water. You can make your own simple but effective recovery drink using sugar and water measured with a special hydration spoon.

DIGESTIVE PHYSIOLOGY

In order to appreciate why some foods make better fuel than others, it helps to have a basic grasp of what happens to each mouthful from the moment you start chewing it to the moment it exits the other end. So here's a quick biology lesson.

The digestive process begins in your mouth. Often the mere thought of food is enough to get your salivary glands going. Saliva contains a cocktail of **digestive enzymes** that attack chemical bonds within foodstuffs. Chewing pulps your food and mixes the saliva in, ensuring the complex carbs in your food have begun to disintegrate chemically before they reach your stomach. Chewing well will speed the whole process of digestion along, while bolting your food will actually slow things down – worth remembering if you want to refuel fast.

Once swallowed, a mouthful of food is pushed and squeezed down your oesophagus to your stomach. Small swallows slide down more easily and disintegrate more quickly than large ones. The stomach is a simple bag in which food and drink sloshes around in a marinade of **acidic juices** containing more digestive enzymes. Low-fat meals will empty from the stomach much faster than fatty ones (in about two hours), so it's wise to eat high-carb, low-fat meals along with plenty of fluid two to three hours before strenuous exercise.

Food pulp leaving the stomach is extremely acidic, so it's time to add some **strong alkali** to the mix. This comes in the form of bile, produced in the gall bladder, which nestles next to the liver and leaks its lurid green secretions into the top section of the small intestine, the duodenum. Bile neutralises the pulp and aids the breakdown of fats. Also released into the duodenum are secretions from the pancreas and intestine, which help the digestive process along. At this stage most of the useful components of your food start to become available for absorption into the bloodstream.

The cells lining the gut have ultra-fine membranes, which useful compounds such as water, sugars, amino acids and fatty acids can cross. Some pass through by virtue of extremely small size, others are internalised by the gut cell within tiny membrane bubbles. Your body recognises each different type of compound, sorting and dispatching the useful stuff as appropriate. Sugars,

---

ENERGY REQUIREMENTS

An adult brain burns 300–400kcal a day on its own. A heart uses another 150–200kcal, and a liver burns a whopping 500kcal. If you stay in bed all day, your body may burn in excess of 1000kcal just keeping systems ticking over. As soon as you get up and start moving around, this increases, and even if you have a sedentary lifestyle without any formal exercise, you'll be looking at an expenditure of over **1300kcal a day for an average woman**, and **2000kcal or more for a man**.

An hour's hill walking with light pack will burn off 400kcal or more – make the pack a heavy one and you're looking at 500–600kcal, similar to the expenditure for running or mountain biking. A full day of any of these activities and you'll easily double, or even treble your normal daily energy expenditure.

Often in the UK you'll be burning calories keeping warm too. Winter kayaking, mountaineering, or just being out and about in exposed locations, can be energetically far more expensive than you might imagine. If all of that ends with a cold night in camp, and you want to continue performing at the same level the next day, you'll need to give serious thought to how you're going to take in enough fuel to sustain yourself. For a mountain marathon, or similar endurance event, competitors will be using well in excess of **6000kcal a day**, though few will actually manage to consume this amount, especially given that all food has to be carried, and heavy packs are a competitive disadvantage.

CALORIE EXPENDITURE FOR ADVENTURE SPORTS

Activity	Kcal/hr
Strolling on the flat	175
Hiking, cross country	350
Hill walking, with light day pack	420
Hill walking, with heavy expedition pack	560
Jogging, 8km hour	490
Running, 10km hour	630
Running, 12km hour	875
Running, 15km hour	1000
Fell running	600–1000
Mountaineering	460+
Canoeing/kayaking, flat water (portaging)	210–280 (410)
Biking – leisure	350
Biking – mountain biking	525
Biking – racing	700+
Skiing/snowboarding	420
Beach games (Frisbee, hackey sac, volleyball, juggling)	200–250
Rock climbing (ascending/abseiling)	700/460
Orienteering	560
Horse riding (walk/trot and faster)	210 (100/380)

This is a rough guide based on a 70kg adult – heavier people burn more calories, lighter folk slightly fewer. (Estimates from www.calorielab.com.)

amino acids and fats are circulated in the bloodstream and taken in by any cell that needs them. The excess is either taken up for storage or excreted via the kidneys as waste.

Meanwhile the remaining pulp is passed further along the gut, making a couple of slow turns about your abdomen in the loops of the small then

Most people completing a long endurance event will find themselves needing to eat more than usual for several days afterwards as their body attempts to recoup its losses.

the large intestine. What remains after all the useful nutrients and water have been absorbed is finally voided via the rectum, usually about 10 to 14 hours after you first ate it.

◀ The annual Three Peaks Race follows a 37km route in the Yorkshire Dales. The gruelling course takes between 3 and 6 hours to complete – slower runners are disqualified at checkpoints en route.

Runner's Belly

For various reasons, the processes described above don't always go exactly to plan. If you eat something your body recognises as toxic, the absorptive function of the gut is switched off to prevent any more toxin getting into your bloodstream and doing serious damage. The food will be sent back up the way it came or rushed through the system in a hurry.

The body can have a similar reaction to stress – be it shock, fright or physical effort, all of which can lead to nausea or loose bowels. Most fell runners and bikers experience this as a dose of 'runner's belly' (vomiting or diarrhoea) from time to time, though some are more prone to it than others. Quite why the body chooses to reject food or water at just the moment it is most needed is a bit of a conundrum, but the reaction probably has its evolutionary roots in the 'fight or flight' response required by our ancestors. Non-essential body functions, digestion included, are put on hold so that oxygenated blood can be diverted to the running muscles. Oxygen-starved bowels can't operate normally, so they let everything go. It's not very nice, but neither is it something to worry about too much – just take it as a request from your body to ease off a bit.

SPECIAL DIETS

Camp meals can be modified to suit most specialist diets – vegetarians, vegans, diabetics, coeliacs and those with allergies to things like wheat and nuts can usually be accommodated.

Weight Loss

It's important to count calories when planning an expedition menu, but instead of looking to minimise your intake you should be seeking maximum benefit from your food. Being active all day and camping at night means that you will burn fuel at more than twice the normal rate.

We're not fans of diets in the sense of simply restricting calories as a standalone means of losing weight. Going hungry makes people moody and obsessive about food, and dieting often contributes to unhealthy fluctuations in body weight and self-esteem – none of these are qualities we'd seek in a camping buddy or expedition companion! Amy tried a weight-loss diet once. She lasted two fretful weeks obsessing about the next meal and lost one measly kilogram before deciding that it was all wrong. It was a particularly sedentary period in Amy's life, when she'd just gone self-employed and spent too many hours sitting in front of the computer. The problem wasn't really her diet, but a lack of activity. As soon as she upped her exercise level, her weight came down to what was about normal for her.

Most fit people see their weight go up and down from time to time, especially when injury, pressure of work or idleness disrupt their normal exercise pattern. Your body knows exactly what to do with the excess, storing it efficiently away as a reserve of fuel to be burned off when you need it.

It's been shown time and again that the only healthy way to lose weight and keep it off is consistent exercise, alongside a balanced diet with plenty of fruit and vegetables, whole grains and lots of water and a moderate intake of anything else you fancy – meat, chocolate, cheese, ice-cream… life is too short to deprive yourself of foods you love. Just try to ensure that burning calories in a way you enjoy is a consistent part of the mix.

Expeditions are categorically not the time for de-tox, low-carb, meal replacement drinks, or any other diet that doesn't involve a healthy, balanced intake of proper food. If you're on a points-style diet, where exercise is rewarded by extra food, award yourself the maximum possible points for every hour you are out and about (remember that by carrying a pack or being out in cold weather, you will burn energy much faster than walking around the shops or on a treadmill at the gym). You'll need to be flexible – the precise food recommended by your diet plan may not be practical to carry or prepare in camp, but with a little imagination you should be able to come up with a substitute.

Classic veggie dishes, including hotpots, curries, dhals and risottos, are delicious, and can be made with optional meaty additions to keep everyone happy. (See chickpea and green bean casserole on p228.)

Vegetarians and vegans

A certain fast-food restaurant chain specialising in spicy chicken dishes welcomes diners with the words 'We love vegetarians. All our chickens are vegetarian.' Our friend Driller often reminds us, 'If God wanted us to be vegetarian, he wouldn't have made animals taste like meat.' Yes, even in this age of diverse and accessible cuisines, being a veggie can be tough.

The vegetarian lifestyle has undoubtedly become easier over the years, though it can still be difficult to get a satisfying, balanced meal without cooking it yourself. That said, many of our friends are veggies, and we frequently cook and eat together in perfect harmony. Many of the recipes in this book are vegetarian, with meat as an optional extra that keeps everyone happy.

In the short term, finding a solution that sees everyone well fed and happy at the end of a meal is just a case of planning ahead. If you're embarking on a trip of long duration, however, a level of pragmatism is required. At the very least it can be difficult to keep pans and utensils used for meat wholly separate. Sooner or later a mix-up will occur, and you're unlikely to endear yourself to your companions if you make a big fuss about it.

Sweet potato chowder, p201

Our friend Kate has been veggie for many years, but on being selected to compete in the Global Challenge round-the-world yacht race, she chose not to insist on special meals. Given the limited galley and storage space, achieving a strict veggie diet from the rations provided for an otherwise meat-eating crew would have been next to impossible. Having made the decision for the sake of harmony, she found that in practice many meals were basically vegetarian anyway, and where meat was included it was often easy for her to pick out what she didn't want.

Staunch veggies might not find this acceptable, in which case they need to take an active role in helping to plan menus that take their preferences into account – it will help group relations enormously if you offer solutions rather than simply digging your heels in. Meat-eaters are often surprised to find that a tasty curry or spaghetti bolognese is meat free (see fifteen-minute soya curry, p219 or Will's famous veggie chilli, p260). Whoever is planning the camp menu needs to do so with the whole party in mind. Faced with a meaty meal or nothing, some veggies may be inclined to eat nothing at all, and in most outdoor contexts this is the worst possible scenario for the whole group. If you avoid certain meats for religious or other reasons, it's usually easier if the whole team abstains from them. Most meat-eaters won't mind going without some meats for a while if they can still eat other kinds.

Most of the above also applies for vegans, only more so. Whatever your reasons for avoiding all animal-derived foods, you may need to re-examine them in the context of expedition food. While it is perfectly possible to eat vegan food in camp (several of our recipes are potentially vegan), it is not always easy. Compromise, pragmatism and patience may be required on all sides.

Diabetes

Diabetes is a condition in which the body's ability to process glucose is impaired. Those suffering from **type I** diabetes cannot produce the hormone insulin, which normally helps cells absorb glucose from the blood. Those with **type II** diabetes produce some insulin, but either it's not enough, or their cells don't respond to it in the proper way. Both forms can be controlled, and neither need prevent people living a normal life and enjoying the outdoors like anyone else.

For sufferers of both type I and type II diabetes, managing their condition is all about trying to maintain healthy blood-glucose levels. They can achieve this by eating carefully, and in some cases by injecting insulin or taking pills. It can be difficult to fine-tune these practices, hence most diabetics occasionally suffer from the effects of too much glucose in the blood (**hyperglycaemia**) or too little (**hypoglycaemia**). There's more on how to deal with these situations in Chapter 10. No food need be off-limits to diabetics, but it's vital that they always have access to a sugary snack should they need it – this means extra emergency rations, clearly marked, just in case someone else gets the midnight munchies! If you are diabetic, make sure your friends understand the condition, and if you use insulin, ensure that you carry some spare in case the trip turns out to be longer than expected.

Coeliac Disease

Coeliac disease is an autoimmune disease triggered by **gluten**, a protein found in wheat, rye, barley and oats. Sufferers will experience a wide range of symptoms as their body produces antibodies that attack their own tissues. Intestinal symptoms such as bloating, diarrhoea and constipation are common, and long term they can lead to severe malnutrition effects – fatigue, hair loss, anaemia, infertility, repressed growth, etc. If your camp buddy is coeliac you need to help them avoid gluten. Use rice, corn and potatoes, instead of wheat or oat products such as regular flour, pasta, bread and porridge.

Allergies, Intolerances and Aversions

An **allergy** is a condition whereby exposure to a particular substance, the allergen (usually a particular protein) causes an immune response. The response can take various forms, such as a rash, itchiness, swellings, headaches and wheezing. In the most severe cases, exposure leads to **anaphylactic shock**, an extreme, whole-body reaction that can lead to unconsciousness and death within minutes. Even mild allergies have a tendency to worsen with repeated exposure, so take them seriously.

A food **intolerance** is any other adverse reaction not mediated by the immune system. Often the exact cause isn't known, but the symptoms can be unpleasant nonetheless – bloating, loose bowel movements or excessive flatulence are common reactions. A relatively large number of people suffer from gluten intolerance and prefer to avoid wheat products in their

Catering for individual dietary requirements and preferences needn't be a headache if everyone speaks up in time for their needs to be considered at the planning stage.

diet. This is not the same as coeliac disease, and the symptoms vary from quite severe bloating and fatigue to just feeling a bit icky. Many people attribute general fatigue or sluggishness to wheat without any real reason for doing so. If you suspect you have an adverse reaction to wheat or any other food, consult your GP and keep your mind open to other possibilities, including lack of fitness or a general imbalance in your diet.

A food **aversion** is really just a strong dislike, and as such it's a psychological issue rather than a physiological one. People with aversions can sometimes convince themselves that the food in question may harm them. It's tempting to dismiss aversions as faddiness, but for the sake of harmony there's little point trying to force someone to eat something they really hate. However, if your 'aversions' extend to a wide range of foods, sooner or later you have to ask yourself two things: are you actually getting everything you need from your restricted diet and, in a camp or expedition context, how does your affectation impact on others?

If you suffer from an allergy or serious intolerance, **brief your companions** on your condition, telling them how to recognize symptoms and what they should do if you have an attack. If you carry medicine, where is it and how should it be administered? This is especially important if your condition is liable to render you unconscious, or if you are planning to camp away from civilisation. Avoiding difficulties is just a case of planning and good communication. Even if you think your companions know about your allergy or aversion, it won't hurt to remind them – they'd probably prefer to be told twice than to deal with your empty-bellied recriminations later, or worse still with a severe reaction miles from medical assistance. If your condition makes conventional meals tricky, as with gluten intolerance, make sure everyone understands what it means, and explain what foods you can eat as well as those you can't – it will help a lot with menu planning and shopping.

CHAPTER 3
Equipment

Outdoor shops offer a dizzying array of camp cooking kit. Nearly all of it is potentially useful in certain circumstances, but that doesn't mean you need it all. With a bit of thought and a careful critique of the items you consider buying, you'll soon find that some items have numerous uses, while others have rather narrow applications.

The ideal piece of kit is the one you hardly notice. It's so well designed for the way you use it that it works first time, every time. You find that it always goes with you on trip after trip and you're reluctant to replace it, even when it's reached the end of its (very long) life. Frustratingly, it can be difficult to know whether a shiny gadget on the shelf is going to be one of these gems, or just an expensive disappointment. Standing in the shop, it's tricky to get a clear idea of how a piece of kit will perform in field conditions – will that little knob be difficult to twiddle with cold fingers, how strong are the eyelets on that tarp shelter, does that folding cup actually have enough volume to hold a satisfying brew?

The good news is that not all quality kit has to be pricey, nor does it have to come from an outdoor shop – many of our basics come from kitchen or hardware shops. These are much the best places to look for things like plates and mugs, wooden spoons, spatulas and tongs, and a huge array of tubs and containers. The thin chopping mats we use come from the budget cooking range at our local supermarket.

We also own a fair bit of specialist camp cooking kit, most of which gets used regularly. We try not to buy expensive items like stoves on a whim – usually we shell out only after having seen someone else using one to particularly good effect.

Here are some things to consider before you buy new equipment.

Functionality
How is this item of kit going to be used? Is it appropriate for all the circumstances in which you are going to camp? Will it work in all the seasons and climates you're likely to encounter? Do you need to buy accessories or consumables, like fuel or batteries, and if so, can you get them everywhere?

Transportability
How will you be carrying this equipment? How heavy is it? Do you have room for it? Does it come with a suitable case or other storage system? Can you take it on an aircraft?

Longevity
How long will the kit last, given your intended use? Would other products give better value?

Robustness

What will happen to this kit if you fail to maintain it, if you drop it or fall on your pack while carrying it, or if you forgetfully put it away damp for three months? Who else will be using it and how expertly will they be doing so?

Ease of Use

Do you know how to use the equipment? Some people are natural tinkers and enjoy working out the intricacies of complex gadgets, but if you're one of the other sort, who find reading manuals and servicing equipment too tedious for words, you might be better off with a more simple, intuitive device.

Value for Money

Even the best bits of kit only represent value for money if you're really going to use them. The best-value kit for you might be a cheap and cheerful device for once-a-year use. Or it might be a classic but more expensive design with simple but reliable technology. You may also be tempted to really splash out on the latest whistles-and-bells gizmo – these have usually been designed by experts and reviewed by various outdoor magazines, but a piece of kit that gathers dust on a shelf somewhere is clearly utterly useless. Gear manufacturers do very well out of impulse buys, so if you're serious about wanting new kit, think about the range of uses you might have for it, do some research and buy accordingly. If you're canny you might even be able to take advantage of someone else's impulse – check out trading websites such as eBay or the classified ads in outdoor magazines.

STOVES

Your stove could be a life-saving piece of equipment in an extreme situation. It is also the item of kit that is most likely to *cause* a life-threatening situation if handled or maintained incorrectly. The ever-increasing variety of camp stoves makes choosing one difficult. The fact is that for any given situation, there is a perfect stove for the job, but the vast majority of us will want to cook under a range of circumstances, and short of buying a different bit of kit for every trip, there always has to be some compromise.

Stoves range from extremely simple to the very complex; from very cheap to mind-bogglingly expensive and (crucially) from the very easy to operate and maintain in the field to those that need considerable know-how and regular maintenance using specialist tools. Many stoves are sold on the basis of **how fast they can boil water**. While raw power does have advantages in some situations, such as when providing drinks for large groups, or when having to melt snow, this might not be what you'll be using your stove for most of the time.

More important when it comes to cooking a variety of interesting meals is the **ability to vary the heat output** from roaring flame to gentle simmer.

Another major consideration is **weight**. Super-light stoves are popular with backpackers and adventure racers, but in most cases the fuel is heavier than the stove, so if your excursions tend to be for more than one night, you might save grams (and cash) by choosing a weightier but more fuel-efficient stove. Lightweight stoves are naturally less robust, too, so bear in mind potential replacement costs.

Your choice of purchase will be a trade-off between these factors and the availability of **fuel**. The most expensive option won't necessarily be the best for you. In some instances you might save money and maximise use-fulness by buying two basic models of different types instead of one top-of-the-range device. There's lots to consider, and if all the information in the following pages seems bewildering, the stove buying guide below and summary table at the end of this section may help.

STOVE BUYING GUIDE

This checklist of considerations will be useful when buying any stove.

✓ **Fuel type** – where are you likely to be using the stove and at what time of year? Understand the limitations of each fuel type, including potential hazards and availability before you choose your stove.

✓ **Burner size and structure** – smaller burner heads mean less even heating and definite hotspots, likely to cause burning.

✓ **Pans** – are they included with the stove?

✓ **Pan compatibility** – does the design of the stove limit the size or shape of pan you can use?

✓ **Pan supports** – slide a pan around on the stove to see how well it grips. Some pan supports are too slippery to be trusted.

✓ **Stability** – cylinder-mounted models are better on small, low cylinders. If you want to use larger cylinders, a spider stove is more appropriate.

✓ **Robustness** – lightweight 'racing' stoves are often a bit flimsy. Decide how often you will be using your stove.

✓ **Field maintainability** – pressure stoves will require more maintenance than other types. You may need to carry spare parts and tools. Some designs are not easily maintained in the field and issues will increase with the use of dirty fuels.

✓ **Packability** – are there sharp edges or fragile elements such as ceramic ignition units that mean you need some kind of protective packing?

✓ **Weight** – if you are going to carry your stove (and fuel), how much can you cope with?

✓ **Efficiency** – how much fuel will you need to carry? Can you improve efficiency by using a windshield or heat exchanger?

Cylinder-mounted stoves are usually lightweight and pack neatly, but they require careful handling due to their inherent instability.

Stove Designs

Cylinder-mounted Burners

These screw-on gas stoves (and some older liquid-fuel stoves) comprise a burner head and pan supports that can be mounted on top of the fuel source. In most cases the supports fold for ease of transport. These stoves are popular with backpackers and racers because they can be extremely light – a range of sub-100g models is available. This category of stove also includes enhanced heat exchange systems such as the Jetboil and the MSR Reactor (see Enhanced Heat Transfer Stove Systems, below)

The main drawback with cylinder-mounted stoves is their inherent **instability**. The act of screwing one to a cylinder creates a structure that is taller than it is wide, and once you put a pan on the burner the whole thing becomes top heavy. Some cook systems get around this problem by incorporating a broad base that attaches to the gas cylinder. Remember that gas and liquid-fuel stoves keep roaring away after they've been knocked over and the consequences can be appalling.

Cylinder-mounted stoves come into their own on short trips, used with small cylinders to cook simple meals.

Consider the **size** and **shape** of the **burner head**. The smallest, lightest cylinder-mounted stoves produce an intense hotspot, making it easy to burn dishes such as porridge or stews, and almost impossible to fry anything without excessive spitting and burning. However, they come into their own when you only need to boil water for hot drinks, to cook pasta, rice or vegetables, or to reconstitute dehydrated meals. A large burner will produce a more diffuse heat, and thus be easier and less limiting to cook on. Naturally, this is at the expense of weight and portability, but for anything other than racing, it's worth the trade-off, especially as slightly larger models are often also more robust and less expensive. Above a certain weight (about 200g), however, you lose the advantage of cylinder mounting altogether, and you're better of with a low-rise 'spider' style stove.

WARNING

Cylinder-mounted stoves can be difficult to use in windy conditions. The arrangement of having the fuel source underneath the pan means the stove cannot be enclosed by a windshield, due to the explosion risk as the cylinder heats up.

'Spiders' (Remote Cylinder Stoves)

Spider-type stoves sit on the ground next to the cylinder or pressurised fuel bottle, to which they are connected by a flexible tube. They are more stable and thus safer than cylinder-mounted burners. The tubing and the built-in base (usually comprising three or four folding legs) means that they tend to be heavier, but because they can be entirely enclosed by a windshield, efficiency is improved to such a degree that the extra weight may be cancelled out by savings on fuel. Of all the stoves we own, our basic gas spider (a very ancient Epigas model) is the most used. It's small, clean, and very easy to operate.

Rarely the most lightweight option, spider stoves are extremely stable.

Integral Windshield (Trangia)

There's really only one commonly available brand in this category. The Trangia design has been tweaked recently, but really has changed remarkably little in 50 years – for the good reason that there is little to improve. All the pans, a stable base, solid windshield and the burner are contained in one robust, essentially maintenance-free package.

Trangia stoves come in three main parts – the base and windshield, both made of aluminium, and a brass spirit burner comprising a fuel reservoir and 23 or 24 pinhole jets. The burner has a simmer ring to provide some heat control, and a screw cap that allows it to be sealed when not in use. The base and burner pack away inside the windshield, along with a couple of custom-fit pans, a pot grab and sometimes a kettle, topped off with a frying pan-cum-lid held in place with a strap.

In its original form the Trangia is a **spirit burner**. You fill the burner with methylated spirits (or any other high-alcohol-content spirit – see *Fuels*, below) and light it. There's no priming, no pumping or other messing around, so setting up takes seconds. You can also buy **gel fuels** in canisters that fit directly into the stove base. Meths and gels burn at a lower temperature than other fuels, so it sometimes seems that you are waiting for things to happen, but the difference is slight, and providing time is not of the absolute essence, it's no real disadvantage.

The Trangia is the stove of choice for many due to its robust design and relatively safe operation. If you want a bit more power, a recent design upgrade means modern Trangias can now take a **gas or petrol unit** in place of the

The stoves in the Trangia range are a miracle of simple functionality, with new lightweight and multi-fuel options adding significantly to their usefulness.

meths burner. The addition of a hole in the base allows the burner to be connected to the fuel canister that sits outside the base, so it doesn't get hot.

You can buy the classic Trangia in two sizes. The larger is adequate for two to four people, the smaller suitable for one or two. New models are made with anodized aluminium and are up to 20% lighter than the original versions. Lightweight backpackers and racers are provided for by the **mini Trangia**. The same robust burner unit is housed in a cut-down pot stand. Also supplied are a small circular pan, pot grab, and a non-stick frying pan that doubles as a lid. As with all Trangia sets, all this nests together in one neat package.

The weight and bulk of the original Trangia mean it isn't first choice for lightweight backpacking or racing. A disadvantage is the messy spill-ability of the fuel – both an inconvenience and a potential hazard. This can be at least partially overcome by using the proprietary fuel bottle, which has an anti-spill safety valve.

Because Trangia windshields are of a fixed size, the stoves work best with the proprietary pans. Other pans can be used, but they may not fit snugly onto the pan supports. This said, Trangia's own range is pretty comprehensive, and we use them with our other stoves too.

ULTRA-LIGHT SPIRIT BURNER

If you are really concerned about pack weight, it's perfectly possible to improvise a lightweight spirit stove using three or four tent pegs and the burner from a Trangia, or lighter still, a home-made burner made from two beer cans and some tinfoil. These super-light alcohol stoves are a bit of an obsession with some – you will find several websites devoted to the subject. With practice they are relatively easy to make, and surprisingly robust in use, though you need to pack them carefully to ensure they don't get crushed in transit.

Solid Fuel Stoves
Another very simple breed of stove, the British Army '**Hexi stove**' and the **Esbit solid fuel cooker**, is popular with military cadets and some lightweight backpackers. They comprise a small metal frame that folds out to

Standard military issue for decades, the hexamine stove, or 'Tommy cooker', is simple and lightweight, but comes with a health warning... don't breathe the fumes.

MOVEABLE FEASTS

hold a solid fuel tablet and support a pan. They work effectively for boiling water and for very simple menus, but lack any means of heat control, other than adding more fuel to increase the heat or letting it burn down for a cooler flame. Hexamine burners are still standard military issue alongside 'wet' (pre-cooked) ration packs in many countries, including the UK. See *Fuels*, below, for more information on solid fuel.

Integral Cylinder Hobs

These stoves are popular because of their **low price** and **ease of use**. For general **family or group camping**, as a stove to leave in the back of a vehicle or keep handy for a power cut, they are marvellous. The flat-bed design means they can't be knocked over, but the drawbacks are size and fuel efficiency. They're certainly not meant for backpacking or putting in your sea kayak, and the cylinders don't last long – you'll get through at least a couple in a weekend.

The next best thing to your kitchen hob, flat-bed stoves are ideal for car camping. The specialist gas cartridges are widely available in the UK.

Multiple-burner Stoves

For car camping and base camps the simplest solution is often a **large, stable, flat-bed stove** with a multiple-burner hob – two burners are adequate for most purposes, unless you're catering for a very large group. Most of these stoves run off large refillable gas cylinders, which are expensive to purchase, but cheap to refill. Because of their bulk and weight, they are often most appropriate in **static camps** for team cooking. After the initial purchase expense they are very cost-effective – and environmentally friendly, as the cylinders are **reusable**.

The choice of many mountaineers and expeditions, pressure stoves require expert handling and careful maintenance.

You can also buy group stoves that comprise a folding frame bearing several burners, each of which runs off a separate small cylinder. We haven't tried one, but their chief selling point is presumably their lightness. They look rather flimsy, however, and would be expensive to run, because you lose the economic benefit of buying gas in large cylinders. We're not quite sure how one of these could be better than two or three single-burner stoves.

Pressure Stoves

Pressure stoves burn a variety of petroleum products. They tend to be the most **expensive** stoves to purchase, and require most **maintenance**, but their saving grace is their **high heat output** and ability to burn **different fuels**. They work efficiently in just about any situation, and unlike gas stoves are **unaffected by cold** (see the box on Sluggish Cylinders, p51).

The higher cost of pressure stoves is due to the technology required to *safely* burn incredibly volatile fuels such as petrol. Poor-quality components or maintenance could be lethal. The multi-fuel versions of these stoves, such as the MSR Whisperlite International and the Primus Omnifuel, are popular with global travellers because of their ability to burn most things derived from petroleum. However, the maintenance, smoke, smell and general grime will increase dramatically with lower grades of fuel.

Enhanced Heat Transfer Stove Systems

A number of manufacturers are now producing cook systems comprising powerful gas stoves teamed with special heat exchanger pans. These have an array of fins on the bottom that prevent heat escaping up the side of the pan and transmit it directly to the contents. In the UK at present you're most likely to come across Primus Eta Power, MSR Reactor or Jetboil systems. We've been impressed by the speed and efficiency of all three – water starts steaming within seconds. These systems have a ceramic piezo spark auto-ignition system, but these are easily broken, so always carry a backup lighter.

Much-hyped as the cutting edge in stove technology, enhanced heat transfer systems are efficient and convenient, but expensive.

The main drawbacks are the limited transferability between systems and the hefty price tag. Primus Eta pans are easily used with other stoves, while the Jetboil and MSR Reactor are very definitely compact, specialist systems. The Eta system is bulkier and heavier overall, but more stable and more versatile. The pans have an extra ring on the fins, meaning they can also be used on conventional stoves. Be cautious though – not all stoves will fit.

Kelly Kettles

Kelly Kettles are named after the Irish family who invented and still produce this ingenious device. A Kelly Kettle is an aluminium flask with a
wide chimney running down the middle. The water fills the walls of the
chimney. To use it you build a **small fire** on the detachable base, then
replace the kettle. The fire heats the water as it draws up the chimney, and
you feed the fire by dropping fuel in at the top as required. Even in bad
weather you can boil a kettleful in three to five minutes. The chief advantage of the system is **the range of materials that can be used as fuel** –
sticks, dry grass, old heather, scraps of rubbish, etc.

*A one-pint Kelly Kettle
will boil water in three
to four minutes, using
only a handful of twigs
or grass.*

Kelly Kettles come in two sizes: the 2.5 pint, good for large groups, and the
more portable 1 pint mini version. In an attempt to address the legitimate
criticism that their kettles aren't for proper cooking, Kelly now also produce
a **cook system** comprising a small pan and a pot stand that fits in the top of
the chimney. If you want to cook often, there are more appropriate stoves,
but if you just want a fresh hot cuppa in minutes, without having to worry
about buying fuel, they're ideal, and a great asset for open canoe excursions, fishing trips, fieldwork or days out on the beach.

Wood Burners

Wood-burning stoves are popular overseas, and while they're increasingly
seen on campsites around the UK, they're not really a mainstream product
and can be difficult to buy. You can fashion one yourself quite easily by
using a metal box (such as a biscuit tin) with one side cut away and a barbecue grill set inside. The fire and the food being cooked are shielded
from the wind. Numerous websites will give you step-by-step instructions
on how to do this.

When buying a stove, you need to factor in the cost of the appropriate maintenance kit, if there is one. Don't skimp on maintenance. Provided you check your stove over regularly you shouldn't need to take a maintenance kit into the field for short trips, but for long expeditions it's wise to carry **a set of spare parts** and **suitable tools**. With liquid-fuel stoves, the first things to fail are usually the rubber 'O' rings that act as seals. It's a good idea to check these when you clean the stove after each trip. Replace them at the first sign of cracking or perishing.

Another common fault with liquid-fuel stoves is soot blocking the fuel tube or the burner jet(s). This will happen faster with some fuels than others. Regular gentle cleaning will help. Make sure you take your jet-cleaner/pricker with you if the stove doesn't have one built in. Trangia burner jets may be cleared using an old toothbrush or an ordinary needle or pin.

High maintenance stoves come with detailed manuals and a maintenance kit. Make sure you know how to use it.

PROS AND CONS OF STOVE TYPES

Cookers	Fuel
Trangia	Spirit (meths or alcohol gel)
Mini spirit burner (mini Trangia, beer-can stoves)	Spirit (meths or other high-alcohol spirit)
Pressure stoves	White gas (Coleman fuel), petrol, paraffin (kerosene)
Kelly Kettle	Virtually any relatively dry organic matter
Heat transfer systems (MSR Reactor, Jetboil, Primus Eta)	Gas or pressurised petrol
Gas spider	Gas

All stoves need protection from the wind, though it's rare to find a gas stove sold with a decent windshield. The marketing blurb often suggests that the burner head in some way forms a windshield – don't be fooled! Decent windshields can be made easily from a few layers of thick foil, but it's well worth investing in a shop-bought one made of thin sheet metal (usually aluminium). They can be rolled or folded easily, and only weigh about 50–90g, depending on thickness and composition. Only enclose your stove if the fuel bottle or cylinder is remote – you don't want it to **overheat and explode**. This can be difficult if you have a cylinder-mounted stove, and it can be tricky to set up a windshield for very tall stoves.

A foil windshield (this one is made by MSR) will significantly reduce fuel consumption. Never enclose a cylinder or fuel bottle with a windshield.

Pros	Cons
Moderate cost, simplicity, low maintenance very robust, highly stable, pans part of compact package, some fuel flexibility.	Bulky, messy fuel, moderate power.
Lightweight, some fuel flexibility, low maintenance, DIY beer-can stoves are a good emergency option.	Low efficiency without windshield, stoves potentially messy, moderate power.
High power, potential for alternative fuels, unaffected by cold.	Expensive, high maintenance, white gas, very expensive, petrol and other fuels are dirty, and dangerous in the wrong hands.
Robust, efficient water heating, great fuel flexibility.	Big, heavy, unsuitable for most cooking.
High power, superb efficiency, pans part of compact package, some pans available separately.	Expensive, relatively heavy, little cross-system compatibility, fine control of low heat difficult, limited cooking options, potentially unstable.
Stable, clean, efficient used with windshield, relatively lightweight, cheap.	Heavier than cylinder-mounted models, sluggish in cold conditions, no fuel flexibility.

continued on pages 50–1

Cookers	Fuel
Gas cylinder-mounted	Gas
Flat-bed hob	Gas
Multi-burner hob	Gas
Hexamine stove	Hexamine
Wood burner	Wood or charcoal

FUELS

Gas

Gas is convenient, clean, potentially very **controllable** and reasonably cheap, but it does have several significant drawbacks. The cylinders are **heavy and bulky** and take up just as much space when they are empty as when they are full – you always have to carry them out again. Most gas stoves will run on gas and only gas, and you can't buy it everywhere, so you need to plan ahead. Gas can be dangerous – faulty stoves or negligence can lead to spectacular and potentially lethal fires or explosions.

Gas stoves can struggle in cold conditions, especially if the cylinder is more than half empty.

When it comes to camp stoves, 'gas' can mean either butane or propane. Both are petroleum products that come in liquid form in a pressurised container, but vaporise instantly at normal atmospheric pressure. In North America, gas can also mean petrol, so be careful what you ask for. Gas can only burn when it is mixed with oxygen, hence it cannot burn inside the cylinder. However, if the cylinder is damaged so that gas escapes faster then intended, or if it is over-heated (for example by being placed too close to a fire or enclosed in a wind-shield), then an explosion is possible. An exploding gas cylinder, even a small one, can be lethal, so don't ever put one near a fire, even if you think it's empty.

There are different types of gas cylinder available. Modern lightweight stoves use re-sealable cylinders that can be separated from the stove for packing. Some very old-fashioned gas stoves run on cylinders that are pierced by the stove. Camping shops in the UK rarely carry these cylinders any more, but they are still available overseas and from hardware shops. Modern cylinder-mounted and spider stoves mostly use one of two types of gas canister – those produced for Camping Gaz (blue) brand stoves, and just about everybody else. The cylinder types are not

Pros	Cons
Lightweight, clean, easy to use.	Poor stability, often flimsy.
Cheap, stable, easy to use, relatively versatile cook options.	Bulky, heavy, relatively inefficient, sluggish in cold conditions.
Cheap to run, ideal for large groups, versatile cooking options. Refillable cylinders.	Bulky, expensive initial cylinder purchase.
Lightweight, compact, very cheap.	Flimsy, no fine control, moderate heat, fumes potentially harmful.
Cheap to run, versatile cook options.	Bulky, limited availability.

interchangeable. A third type of cylinder, currently enjoying a massive boom in popularity, thanks in part to TV chefs taking to the outdoors, is the butane cartridge used in flat-bed integral cylinder hobs.

SLUGGISH CYLINDERS

When gas cylinders are more than half empty, the loss of pressure will start to affect the performance of your stove. The problem is especially acute in cold conditions. You can boost the output of a flagging cylinder by sitting it in a centimetre or two of lukewarm water. If you're stuck for something to do one evening, you can make a cylinder jacket out of old carry-mat foam or thick neoprene. The final solution (for the really reckless) is to tuck a cold cylinder in against the warm skin of one of your sleepy tent-mates first thing in the morning...

Don't throw out empty cylinders with the household rubbish – take them to your local waste facility, where they can be recycled safely.

Petrol

Unleaded petrol is the fuel of choice for many regular backpackers. It's relatively cheap, **easily available** and fairly clean, once the stove is running. However, it can be extremely **smoky and sooty** when the stove is warming up and cooling down. There is also some concern about the additives in vehicle fuel – these are not meant to be inhaled or ingested.

When buying petrol for your stove, remember that petrol stations have **strict rules on dispensing fuel**. There is usually a minimum delivery of 2l or 5l, and you can't just dispense fuel into any old container. It's virtually impossible to fill a small stove bottle from a petrol pump without spilling fuel, and the only safe way (and the method that petrol stations will permit) is to use a proper petrol can. Keep one locked in a cool, ventilated place such as a shed or garage and top up fuel bottles from there.

Paraffin

Many pressure stoves will also burn paraffin or kerosene. This is a traditional stove fuel, used successfully for many years before petrol stoves were available. Paraffin does not ignite as readily as petrol, and requires the stove to be warmed or primed using flammable paste or other material to get things going. Once alight, paraffin stoves are clean and very efficient. Spilt fuel can be very messy and difficult to clean up, though the fire risk is less than from spilt petrol.

Paraffin is generally diminishing in availability as domestic usage wanes. These days it is usually sold in plastic bottles at hardware shops and some petrol stations.

White Gas/Coleman Fuel

White gas is far and away the **cleanest** liquid petroleum fuel and the easiest to use. It doesn't smoke excessively or create much soot and it burns very hot. The downsides are its high cost – generally about 10 times more

expensive than petrol in the UK. It can usually only be bought in specialist camping shops. It is much cheaper and more widely available in the US and Canada and is the fuel of choice for many North Americans.

Spirits

Spirit stoves burn alcohol. In the UK, methylated spirit (ethanol with methanol), known as meths, is available in camping shops, hardware and DIY stores and from chemists. It has an additive that induces vomiting to prevent its use as drinking alcohol and is dyed purple for easy identification. If meths is unavailable, then sterilising alcohol (from the first aid section of a chemist or supermarket) or surgical spirit will do the job. The cleaner and more pure the fuel, the less it will smoke and smell. Some fuels

MULTI-FUEL STOVES

A number of pressure stoves are sold as 'multi-fuel'. Many petrol stoves will burn a range of products such as white gas, unleaded petrol, diesel, paraffin and aviation fuel. This is a huge advantage in outback situations where fuel availability is limited, but each fuel will still need different handling, so a fair amount of expertise is required to make full use of the stove. Some of these fuels are also a last resort – imagine the exhaust fumes from a truck – now imagine trying to cook with diesel. It works – but you wouldn't choose it! The cleaner (more expensive) the fuel you use, the less your stove will smoke, soot and clog up.

Genuine multi-fuel stoves, in other words devices that will burn anything, are still some way off. The closest thing at present is a range produced by Primus. Some of their stoves can burn any liquid petroleum-based fuels and can also be quickly converted to use a gas cylinder. The payoff for this flexibility is the weight of your stove and the cost. For a belt-and-braces approach, we sometimes pack one of these stoves and a mini Trangia, or even just the Trangia burner. This combination covers just about any fuel.

Spirit stoves will burn a range of fuels with high alcohol content, but beware of additives that may clog your stove or produce nasty fumes.

leave an oily coating on your kit. Surgical spirit is especially bad for this – only use it as a last resort. *Never* try to burn petroleum-based fuel in a spirit stove, or vice versa. **Note** White spirit and turps or turpentine substitutes are *not* alcohols, so never try to use them in a spirit stove.

Solid Fuel

In most instances solid fuel means hexamine. Hexamine is made from formaldehyde and ammonia. In its crystalline form it's greasy, white and flammable. In other forms it is used as both an antibiotic (methenamine) and a food preservative (E239). Hexamine and its fumes are **toxic** – the compound can be absorbed through the skin and can cause rashes. It's banned in some countries, but the UK is not one of them. To be used safely, a hexamine stove needs plenty of ventilation – don't use one in an enclosed space.

Gel Fuels

Gel fuel canisters are another innovation in fuels. The alcohol gels are **clean**, don't smell and are probably the **safest** fuel of all. If you can over-look the air miles involved in importing them, they're also very **environmentally friendly**. Once cooled, the canister can be resealed for transportation. The disadvantages are that the heat output is relatively low and can be inconsistent. Also they can be difficult to light once the canister is nearly empty. The gel needs to be smeared up the sides of the tin with a twig to bring it within reach of a match or lighter (if you use your fingers make sure they are wiped completely clean before you strike a match!).

'Natural' Fuels

Wood, coal, charcoal and peat fires can all be wonderful for cooking on. All can be purchased from garages and general stores and sometimes from farms (in the UK peat fuel is usually only available in areas where it is still used domestically, mainly in Scotland and Ireland). Unless you are using a specialised wood-burning stove or BBQ, see *Open Fires*, Chapter 7.

Fuel availability varies from country to country. If you are planning a camping trip overseas, do some research to find out what fuels are available there and what name they are sold under. Be prepared for familiar-sounding names to refer to completely different substances.

To store and transport fuels safely you need to use an appropriate container. Pressure-stove bottles have thicker walls than drinks bottles. The seals used on individual bottles may also be designed for a particular use and particular fuel types.

Fuel bottles can look similar to each other and to aluminium drinks bottles, but they are made to different specifications. To be safe, only use them with the stove and fuel type for which they are sold.

Barbecues

Disposable BBQs that come in a foil tray are convenient, but they get extremely hot. Stand them on something that won't burn – a flat rock, a heap of sand or a couple of bricks will prevent damage to the ground below. **Disposables** are overrated – they seem cheap, but they don't burn for very long and often you need to use more than one. For about four or five times the cost of a single disposable you can buy a **budget portable** BBQ that will give you several years service. The kind with folding legs and a fire tray that shuts like a suitcase are easy to pack and transport without leaving a scattering of ash and charcoal smudges everywhere. Some sites and picnic areas have permanent BBQs – you just bring your own charcoal. A handy tool for such occasions is a grill scraper which you

Where a camp fire is inappropriate a small BBQ adds an extra dimension to camp meals, with the option to grill or bake foods in the embers.

Where a low heat is required – such as for a fondue or just to keep something warm – a bit of candle power is often all you need. Our fondue recipes start life on a stove, but move to a cluster of four or five tea lights and a pot stand made of tent pegs. We also use our three-candle Candelier lantern for keeping things warm inside the tent – the flat aluminium top is designed with this in mind.

The low heat from tea lights is ideal for keeping food warm. Make sure they are placed on a non-flammable surface.

can use to remove the worst of any rust, or the grease or burned-on food left by the last users.

You can turn an open fire into a barbecue by raking out some hot coals and mounting a wire grill above. You can buy camping grills with folding legs, but a large cake cooling rack mounted on a couple of logs, bricks or stones will do the job.

No stove required: heater bags and self-heating meal packs use the heat of reaction between water and lime to warm food through.

Heat Without Fire

One final way of generating a hot meal is to use **chemical heat packs**. These exploit the heat produced when certain chemicals react. Flameless heater bags are designed to be used with pouches of ready to eat food (known by the abbreviation MRE for 'meals ready to eat'). The heater bag contains sachets of powder (10% aluminium, 87% lime and 3% other chemicals), which react vigorously to the addition of a few tablespoons of water. Untreated water or even seawater will do, since it does not make contact with the food. Within seconds the pack is too hot to hold, and a food pouch placed inside will be heated in 10–12 minutes. The reaction gives off a small amount of flammable gas, so the pack should not be used in an enclosed space close to a naked flame. For more information, or to purchase heater bags in the UK, visit www.expeditionfoods.com.

It is also possible to buy food ready packaged inside a reaction pack. To heat it, you break a seal between a reservoir of water and a sachet of powdered reagent – the resulting reaction heats a small portion of food inside. These packs are sometimes stocked as emergency rations on boats or in bunkers, but are not intended for routine use, and only come into their own in situations where actual cooking is out of the question. They are too heavy for backpacking and the amount of food involved is very small – more a comforting snack than a meal.

FIRE STARTERS

Our golden rule for lighters of any kind: **carry lots, and spread them about**. Ideally every member of a group should carry one or even two, carefully packed in different places. Overkill is fine. Getting to camp and having a row because everyone thought someone else had the lighter, or discovering that the only one doesn't work, is very far from fine. We keep a couple of lighters with all our stoves and a liberal selection in various coat and rucksack pockets – there's one in the first aid kit, a couple in the glove box of the car, and Amy usually packs another with the food too. It's also worth carrying matches as a backup, especially in very cold weather. Lighters can freeze up, or become difficult to operate with numb or wet fingers.

Disposable Lighters

The easiest and cheapest way to start a fire or light a stove is with a bog-standard butane lighter. Buy them in multipacks every so often and distribute them throughout your kit so you're never caught without.

Turbo Lighters

Whatever type of lighter you carry, it's always wise to have at least one backup.

Various lighters are available with air-intake holes in the side of the burner nozzle. Just as opening the baffle on the old Bunsen burner in your school lab turned the sooty yellow safety flame to a noisy blue inferno, a lighter such as a Turboflame will produce a roaring blue point, much hotter than anything you get from a regular lighter. This is pretty unnecessary if all you want to do is light a stove, but a turbo lighter is a bit more directable and less likely to be blown out. It's easier to light a candle in a lantern with one of these, or to reach the fuel in a half-empty gel fuel canister. (Ours gets more use as a welding torch when repairing plastic kayaks and canoes.)

Matches

Brown-headed safety matches will only ignite when struck against the side of the box. Safety matches must be kept dry, and so must the striker. There's no point carefully wrapping your matches in plastic if the striker is wet. **Red-headed matches** can be struck on any surface rough enough to generate friction, but not so rough it tears the head off the match – a stone, a house brick, tough canvas. Even wet surfaces will do the job. Strike-anywhere matches are classed as dangerous goods and not permitted on aircraft.

Wind and waterproof **expedition matches** are a bit expensive for routine use, but a small pot is a useful addition to your emergency repair kit. Be careful using and disposing of them as the head stays red-hot for quite a while.

Fire Strikers

Getting a spark out of a steel and flint such as the Light My Fire Firesteel is just a matter of firm pressure and a confident strike. The sparks are short-lived but incredibly hot (about 3000°C), so the trick is to have tinder that catches very quickly. This may be very fine dry seed heads, pocket fluff, newspaper, shredded birch bark, very dry leaves, grass or pine needles. You can help things along with fine shavings of resinous wood sold as 'Maya Dust', also from Light My Fire.

COOKWARE

Big is Beautiful

One of the reasons camp cooking is often seen as fiddly and difficult is because people assume that camp equipment has to be small. For obvious reasons, you want to keep weight and bulk to a minimum, but you can make life much easier with a few well-chosen items of reasonable size. The extra 100–200g of weight incurred carrying a larger lightweight pan, a large chopping mat and a decent-sized sharp knife can be well worthwhile when it comes to preparing food.

When it comes to equipping yourself, your first recourse is to your kitchen at home. When faced with the shiny arrays of camp-cooking equipment you'll see in outdoor shops, you might be lured into thinking that a mini can opener and mini cutting board are essentials, when in fact they are gimmicks. Most penknives have a can opener, and there is little point in a tiny chopping board if you already have a plastic plate. If you want a cutting and preparation surface, take a decent-sized mat (see *Cooking Utensils*, below) rather than a postage-stamp-sized board.

Pans

To some extent, the type of pans you need will depend on your choice of stove. If you opt for something like a Trangia, you'll find all the pans you need come as part of the set – usually one small, one large, one lid-cum-frying-pan, one pan grab and a kettle. We rarely bother with the kettle, but the rest make a good basic set that can be used on most other small stoves. For many years our pans have all been Trangia, the latest addition being a very large billy that works on top of a small Trangia but is also

This large, lightweight aluminium billy packs easily with the regular Trangia stove set inside it. It's one of our favourite pieces of kit.

large enough to contain the whole stove when packed. If you're buying pans separately from a stove it's a good idea to get them as a set, as they'll nest together neatly and be easier to pack. Check that the outside surface of the pans is not too slippery.

Most lightweight pans are **aluminium**, some are **stainless steel**, and the really swanky ones are **titanium**. To some extent they all have a similar problem, in that if you're cooking over a small heat source, one part of the pan will heat up more than the rest. If you're cooking something like sauce or porridge, you need to stir constantly to prevent burning around this one spot. Food burned onto an aluminium or titanium pan is a devil to scrub off. Aluminium is better at distributing heat, while stainless steel is easier to clean.

Some people worry about a possible link between aluminium and Alzheimer's disease. In fact the doses you'll absorb from a meal cooked in aluminium are relatively small compared to those you might take in from other sources, but if you want to be certain, make sure the pans you buy are anodised, to minimise leaching of aluminium into your food. **Composite pans**, made of aluminium with a stainless steel lining, are a very good compromise – easier to use and care for than plain aluminium or steel, and cheaper than titanium.

Always take the biggest pan you can manage, even when backpacking. Because a pan can be stuffed with other kit, the difference in volume between a large pan and a small one can be negligible in terms of packing. There is a weight difference, but it can be surprisingly little. Pot shape also makes a difference. A tall narrow pot may be great for storing the stove inside if you're backpacking, but it makes heating evenly and stirring the contents more tricky.

WORTH THEIR WEIGHT – PAN SIZE/WEIGHT COMPARISONS

Big Trangia pan and lid 400g, vs mid size 290g, vs mini 170g.

Detachable pot grab handles are excellent for several reasons. Pans without fixed handles are easier to pack. Attached pan handles tend to get very hot – and those insulated with plastic or wood have a tendency to melt or burn if you're not very careful. Provided you don't leave a pot grabber attached when the pan is in use, it never gets hot, so you won't burn your hands.

Many stove kits come with a pot grabber, but if your pan has a loop handle it's still worth buying a separate pot grab – the loop is fine for lifting the pot off the stove, but when you want to drain the contents you'll find you need three hands – one to hold the loop, one to tip the pot and another to hold the lid or strainer. Using a pot grabber, you can hold and tilt the pan with one hand.

If weight isn't an issue and you're using larger camp cookers or an open fire, you have more options, and most sturdy pans will do, though beware those with metal handles, which get very hot, and plastic ones, which melt! Cast-iron cookware is great – virtually bombproof, and produces a lovely even heat, which is excellent for cooking.

Non-stick Pans

Many pans now come with a non-stick surface. As long as you are prepared to be a little more considerate to your kit, and only use wooden or plastic utensils and soft scourers, then these are generally a good idea. If you're cooking with other people, confiscate metal utensils and scrubbers, or accept that damage from over-zealous stirring, scraping or scrubbing will occur.

Caring for Pans

Washing the blackened bottom of a pan is a bit of a waste of time on a short trip. When cooking with a smoky fuel such as meths, or on an open fire, some people rub a little washing-up liquid onto the base to make the pan easy to clean afterwards, but it also means the black will rub off very easily onto anything else the pan touches. Wash and dry pans properly at the end of each trip – we put ours through the dishwasher even if they've been washed in camp.

Camp Ovens

Camp ovens (sometimes called Dutch ovens) come in two basic types: those designed to sit in an open fire, and those for stove-top use.

A conventional camp oven is a large cast-iron container with a loop handle and sunken or lipped lid; often the base has little legs. The idea is that the pot nestles directly into the fire and the sunken lid is heaped with hot coals. This generates an even heat inside, allowing you to roast or bake anything from lamb casserole to whole chickens, bread or even fairy

cakes. This is a very popular method of camp cooking in Australia, where huge distances mean many long-distance car journeys are often broken with an overnight camp in the middle of nowhere.

Traditional camp ovens are heavy, but if you're camping with a vehicle the weight doesn't matter. They are pretty much indestructible, and if properly looked after will last several lifetimes. A traditional camp oven also makes excellent open-canoe ballast for expeditions on the water – just make sure it's packed securely enough to survive a capsize.

Stove-top camp ovens are usually much lighter than the traditional cast-iron type. We love our Optimus Mini Oven (available from www.base-camp.co.uk) for all kinds of bread, cakes, and especially toad-in-the-hole, which it cooks so well we even use it at home in preference to the kitchen oven. It's made of aluminium so it's light (a shade over 500g), although too bulky for backpacking over any distance.

The Optimus Mini Oven has three parts: a doughnut-shaped base, a doughnut-shaped cooking pan and a lid. The base protects the cooking pan from direct heat, thus avoiding burning. The holes in the middle of the base and pan allow heat to circulate inside, so the food cooks from above as well as below. The only disadvantage is that it can only be used on clean-burning stoves, ideally gas – soot from dirty fuels would spoil the food.

The Outback Oven from US outfitters Backpacker's Pantry (www.backpackerspantry.com) is a folding stove-top camp oven made of tightly woven mesh, which folds for storage. In use it encloses a lidded pan, which sits over a diffuser plate that allows for very even baking of its contents. Although we haven't tried it, it comes highly recommended by those who have. At about 700g the original is about 185g heavier than the Optimus, but it isn't restricted to clean-burning stoves.

There is also an ultra-light version without a dedicated pan that weighs only about 270g. The idea is that you use it with your regular camp pans. The overall weight saving and collapsibility makes this system potentially more transportable than others.

You don't have to buy a purpose-built camp oven – they are surprisingly easy to **improvise**. You just need two different-sized, lidded pans that will fit inside one another without touching at the sides. Separate the base of the inner pan from the outer one with a handful of fine gravel or with water. Gravel creates a hot, dry heat, perfect for baking bread or roasting meat. Water limits the temperature, and of course generates a lot of steam, which can be disastrous for bread, but is perfect for gooey sponge puddings (see sponge pudding, p272).

◀ *The stove-top Optimus Mini Oven creates an even heat ideal for cakes, pies, bread and batter puddings.*

Big supermarkets and kitchen shops stock cooking bags that minimise washing up. They work brilliantly for reheating wet food such as reconstituted stews, and you can use them to make excellent scrambled eggs (see p192). They are made of heat-safe plastic, so you can put your food inside, tie off the top and lower them into a pan of boiling water. After the food is cooked or heated you can use the water to make a hot drink, and the pan stays spotless.

COOKING UTENSILS

Knives

Don't be tempted to buy the smallest knife you can find for camping – cutting steak or potatoes with a flimsy little vegetable knife is difficult, and far more likely to end in injury than if you use a large, sharp, quality blade. When car camping we always take a **big kitchen knife**, wrapped in a cardboard sleeve or a clean tea towel for protection, and stored in a plastic box. When backpacking we use a **decent-sized penknife**. Whatever kind of knife you use, treat it with care and sharpen it from time to time. A blunt blade is more difficult to use and more likely to skip and cause injury.

The tiny Victorinox Classic penknife gets used time and again, but for any serious chopping, a larger, lockable blade is essential.

Penknives and Multitools

If you want a knife that will perform and last, buy a decent make. The original Swiss Army knives are made by Victorinox, so beware of cheap imitations. Other good-quality knives are made by Gerber and Opinel. We have a selection of these between us. Our tiny Victorinox Classics, which hang on key rings, go everywhere we do (except cabin baggage – we've lost a couple to airport security that way). They have a small blade (useful for cutting cheese, apples, cord, etc.), a set of scissors (good for trimming nails), a flat-head screwdriver, a file, a set of fine tweezers (ideal for splinter removal) and a toothpick. Our bigger penknives have **locking blades** – this makes them safer to use for more heavy-duty tasks as well as routine food chopping.

Penknives that come with a colossal array of ancillary gadgets are often simply too big, heavy and unwieldy to be handled easily. The range is huge and there are knives tailored towards many different activities, so choose whichever is likely to be most useful for your purpose. Ours have can- and bottle-openers, corkscrews, screwdrivers and files. For camping we've never needed more than that. As with many things designed for the outdoors, quality teamed with simplicity is the best solution.

We use folding knives because they're easy to carry. Bushcraft and survival specialists usually prefer a stronger fixed blade, but for our purposes it's not really necessary. Remember that you need a very good reason to be carrying any kind of blade in a public place – sadly, in urban areas it's enough to get you thrown out of pubs, arrested, or attacked – so beware, be discreet, be careful.

The classic multitools are made by Gerber and Leatherman – the integral pliers are what make them must-have gadgets around camp. Don't buy anything too big – it's better to work cleanly with a simple, well-chosen tool than clumsily with an unwieldy monster.

Cutting Board/Mat

Chopping anything is made immeasurably easier if you have a large board or mat to do it on. We use a couple of inexpensive plastic mats bought from a supermarket. They need replacing more often than a rigid board, but they're light, and slip easily inside a rucksack. Tiny chopping boards are pretty hopeless – virtually any normal-sized vegetable will end up spilling off the board as you chop.

Wooden Spoon

As simple as it gets. We have a couple of wooden spoons in the camp box, one with a long handle, for stirring big vats of stews and suchlike, and the other very small, for backpacking. Being wooden, they don't damage non-stick pan coatings and they don't get as hot as metal if you leave them in the pan (though they will burn).

Tongs

Ideal for campfire and BBQ alike. Wooden tongs don't heat up as much as metal ones. They're light, cheap, and very useful for fishing out beans or pasta twists to see whether they're cooked.

Can Opener

We have can openers on our penknives, so in theory we're never caught without. Another failsafe is to keep a miniature army-style can opener in your camp basics box, or even in with the stove. For car camping we use a regular-sized kitchen one, with nice comfy handles.

Corkscrew, Bottle Opener

Again, these essentials might be on your penknife, which makes them difficult to forget. Bottle-opener key fobs are useful, or choose bottles that have screwtops.

EATING WARE

Cutlery

For lightweight camping we usually carry one Lexan spoon each. If you can afford a bit more weight, a knife-fork-spoon set is nicer to eat with. Sporks (spoons with short fork tines at the tip) are popular with lightweight backpackers. They're one of those slightly gimmicky items that most people seem to buy or get given at some point. Their actual usefulness is debatable, but they weigh the same as a spoon, so carrying one does no harm. Choose a Lexan spork if you want to cook with it. Sporks with a knife blade at the other end are fairly pointless – the knife isn't sharp enough for chopping, though you might use it for spreading, and you still need two sporks if you want to eat knife-and-fork style, otherwise at some point you end up holding the mucky end. We use a 7ml Lexan camp spoon as a standard measure in our recipes.

Mugs

If you're really travelling light, a good mug can serve you in a multitude of ways – you can drink from it, eat out of it and cook in it. If you want this kind of multi-purpose mug, it'll have to be metal – either stainless steel, titanium, aluminium or enamelled tin. The disadvantage of metal

MATERIALS FOR EATING WARE

Stainless Steel

It's indestructible, easy to clean, and can usually be found in abundance in your kitchen drawer or purchased for a song in charity shops.

Plastic

A cheap and cheerful material for plates, mugs and bowls, but it scratches easily, and will soon need replacing if you use it for cutting on, since deep score-marks are unhygienic. As cutlery it won't last long – it's easily melted and broken.

Lexan resin (lexan polycarbonate)

This stuff is impact and flame resistant – it's often used as an alternative to glass in secure buildings or in bus shelters prone to vandalism. It makes excellent everyday camp cookware – cutlery, plates, bottles and cups, as well as 'luxury' camp items such as filter coffee makers and wine glasses.

Enamelware

Very traditional and robust, enamel mugs and plates are great for car camping or backpacking if you don't mind the weight. They can be used for cooking too, but beware of grabbing a hot handle. Avoid using them for chopping on – once the enamel is chipped or scratched, the metal may rust. You can buy enamelware extremely cheaply in old-fashioned kitchen and hardware stores, or very expensively in trendy homeware and gift shops – you choose!

Titanium

This super-lightweight metal is strong and durable and makes superb utensils, but it comes at a high price, roughly three times that of Lexan. Titanium pans are one thing, but for most purposes, titanium cutlery is overkill. The weight saving is negligible… but then again they are very pretty!

mugs is weight and thermal conductivity – leave a steaming cuppa standing in the cold and it'll be chilled in no time.

Insulated mugs will keep hot drinks hot (and cold drinks cold) for anything up to an hour, longer still if they have a lid. Many outdoor retailers now sell insulated mugs with a narrow base. These fit neatly in car cup holders, but elsewhere they're top heavy and easy to knock over. Some camp mugs are shaped the other way, with a broad base to improve stability, but this shape makes them trickier to pack.

We reckon most mugs are mug-shaped for the good reason that they work best that way. It's hard to improve on something that does the job as well as a stout cylindrical insulated mug with a lid, but be aware that most insulated mugs tend not to be dishwasher safe and cannot be boiled for sterilisation purposes in camp.

We use our mugs for **measuring ingredients**. Most standard camping mugs hold about 400ml. We've marked off 100ml increments on several of ours to take some of the guesswork out of cooking. Our recipes assume a standard mug contains about 400ml.

Plates and Bowls
If you're only going to carry one plate, a deep one will allow you to eat both dry and sloppy foods. Plastic plates insulate food slightly better than metal ones, but are not quite as robust. If plates are used for cutting, the deep scratches can become unhygienic. If you have a dishwasher, run your plates through it at the end of each trip and make sure they are put away dry.

A bowl is potentially more useful than a plate. It will keep food warm longer and can be drunk from as well as eaten off. For wild camping, we rarely bother with either plates or bowls. Eating straight from the billy saves washing up, and metal can be cleaned without detergent then sterilised over a flame.

Flasks
The **stainless-steel flask** is a wonderful invention – although big, bulky and heavy, it allows you to have hot food or a drink just about anywhere. A stainless-steel flask is invaluable when out for long periods in winter, and we use them for winter walking, kayaking and canoeing. However, not all stainless-steel flasks are the same. Cheap ones may not be terribly effective, but expensive 'executive' style ones can be rubbish too! Buy an outdoor-specific flask from a brand you trust. Our battered 1l Camping Gaz flask is over 10 years old, but it keeps contents hot for at least 24 hours.

Remember that a vacuum flask will keep fluids cold as effectively as it keeps them hot – a small flask can keep milk fresh for several days.

Wide-necked flasks are useful for chunky soups or recipes like lentil kedgeree, but they don't keep the contents as hot as narrow-necked ones. The bigger the volume of the flask, the hotter it will keep the contents. The small **beaker-style flasks** we use for walking or kayaking are fine for a lunchtime drink, but in cold weather only keep things hot for three to four hours.

Once a flask has been opened and the contents partially drunk, the remaining liquid will cool down much more rapidly.

Water Bottles and Carriers
See Chapter 4.

In cold weather, a flaskful of a hot sugary drink serves multiple functions, providing hydration, energy, warmth, and boosting morale. Don't leave home without one.

Furniture
Because we do most of our camping with small tents (our largest sleeps three to four in one dome), we don't use much furniture, although we have some **full-size folding chairs** for use when car camping. If you're short on space, buy chairs with no arms, as they are much lighter and pack smaller. We also sometimes use a folding table.

Cooking and eating at a **table** is potentially safer and more hygienic than cooking on the ground. Larger camp shops usually stock a range of folding tables, some with integral seats. The most space-efficient ones we've seen have detachable poles for legs and a top made of slats that concertina for storage, but these are surprisingly heavy. The lightest option is a flimsy coffee table with short folding aluminium legs, suitable if you are sitting on the ground.

For backpacking in comfort, the **chair kits** designed for use with Thermarest inflatable mattresses are a worthwhile investment. They give you a nice comfy seat (at ground level) and some back support, which can be very welcome indeed.

USEFUL ANCILLARIES

Sit Mat/Stove Mat
A small square of foam to sit on can make cooking much more comfortable. Some lightweight rucksacks have a back pad which doubles as a sit mat. You can use a smaller mat, stiffened with a few layers of gaffer tape, to create a stable platform for your stove when cooking in snowy or boggy locations.

Plastic Sheet
A clean plastic rucksack liner or survival bag makes an excellent cold-food preparation surface. Ideally it should be labelled so you always use the same side. Don't put hot pans on the plastic, and make sure it is cleaned and dried after use.

Dry bag
A fully waterproof bag with a roll top, available in most outdoor shops.

Aluminium Foil
Foil is almost endlessly useful. You can use it to wrap foods for cooking directly in or on a fire, for improvising a pan lid, or for wrapping food-stuffs for storage. Don't use it for any food with a high acid content (fruit, tomatoes, cabbage, etc.), as the foil will taint their flavour.

For most camp purposes, thick foil is best – turkey foil is good and worth stocking up on at Christmas (not all supermarkets stock it all year round). To save space, tear a few sheets off the roll and fold them carefully for packing. Clean foil can be recycled.

Muslin
A few squares of muslin are useful for keeping flies and dirt off food, and we sometimes also use them for cooking dumplings or suet pudding. Make sure they are always washed after use – boil them up for a few minutes to make sure they stay sterile.

Cool Bag with Ice Blocks
Any kind will do. Rigid ones are sturdier and usually have better insulation, but they take up more space and can't be stuffed as easily. The more food you keep in a cool bag, the better it works. See Chapter 6 for more on keeping food cool.

Cordage and Small Karabiners

We keep a few of these in our camp box. They're very useful for hanging food or lanterns, for rigging up drying lines and tarp shelters, or just clipping rubbish bags to guy lines so they don't blow away. You'll find all sorts of other uses for them too.

Wire Twist Ties, Plastic Zip Ties and String

Twist ties are handy for closing bags and packets, while zip ties can be used to make permanent repairs to anything from guy lines to rucksack straps. String is used to wrap food in some recipes – use the undyed, natural stuff.

Wooden Clothes Pegs

Amy uses these by the dozen at home and in camp. If it doesn't move, it gets pegged open, closed, up or down. They're very cheap.

Scotch Tape

This is the stuff you can stick and unstick several times (sold as gift-wrap tape because it's almost invisible when you press it down well), and is really useful for resealing opened packets and sachets. Stick a length to every packet before you set out.

Gaffer Tape (Duct Tape)

Another indispensable item! It tears easily so you don't need a knife or scissors. It sticks to most things but peels off again quite easily. It's waterproof and very strong. Where carrying the whole roll is impractical, we wind lengths of it around other items, such as kayak paddle shafts, walking poles and drinks bottles. We've used it to build shelters, fix tears in groundsheets and waterproof clothing, insulate wire pot handles, re-attach car wing mirrors and even hold together cut skin.

Containers

See Chapter 6 for lots more information on jars, bottles, tubs and other reusable containers.

Washing-up Liquid

You can buy specialist camp washing-up liquid that boasts biodegradability along with effective cleaning, and no doubt all sorts of other desirable qualities, but at a price. Most people would baulk at paying anything like as much for household dish detergent, so why should camping products be different? Biodegradability is important whether you're in the wild or at home, so switch to an eco brand for general use and just

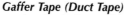

decant a small amount into a reusable bottle when you go away – you'll save money and do your bit for the planet. If you do choose a specialist outdoor brand, get one that can wash everything – you, your clothes and your dishes.

Scourers
Sponge scourers are handy. Choose the soft variety if you have any coated cookware; if not, go for a bit of extra-coarse scrubbing power. Either way, it's important to rinse the scourer clean after use and to let it dry out whenever possible. Soap-pad scourers (such as Brillo pads) produce lots of unpleasantly scummy waste water, continue to leak soapy goo after use, and go rusty. By all means keep a stock of them at home for post-trip cleaning, but we wouldn't recommend taking them with you.

Washing-up Bowl
You can buy collapsible ones, but there is a risk of damaging these with sharp utensils. A small rigid one or a bucket is great for car camping. See the *Hygiene and Washing Up* section in Chapter 7 for more information and ideas on hygiene kit.

TRAVELLING LIGHT, OR EVERYTHING BUT THE KITCHEN SINK?

The absolute minimum requirement for cooking outdoors is a sharp knife and a whole load of knowledge – this is the realm of the serious survival expert, and beyond the scope of this book. But with the increasing popularity of multi-day mountain marathons and other adventure racing events, there is a burgeoning demand for lightweight, no-fuss cooking equipment and meals.

If washing-up kit is required, keep it simple and use biodegradable detergent.

In the UK, where areas of true wilderness are small and you have to try quite hard to walk for a day and not see a road, car camping is very much the norm, and let's face it, who can really say they don't enjoy the extra luxuries that a boot full of kit can offer? If you are camping from the back of your car, there's no point travelling very light – you can enjoy some home comforts, and get away without a lot of the specialist kit that can make wild camping expensive.

For example, we often use duvets and rugs instead of sleeping bags and groundsheets on this sort of trip. When it comes to cooking, the lack of restriction on weight and bulk means you can really go wild. Most electric gadgets aside, you can pretty much transport your whole kitchen if you choose.

The following three kit lists represent three 'weights' of camping.

This is the **ultra-light** set of kit we'd reserve for racing, or camping overnight from a 25–30l pack, or from a kayak. We've also used this kind of kit on one or two overseas trips.
- ✓ Lightweight stove, either gas or spirit burner
- ✓ Fuel in suitable container
- ✓ 1 billy with handle
- ✓ 1 billy lid (or a piece of thick foil)
- ✓ Lexan spoon (per person)
- ✓ Light plastic mug (per person)
- ✓ 2 plastic water bags (ziplock)
- ✓ 2 lighters
- ✓ Rubbish bag

For **backpacking** with a 35–60l pack we'd consider the following kit (items in brackets would be eliminated at the lighter end of the spectrum).
- ✓ Easily packable stove and maintenance kit
- ✓ Windshield
- ✓ Fuel in suitable container
- ✓ (Plastic sheet (clean rucksack liner) for food prep)
- ✓ Nesting pans with handle
- ✓ Pan lid/frying pan
- ✓ Deep plate/bowl (per person)
- ✓ Insulated mug (per person)
- ✓ Penknife with locking blade, can opener and bottle opener
- ✓ Lexan spoon (per person)
- ✓ (Small wooden spoon)
- ✓ (Folding MSR spatula)
- ✓ (Fork (per person))
- ✓ (Knife (per person))
- ✓ (Cutting mat)
- ✓ Washing-up sponge
- ✓ (Washing-up liquid)
- ✓ (Steripen or other water-purification device)
- ✓ 2 lighters
- ✓ (Matches)
- ✓ (Lightweight gas or candle lantern)
- ✓ Antibacterial hand gel
- ✓ Water bag
- ✓ Rubbish bag
- ✓ (Sit mat)

For **car camping**, pretty much anything goes, but this is a fairly normal list for us for, say, a long weekend in the UK or a week in the Alps. Often on these trips we won't decide the full menu until we arrive, so we don't always need everything we take.

- ✓ 2 large plastic stacker crates
- ✓ Cool bag or box with ice blocks
- ✓ Flat-bed stove
- ✓ Spider stove
- ✓ Fuel in suitable containers
- ✓ Selection of large pans and lids
- ✓ Non-stick frying pan
- ✓ Griddle
- ✓ Stove-top camp oven
- ✓ Spatula/fish slice
- ✓ Wooden spoon
- ✓ Wooden tongs
- ✓ Slotted spoon
- ✓ 2 large kitchen knives
- ✓ 2 large cutting mats
- ✓ Plastic sheet
- ✓ Penknife with can and bottle opener and corkscrew
- ✓ Kitchen can opener
- ✓ 2 large plastic mixing bowls
- ✓ Full set of eating utensils for each person
- ✓ Insulated mugs, plastic beakers, Lexan wine glasses
- ✓ Candles and/or lanterns (citronella if it's buggy)
- ✓ Bag of tea lights
- ✓ Several lighters
- ✓ Furniture – folding chairs and maybe a table
- ✓ Tarp cooking shelter and cordage
- ✓ Washing-up bowl/bucket
- ✓ 10l collapsible water-carrier
- ✓ Millbank water filter
- ✓ Steripen (or other water-purification device)
- ✓ Sponge scourer
- ✓ Washing-up liquid
- ✓ Tea towel
- ✓ Antibacterial hand gel
- ✓ Rubbish bags
- ✓ Spare ziplock and carrier bags
- ✓ 3 or 4 cloth shopping bags
- ✓ Lunch boxes and bags
- ✓ Roll of kitchen paper
- ✓ Roll of aluminium foil
- ✓ Roll of gaffer tape
- ✓ Bag of miscellaneous bits – wooden clothes pegs, mini karabiners, lengths of cord and a ball of cotton string

...and perhaps the kitchen sink.

CHAPTER 4
Water and Drinking

It's difficult to overestimate the importance of water – it is vital to life and well-being, the one dietary component that we simply cannot do without in the short term. All in all your body is **50–60% water**, and sensitive to quite small fluctuations in this volume. Neglect to drink for a few hours and you'll start to feel the effects. Go without for a few days in some climates and you could be decidedly dead.

Unfortunately for the outdoor enthusiast, water is one of the heaviest things you're obliged to carry. Fresh water weighs exactly **1kg per litre**, and on a spring day in Britain, an average person engaged in moderately strenuous activity, such as hiking, should drink about 4l. Increase the severity of the weather to hot summer sun, strong winds or winter snow, and this requirement increases. In extreme circumstances, such as endurance races in hot climates, competitors must drink almost continuously. Athletes taking part in the seven-day Marathon des Sables (Marathon of the Sands) in the Sahara are advised to take on at least 7l during each day's run.

WHERE DOES IT ALL GO?
Water is lost from the body in a variety of ways, some of which are more obvious than others.

Urinating is the body's way of clearing the waste products of metabolism, most notably ammonia, which is toxic if allowed to accumulate. If you become dehydrated your kidneys will reabsorb water, making the urine that does reach your bladder more concentrated and a darker shade of yellow than normal. Anything darker than a very light white-wine colour means you are dehydrated. Drinks containing caffeine and alcohol interfere with the signals that tell your kidneys to conserve water, and this 'diuretic effect' means you pee more than is good for you. So while tea, coffee and beer all contain water and make tempting refreshments (and obviously they're better than nothing), plain water or dilute, non-caffeinated, non-alcoholic drinks are better for hydration purposes.

The amount of water lost in **faeces** is also variable, and bowel movements will become much less moist if your body is under water stress. While some people on camping trips may regard constipation as preferable to squatting *au naturel*, a disrupted pattern of bowel movements is a sign that all is not as it should be with your body. In cases of diarrhoea, water loss is considerable and can be very dangerous. If you or your camping comrades are suffering from the 'squits' for more than a few hours, you're better off heading for home before the condition becomes debilitating.

◀ *Remembering to drink on the move is crucial in maintaining physical performance – don't wait until you feel thirsty.*

Another highly variable form of water loss is **sweating**. It's perfectly possible to sweat a litre or more an hour when exercising hard on a hot day. Over-sweating isn't normally harmful, as long as you replace the water you're losing. It's also worth remembering that losing heat also means you're burning calories. Water is also lost by **evaporation** from moist surfaces such as eyes, nose and lips. A few hours on a cold windy hill can give most people streaming eyes and a nose running like a tap. A surprising amount of fluid can be lost in this way, so have a couple of extra swigs for your eyes and nose. In very hot, dry or windy conditions, Vaseline on your lips and around your nostrils will stop the skin chapping.

Vomiting can be both a cause and symptom of dehydration. In the latter case it contributes to a dangerous downward spiral, and needs urgent medical attention involving the administration of fluids intravenously (via a drip).

Finally, water can be lost through bleeding, though in such instances dehydration is probably of secondary concern. Being seriously injured can change the rules of nutrition considerably, and a basic first aid course is a good idea for anyone planning to spend time in the great outdoors.

WHEN YOU'VE GOT TO GO...

There are times when going for a pee is inconvenient. In the middle of the night when the wind is lashing rain or snow against your tent, for example, or when roped into a climb, or zipped into a drysuit. For men, the solution is simple – peeing into a bottle (carefully marked of course) is easy enough, and most drysuits have a 'relief zip' that make things fairly straightforward. It's much more difficult for the lasses though, and there is often a temptation to stop taking in fluids in order to avoid the inconvenience of getting up in the night or having to get undressed. Women can be particularly prone to dehydration as a result. If this sounds familiar, check out the various funnel-like gadgets available from manufacturers like Whiz and Shewee, which allow you to pee standing up, into a bottle, or through a relief zip. If you're wearing a lot of clothing layers, you might need a longer tube – extensions are available!

DEHYDRATION

The consequence of not drinking enough to replace lost fluids is dehydration. Even mild dehydration (1–2% of your body weight) can make you feel ropey and will impair your performance if you're competing; more than 5% and you will become unable to function normally; 10% dehydration could put you in serious danger.

The effects of dehydration are **cumulative**, which can make it hard to recognise the problem. Imagine you're trekking in hot weather for several days. Each day you drink roughly the same amount – say a couple of a litres. You feel OK for four days, and suddenly on day five you experience classic symptoms of dizziness, lethargy and a thumping headache. You think, 'I can't be dehydrated because I've drunk the same as yesterday and the day before, and I felt OK then.' Try drinking more – nine times out of ten it will sort out the problem. The same applies in everyday life – it's easy not to drink enough during a busy day.

Water should form an important part of planning your camping trip. If you're staying on a campsite, or somewhere else with access to mains water, you still need some means of transporting water from tap to cooking area, and containers for carrying water during the day. If you're camping wild, or travelling in an area where tap water cannot be trusted, you need the wherewithal to treat water before you use it (see *Water Treatments*, below).

BE A BUDDY

In hot or challenging conditions, make it your business to check on your companions' hydration state. If you don't see them drinking often, remind them – some people just forget. (Don't be bashful – starting a conversation about pee colour is a great way to break the ice!)

WATER SOURCES

Tap Water
On official campsites, drinking-water taps will usually be labelled clearly, but water from unmarked taps (such as in washrooms or at water troughs) may well come from a standing tank, a rainwater butt or a stream, and thus will only be suitable for washing or watering livestock. If you're camping on a farm, ask about the water supply. If in doubt, treating water anyway is a wise precaution.

Springs, Streams and Rivers
If you are on high ground, water bubbling up from the ground is usually about as clean as you could wish for. If you can't see the actual source, at least check as far **upstream** as is practical to ensure you're not collecting water in which a dead and bloated sheep has been marinating. Any water from a stream that passes through pasture should be treated. At lower altitudes, almost all water should be regarded as suspect, even if it appears to be coming from underground. In limestone country especially, streams frequently appear and disappear more than once, flowing through caves and sumps containing who-knows-what festering flotsam.

Drinking untreated water from a lowland stream is usually a bad idea in any part of the world. Upland streams well away from pasture are a safer bet.

Reservoirs usually contain what will become safe drinking water, but only after treatment.

If you're collecting water from anywhere other than the head-waters of a river, there's a good chance it will contain a suspension of silt. Water from fast-flowing areas will often be turbid, with more stirred-up silt and other muck, while that in large eddies or areas of very sluggish flow could be clearer, but is also more likely to be warm, stagnant and teeming with bacterial and algal life. Our advice is to look for somewhere with a steady flow but no real turbulence.

Lakes and Reservoirs
The water in natural lakes and in reservoirs should be reasonably clean, but it will definitely need treating or boiling before drinking. In lowlands, a glance at the map should alert you to any obvious sources of pollution, such as agriculture or industry.

Rainwater
Rainwater is normally good to drink. In very polluted regions it may collect dust from the air, but these tend to be populated areas where you'll have access to other sources of water anyway.

Collecting rainwater efficiently means creating as large a catchment as you can. The catchment needs to be non-porous, impermeable and clean, or you'll contaminate an otherwise pure supply. A clean tarp, survival bag or shelter can make a fine collecting device.

Melted Snow and Ice
Start the melting process slowly, with just a handful of snow or some well-crushed ice in the bottom of a pan. Heat it very gently – if you blast it with heat the water will **sublimate** (in other words it'll turn directly from snow/ice to steam). When it has melted and become very slightly warm, add another handful. Be patient and you'll achieve quicker results in the end. Once you have an inch or so of water in the pan you can turn up the heat. Freezing is by no means guaranteed to kill harmful bacteria and other nasty bugs, so water from melted ice and snow still needs **treating**.

WATERBORNE DISEASES

You can catch some really delightful illnesses from bad water. In fact, about four out of five human diseases are waterborne. While the majority of these are endemic in the tropics, British water still has its fair share of nasties.

Many of the best-known diseases are caused by protozoan parasites. **Protozoa** are single-celled organisms – way too small to see in most cases – but with the potential to wreak havoc on your insides, by multiplying fast and exuding toxins that will make you very unwell. One of the commonest protozoan infections afflicting outdoor types is giardia.

Giardia lamblia is a flagellate protozoan – basically a single-celled animal that swims using a long whippy tail. It lives and reproduces in the digestive tract of all kinds of wild and domestic animals and in humans. The progeny develop into cysts, which are excreted along with faeces. The cysts can survive months in cool, moist conditions, waiting to be taken in by another host, then they spring to life and begin the cycle over again. A person infected with this charming beastie will experience an array of symptoms, including fatigue, bloating, stomach cramps and diarrhoea, starting a week or more after infection and often continuing off and on until they are successfully diagnosed and treated with powerful antibiotics. The condition is known as giardiasis, 'beaver fever' or 'hiker's fever', and incidences appear to be increasing in the UK.

Broadly similar gastroenteric symptoms are also caused by various other protozoa, including species of *Cryptosporidium* and the amoeba *Entamoeba histolytica*. These can all be transmitted in water, but are probably caught at least as often from food contaminated by the touch of an unwashed hand.

Another nasty little waterborne organism is *Leptospira*, responsible for the potentially life-threatening condition known as leptospirosis or Weil's disease. Infection is through water contaminated by animal urine – in the UK rats usually get the blame. Symptoms may develop anything from a few days to three weeks after infection, and at first are much like those of 'flu. Patients then usually begin feeling better before deteriorating into a more serious condition. At this stage it's very important that medical staff are alerted to the possibility of Weil's disease, since it is usually fairly low down on the list of possible diagnoses. (Our friend Jon contracted leptospirosis when caving, and was near collapse when he went to accident and emergency. Knowing that he had been in contact with dodgy water gave the doctors something to go on, and allowed them to diagnose the problem quickly, despite Jon's delirious state.)

Not all waterborne parasite infections are microscopic. Drinking untreated water is also a great way to pick up a rather splendid variety of worms and flukes that will cause anything from itchy rashes and diarrhoea to incapacitating fatigue and chronic weight loss. The worms develop, attached to the gut lining, from eggs or cyst-like entities and can grow disturbingly large.

You can catch viral diseases such as hepatitis and polio from untreated water, and the list of waterborne bacterial infections is daunting – typhoid, cholera, botulism and Legionnaires' disease, plus many others without common names. Most are contracted from untreated water, especially in parts of the world where raw sewage is discharged into river systems. It is possible to be **vaccinated** against some, and if you are contemplating a trip overseas, you should consult the practice nurse at your doctor's surgery for advice. For others, **vigilant hygiene** and careful treatment of all drinking water are the only practical preventative.

Another group of potentially troublesome single-celled organisms are blue-green algae or **cyanobacteria**. Species such as *Microcystis* occasionally form bright-green blooms in rivers and lakes, usually in summer. The toxins produced will poison other lake organisms and animals drinking the water, although in the UK at least, *Microocystis* blooms are usually well publicised.

If all this is starting to make the outdoors sound just a bit too perilous, rest assured that all these conditions are relatively easy to avoid. There are a number of simple and effective ways to treat water that will make it perfectly safe to cook with, wash with and drink.

WATER TREATMENTS

There are five main types of treatment – heat, filtration, chemical purification, irradiation and distillation. Under most circumstances, boiling is the only treatment guaranteed to make water safe on its own, but if the source water contains sediment you'll probably also want to filter it before using any other treatment. At the very least, this makes the water more pleasant to drink.

Boiling

To treat water by boiling you must bring it to a **full rolling boil** and keep it there for at least a minute, preferably two. This will kill bacteria and other organisms in the water and destroy toxins. The distinctive 'flat' taste of recently boiled water is a result of lost oxygen. If the water is left to stand for an hour or two, oxygen dissolves back in and the taste improves. You can speed up the process by shaking the water in a clean container.

At altitude, water boils at a lower temperature than at sea level, so to be safe, you should let it boil for longer – up to five minutes is recommended. Purifying water by boiling can work out expensive in terms of fuel. Don't forget to cover the pan to increase the efficiency of heating, and use a windshield around the burner (don't enclose a gas cylinder or fuel bottle within a windshield, see Chapter 3).

Combined with boiling or chemical purification, water filtered through a Millbank bag is very safe.

There is little to be gained in terms of safety by the belt-and-braces approach of boiling and filtering, but water without grit and floaters is much more pleasant to drink. Boiling does not remove harmful minerals or inorganic toxins such as heavy metals.

Filtration

At it's simplest a water filter is a fine mesh that allows water to percolate through, while retaining particulate matter. Almost any woven, non-water-proof fabric can serve as a filter – a clean tea towel or t-shirt will do if you have nothing else. But the minimum size of particle that passes depends on the size of the mesh, and if you're relying on filtration alone you want that mesh to be as fine as possible. Most 'rough filters' are only useful in combination with a second form of treatment, such as boiling, chemical purification or further fine filtration. Only the most expensive filters can be relied on to render water safe to drink on their own.

A Millbank bag is a filter made of very tightly woven canvas, designed to be hung from a branch or fence. A Millbank bag costs about £10, weighs about 100g, rolls up to fit in a pocket and, if well cared for, will last indefinitely. Brilliant, simple technology. (**Note** A brand-new Millbank bag can appear to be completely watertight – running it through a couple of washing machine cycles will help the breaking-in process.)

Modern high-grade filters incorporate a replaceable cartridge with a limited life, or a more expensive cleanable cartridge. The cartridge may contain fine mesh or special granular media, both of which retain silt, bacteria, algae and protozoan parasites. Because filtration can be slow, many systems have some sort of pump to speed the flow of water through the system. The Swiss manufacturers Katadyn are the market leaders in these devices. Their product range is extensive, and includes filters of all sizes and shapes, designed for use in a wide range of circumstances. Some will filter the smallest of pathogens, such as viruses.

The latest filtration systems appearing on the market combine a Millbank-type setup with modern granular filters. Water flows from one bag to another through a hose fitted with a filter cartridge. Examples include the MSR Autoflow and the Platypus Clearstream. Known as **gravity filters**, they remove bacteria, algae and protozoans, but cannot guarantee to remove viruses.

Filter Straws

Drinking straw filters are best carried for use as backup rather than a primary means of obtaining safe water.

Several manufacturers use the granular filtration principle to produce pocket-sized emergency drinking straw filters. With one of these, they claim you can drink safely from a mucky puddle. But before you make this your regular party trick, remember that the straw stops working when the filter is full, so the worse the water quality, the less usage you will be able to get out of one straw.

You can pay up to £20 for one of these devices, but the one we have cost just £5 from the Filtastraw Project, which sends one drinking-straw filter to help people in the developing world for every one we buy here – a bargain with a bonus. For more information visit www.filtastraw.org.uk.

Chemical Purification

Chemical treatments are appropriate for clear water. If particulates are present in the source, it will first need filtering. Most chemical treatments are based on iodine or chlorine, which are added to water in the form of drops or tablets. Both are capable of destroying bacteria and most protozoan parasites, provided the correct dose is used and the water is left to stand for long enough (half an hour is usually advised).

Chlorine tablets (puritabs) are not always as effective as iodine, and neither is as reliable as boiling. Under certain circumstances (such as in very cold water) giardia cysts and some other protozoa with dormant phases have been know to survive several hours' treatment.

Below and left: Two commonly available means of chemical treatment – iodine drops and chlorine purification tablets.

Miox

The proprietary mixed-oxide treatment system developed by the Miox Corporation has been used in large-scale commercial and municipal plants all over the world, and is now being marketed for domestic and portable use, in partnership with MSR. In very simple terms, the new Miox purifiers use an electrical charge to turn tiny quantities of salt (sodium chloride) and water (dihydrogen oxide) into a cocktail of chlorine and mixed oxidants that kills all waterborne pathogens. We haven't yet seen one of these systems in action, but with a long battery life and the potential to treat large volumes of water at a time, there is clearly enormous potential here. The only drawback we can see is that treatment takes about half an hour – comparable to other chemical treatments, but slower than boiling, UV and faster filters.

UV Irradiation

Sewage treatment plants have been using ultraviolet light to sterilise water for many years. Now you can buy a pocket-sized battery-operated device that will do the same. A Steripen (www.steripen.com) looks like a torch with a long bulb. Clear water (pre-filtered if necessary) is most easily treated in a wide-necked bottle. The bulb is immersed and the UV bulb lights up. UV kills bacteria and viruses by messing up their genetic material, and has been shown to be particularly effective at destroying giardia. It takes about a minute for a Steripen device to treat a litre of water. The downside of this treatment is that if there is contaminated water lurking in the drinking nozzle or the screw threads of the cap, pathogens could still find their way into you.

Quick and convenient to use, the Steripen is a good option for long treks, best used in conjunction with a simple filter.

Distillation

This is a means of extracting fresh water from brine or other non-potable mineral waters. In camping terms, it's pretty much an emergency measure, or something to try just for fun. To de-salinate water you need to build a still, a device in which you can heat the water, collect the steam and condense it back into water.

Clean Containers

Remember that anything you rinse in or use to collect untreated water is **potentially contaminated**. If you use a mug to help fill a kettle, it will also need treating. A metal mug can be heated over the stove, a plastic one can be dropped into the boiling pan. Alternatively it can be dried and left in direct hot sunshine for a few hours – the combination of complete desiccation and solar UV will finish off most bacteria and viruses.

Likewise, there is little point sterilising water if you then transfer it to a non-sterile water bottle or hydration pack. Where possible you should avoid rinsing these out in untreated water. Use **sterilising tablets** to ensure they are clean, or fill them with boiling water and allow to stand for several minutes. Be warned that some hydration packs (usually the cheap imitations of reliable brands such as Platypus or Camelbak) won't take boiling water, and these are best avoided if water safety is likely to be an issue on your trip. It's also important to remember that with most treatment methods, only water inside the bottle is treated – make sure you wipe the outside of the bottle dry before drinking or pouring from it, and ensure that hoses, drinking nozzles and bottle threads are rinsed in clean water and allowed to completely dry out regularly.

FINDING WATER IN THE WILDERNESS

Begin your search for water on your map. In the UK, Ordnance Survey and Harveys mapping shows water in blue. As a basic rule of thumb, if you want to find water you should head downhill. If you do so at an angle to the fall line (in other words walk diagonally across a slope rather than straight down it) you are more likely to intercept small streams running down. Pay attention to clues in the vegetation – clumps of small trees or spiky rushes often indicate damp ground.

CARRYING AND STORING WATER

Bowsers and Canteens
If you're catering for a large group, or camping some way from your water supply, it's useful to have a big water container. A 15l plastic bowser is about as much as you'll be able to carry from tap to tent.

Bags
Many camp stores sell reinforced water bags with a tap. These are easier to pack than rigid containers, but far less robust. We've had a few, but they always seem to end up leaking, so for backpacking purposes we usually just use bottles, bladders or **plastic food bags**. The latter are an ideal lightweight solution, because they weigh next to nothing when empty. Ziplock types work best, as they are easier to pour from and reseal. Tie-handle bags can work too, but you need to make sure they stay upright, for example by tying them to a guy line. Be warned that plastic bags rupture easily (watch out for spiky grass) and usually only survive one night's use. You can't carry water very far like this – it's a means of storage in camp, not a solution to hydration on the move.

Above: A large expandable plastic canteen with a tap minimises water-collecting trips. Dry it out between uses and store with the lid off.

Below (top): Some wide-necked bottles come with an insert that stops the liquid rushing out too fast.

Bottles
A discarded soft-drink or mineral-water bottle makes a perfectly serviceable water-carrier for hiking, but it might not survive being dropped or fallen on, so if you spend a lot of time on the move it's worth investing in a robust drink bottle. The more off the beaten track you go, the more reliable you need your water bottle to be.

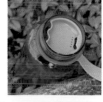

Sports-top bottles are easy to drink from on the move, but also potentially unhygienic unless the teat has a cover. A safer option for a bottle carried on a bike, on the outside of your pack or knocking about the bottom of a boat, is a **screw top**, in which the lip of the bottle is protected by the lid. **Wide-necked bottles** are quicker and easier to fill than narrow ones, but trickier to drink from on the move.

Don't share drinks bottles with others unless you want to share whatever germs they might have. Nine times out of ten you'll be fine, but if you're a few days out from civilisation there's no point in you both getting sick. Label your bottle clearly.

Hydration Packs
Most rucksack manufacturers now make backpacks and bumbags with hydration systems. These were developed by Camelbak and Platypus, who still dominate the quality end of the market, but there are dozens of similar designs out there too. Both systems require a pack with an internal

---

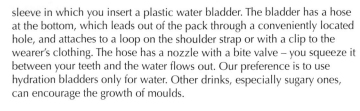

sleeve in which you insert a plastic water bladder. The bladder has a hose at the bottom, which leads out of the pack through a conveniently located hole, and attaches to a loop on the shoulder strap or with a clip to the wearer's clothing. The hose has a nozzle with a bite valve – you squeeze it between your teeth and the water flows out. Our preference is to use hydration bladders only for water. Other drinks, especially sugary ones, can encourage the growth of moulds.

As with the sports-bottle teat, it can be difficult to keep the nozzle of a hydration bladder clean, especially if you're biking or running in the muck. Some systems come with a **nozzle cover**, or you can buy them separately. They'll help keep your nozzle clean, but do make getting a drink a bit more fiddly.

Most small rucksacks now come with an internal sleeve, hose hole and shoulder straps to accommodate a hydration bladder.

GOING WITHOUT – A LIGHTWEIGHT SOLUTION?

Many mountain marathon runners and adventure racers don't carry water – they carry a mug or cup and drink from streams when the opportunity arises. A popular choice is the type of trainer cup designed for babies. This has a lid and a 'beak', which gives a bit of short-term portability – the athlete can fill the cup in a matter of seconds, then sip the water over the next few minutes while continuing on his or her way. Adopting this strategy may mean taking a chance on going thirsty for a while, or being forced to drink from less-than-ideal sources. This might be an acceptable gamble in a well-marshalled event where someone will miss you should you be much delayed, or have to make an enforced stop, but it's really not a wise choice if you're out alone. Even in the UK something as simple as a sprained ankle could become really serious if you're not carrying water with which to stay hydrated on a hot day or make up a brew on a very cold one.

CLEANING A HYDRATION BLADDER

A home-made alternative to proprietary bladder-hose cleaning kits – a scrap of rag on a cord.

Both Camelbak and Platypus product ranges now include bladders with wide openings, making them easier to fill and clean. We clean ours using the sterilising tablets intended for babies' bottles. The trickiest part to clean is the hose. For this you can buy a special proprietary wire brush. Alternatively you can use a thin strip of rag, or a thickish shoelace threaded onto a thinner cord a bit longer than the hose itself. Flush the tube with hot soapy water, then drop the free end of the cord through the tube, and use it to drag the rag or the shoelace through a couple of times. Rinse the tube and sterilise along with the bladder. Leave both to dry in a warm spot. Wash and dry the rag/shoelace thoroughly between uses. Keeping your empty hydration bladder in the freezer between uses is another good way of keeping the bugs at bay.

CHAPTER 5
The Camp Larder

If you camp regularly it really helps to have a stash of **long-life ingredients** from which you can select what you need for each trip. This saves having to raid all your other kitchen cupboards and repeatedly decant small amounts of various ingredients. If you camp less often it's not worth stocking a full camp larder with stuff that could go off between trips, but we'd still recommend a basic camp pack of things like seasonings, tea, coffee and sugar, ready packed in small quantities.

Some dried long-life goods appear time and again in the meals we cook on camp trips, and we keep these in our **camp basics box**. It makes packing quicker, and means it's easy to get away for a spontaneous weekend without having to do any special shopping before we leave. Some of the ingredients listed on the following pages are things we use all the time at home too, but keeping a separate camp stash means there's always some handy even if the kitchen larder has run out.

The camp box also contains things we're unlikely to use at home – tubs of milk powder, instant potato flakes, packets of dried onions and other vegetables, single servings of jam or honey (left over from cafeteria or airline meals) and sachets of salt, pepper and sugar (from service stations, cafés and pubs).

If you have a store like this, try not to let it become a graveyard of out-of-date and half-empty packets. Get everything out every couple of months and check for packs of food going past their prime. For most tinned and dried goods, the 'use by' date is a rough guide rather than a hard-and-fast deadline – if something is packaged to last two or three years, there's no real reason it won't last four. A **regular check** of your stocks means you can put the things that need using to the front.

It's easy to forget things that aren't kept together. More than once we've left certain items in the fridge, intending to collect them and add them to the cool bag at the last minute. Distressingly, this has sometimes meant no cheese, no bacon, no chocolate, and worst of all, no beer! So now, as a reminder, we leave the cool bag where we have to literally step over it to leave the house.

If you camp regularly it's convenient to keep a box of basics stashed away. This means you don't have to spend ages making lists, shopping, decanting and packing before you leave – most of the essentials are there ready to go. Here's the usual contents of our basics box, which lives alongside the non-food camp ancillaries (see Chapter 3 and Chapter 6).

- ✓ Couscous
- ✓ Dried fruit (sultanas, cranberries, apricots)
- ✓ Herbs and spices: chilli powder, curry powder (a mix of chilli powder, ground cumin, ground coriander and garam masala), mixed herbs, ground mixed spice, nutmeg and nutmeg grater
- ✓ Hot chocolate/cocoa powder
- ✓ Instant coffee
- ✓ Instant mash
- ✓ Instant soup
- ✓ Long-life skimmed UHT milk
- ✓ Noodles
- ✓ Moreish seeds (see p196)
- ✓ Pasta
- ✓ Pine nuts
- ✓ Plain flour

- ✓ Powdered milk
- ✓ Quick-cook oats
- ✓ Seasoning (salt and pepper sachets and cruet)
- ✓ Single-serve jam pots, Marmite, etc.
- ✓ Single-serve sauce sachets
- ✓ Soy sauce (bottle and the little single-serve capsules you get in some Asian restaurants)
- ✓ Stock cubes
- ✓ Sugar
- ✓ Tabasco sauce (we use the mild jalapeno version as it's easier to control the heat)
- ✓ Teabags: regular, fruit and herbal (keep peppermint tea wrapped separately to prevent it making other foods taste minty)
- ✓ Vegetable oil

A-Z OF GREAT FOODS AND INGREDIENTS

Apples

A fresh crisp apple is one of easiest ways to eat fruit. Choose firm varieties over softer ones, as they're juicier and last longer in warm weather – up to a week if you can stop them getting bruised. Some people eat the core, which solves the problems of disposal neatly. Tempting though it is to chuck the degradable core away, this is still littering. Cooked apple makes a great accompaniment to breakfast cereal, pancakes or cooked meat, or a good dessert in its own right.

Dried apple comes in various forms – the chewy rings are good for snacking, while apple crisps and flakes can be eaten as they are, or rehydrated to make sauces, crumble fillings or fruit stews.

Apricots (dried)

See Dried Fruit

Bacon

See Cured Meats

Bananas

Ripe bananas are packed with fruit sugars that have a relatively low GI and thus provide a nice slow release of energy. The riper the banana, the greater its sugar-to-starch ratio (though the squishy black 'drinking bananas' Roy loves are an acquired taste!). Bananas lack the acidity of other fruits and are thus easy on the stomach. They also contain high levels of potassium, which is essential for healthy nerve and muscle function. If you don't mind a bit of extra weight, you can buy a Banana Guard, a rigid plastic box shaped like a boomerang that will accommodate a banana whichever way it bends. Alternatively, you can slip bananas into the mesh pockets of a rucksack, where they're visible and you'll notice when they need eating. Banana chips or chewy air-dried whole fruit won't go down as easily as a fresh banana, but the nutritional benefits are comparable and they're much easier to carry and store.

Berries
Fresh berries are one of the treats of late summer – blackberries, bilberries and occasionally wild strawberries all add to a meal in camp (if you can resist the temptation to eat them on the spot!). Carry them in a mug wrapped in a plastic bag to prevent squashing, or make a rigid container from plastic milk bottles, as described in *Recycled Packaging*, Chapter 6. See also Dried Fruit.

Beans
Fresh Green beans are among our favourite camp vegetables, especially in summer when UK-grown varieties are in season. They're very easy to carry in a mug or recycled box (see *Recycled Packaging*, Chapter 6), and provide a dense source of the good green stuff. French or fine beans are the easiest to process, as they just need topping and tailing. Runners are great, but the fine slicing required can be a bit of a faff.

Tinned Baked beans have been a camp favourite since the first tins appeared on grocers' shelves at the beginning of the 20th century. Also check out your local supermarket for tins of mixed beans. These come with various dressings and flavourings and make a good basis for bean casseroles or veggie chilli.

TOXIC BEANS

Most beans contain a toxic protein called phytohaemagglutinin, which is destroyed by cooking. In fresh green beans the concentrations are low, so a quick boil or steam is all they need. Uncooked kidney beans contain high concentrations of the toxin, and can make you very sick indeed. Fortunately raw kidney beans are very hard and dry and you wouldn't want to eat them anyway. Most cases of kidney-bean poisoning result from people eating inadequately cooked beans (cooking at very low temperatures actually increases the toxicity rather than decreasing it). Tinned beans are already cooked, and perfectly safe. If you have a dehydrator (see Dehydrating at Home, below) you can re-dry cooked beans – they can be reconstituted in camp by soaking for a couple of hours and are safe to eat.

Beansprouts An excellent little book by Marcelle Pilkington (see *Further Information* at the end of this book), loaned to us in New Zealand, recommends taking mung beans on summer backpacking trips. If you're staying put for more than one night, there's time to get them sprouting – they're sweet and edible after 12 hours. After 48 hours in warm weather they're proper bean sprouts, bursting with protein, sugars and vitamin C. What a great idea.

Bread

Pittas keep for weeks if the pack is unopened, and they're really easy to carry because they pack flat. But they can be fiddly to fill, splitting easily and falling apart when you try to eat them. Standard bread rolls go stale fast and take up more pack space but are more robust when you come to tuck in. Soft tortilla wraps are easy to carry rolled up, more fiddly than bread rolls, but less prone to falling apart than pittas. Wholemeal bread tends to keep better than white, an extra day at least. Bread fresh from a bakery is lovely, and often boasts a lack of preservatives… so don't be surprised when it's stale in two days. French bread is stale by the end of the day, but still edible. Pre-packed sliced bread lasts up to a week – preservatives aren't necessarily a bad thing! Black rye bread lasts longest of all. Take your pick of these, or use one of the recipes in Part Two to make your own bread in camp.

Bulgar Wheat

Like couscous, bulgar wheat doesn't need to take up stove space. You simply pour on boiling water and leave it to stand for 15 minutes or so while you prepare the rest of your meal. It can be eaten hot as part of your main meal or cold in a tabouleh-style salad. It travels very well raw or cooked, and can be  flavoured with whatever else you fancy – a great camp-larder staple.

Butter, Margarines and Spreads

Butter and margarine are solid fats that can be used for spreading as well as cooking. Low-fat spreads are no good for frying, though some claim to be OK for baking. There's usually a list of suitable uses on the tub, so check before you pack. This said, for cooking, most chefs would choose butter over margarine any day, and so would we. The main disadvantage of both butter and margarine is that they melt.

Traditional blocks of butter stay firm longer than soft margarines or 'spread-from-the-fridge' butters, which are developed to have a lower melting temperature. In winter you might be better off with the soft stuff if you're going to be using it for spreading. Both butter and margarine go rancid if kept too long, and this happens a lot quicker if they are not refrigerated. You'll know if your butter or margarine is off – it'll have an unpleasant, slightly metallic smell. Salted butter keeps a bit longer than unsalted.

Cabbage

The solid red or white 'cannonball-like' varieties (not the loose, crinkly, Savoy type) are about the only leafy fresh vegetables we'd recommend for longer backpacking trips, as they're not as prone to wilting as other greens. They're heavy, but you probably don't need a whole one – just carry as much as you need in the form of a wedge wrapped in cling film or a plastic bread bag. It should keep at least three days.

Cake Mix

So it's cheating. But packets of cake mix make a very easy and reliable alternative to proper home/camp baking. You still need to bring eggs or egg powder, but there's no messing about measuring dry ingredients and the results are usually pretty good. Make sure you can measure liquids accurately by marking off the required levels on a mug or pan before you leave home. Where the instructions call for milk, use pow-

dered, and water. If butter is needed, you can use vegetable oil, though you'll need less than the recipe asks for – about 20ml oil per 25g butter. Avoid olive oil for baking sweet things – its flavour is too strong.

Carrots

Root vegetables are a plant's way of storing surplus energy, and thus they're very nutritious.

We wrapped three carrots in plastic, cloth and paper and left them outside. After three days, the plastic-wrapped carrot was the only one still fresh, crisp and lovely.

Carrots add a kind of sweetness to all kinds of recipes, and they're robust enough to survive a few days in your pack. Try and keep them dry. They'll keep three days, longer in cool weather.

Cheese

Hard Cheese A good hard Cheddar or rubbery Edam or smoked cheese will survive pretty well in camp, as will waxed cheeses. Avoid crumblers like Cheshire or Wensleydale unless they're encased in wax – they're tasty but don't travel very well. Cheese can get sweaty if you carry it in plastic in warm weather – it's best wrapped in greaseproof paper or a cotton cloth then put in a plastic bag or tub. Aim to use cheese within two or three days. Halloumi (a salty cheese from Cyprus) is brilliant, as it doesn't melt and can be cooked like meat on a grill or in a frying pan.

For convenience you can buy snack-sized portions of cheese – supermarkets often do them as pick 'n' mix selections. These are pretty handy for lunches and snacks, but if you're planning to use more than a tiny amount you're better off buying a proper block and cutting it up yourself. If you buy from a deli counter or market you can buy exactly the amount you need and avoid having to discard or carry excess.

Soft Cheese Ripe, runny Brie is a favourite lunch snack when we're in the Alps, but sadly it's not really backpack friendly. Your best bet for backpack-able soft cheese is the squirty stuff in a tube. It tastes a bit artificial, but it's a great standby for simple lunches or as the basis of a cheese sauce, and it's simply too easily packed and transported to be sniffed at. It keeps for weeks when sealed and about a week once opened, as long as it doesn't get too warm. Cream cheeses like Philadelphia are useful, and appear in some of our recipes, such as cheesecake. The tubs are not leak-proof, so to be on the safe side, carry them inside a plastic bag, or transfer the contents to a more secure container – a double layer of ziplock bags will cope with most eventualities, barring being sat or fallen on. Use within two days in warm weather.

Chickpeas

Buy these tinned – dried ones require overnight soaking and long boiling to render them edible. They're an excellent alternative to meat if you're cooking for vegetarians.

Chillies

Fresh chillies are small enough to be carried easily and give lovely flavour. Bear in mind that the smaller the chilli, the hotter it will be. Rub a little oil into your fingers before chopping, to prevent the juices soaking into your skin, wash your hands afterwards, and try really hard not to rub your eyes. Chilli seeds are hotter than the flesh, so unless you're cooking for a team of fire-eaters, leave them out. Not to everyone's taste, so check before you add chilli to any dish.

Dried whole chillies can be just as potent as fresh ones, but easier to prepare. Chilli powder is easiest of all. We use the mild stuff, as it's easier to control the heat that way.

Chocolate and Cocoa
Considered by some to be an essential food group. Dark chocolate isn't to everyone's taste, but weight for weight it's more chocolatey, so you use less in recipes, and in theory you need less to sate that craving. If you're eating it for raw energy, however, milk chocolate bars contain more sugar and fat.

Store chocolate wrapped in plastic to prevent leaks. Cocoa powder is the lightest way to carry chocolate, good for drinks, sauces and cakes, but somehow never quite as satisfying as the real thing.

Coconut
Desiccated Useful for curries and cakes, it weighs very little and keeps well.

Cream A vital ingredient in Thai-style curries, coconut cream adds delicious sweet richness. You can buy it tinned, in cartons, or in boxes containing one or two sachets. Sachets are easiest to transport, and more useful if there are just one or two of you.

Cream Powder Asian supermarkets sell powdered coconut cream, which just needs making up with water.

Condensed Milk
Not to be confused with evaporated milk, which is much runnier and not nearly as sweet. Don't buy it in a tin unless you're planning on using the whole lot – larger supermarkets stock it in useful re-sealable tubes. We use it in lots of our puddings and as a topping for things like oatcakes.

Coffee
An essential for some. If you're happy with instant, your life is easy, but even if you prefer fresh, the added hassle is fairly minimal (see camp coffee, p278), and

nonexistent if you use coffee bags, though these are expensive. Either way, it's vital to keep your coffee dry. Mini ziplock bags or little screwtop Nalgene jars are ideal containers. (If you stay in hotels or bed and breakfasts, or go to a lot of meetings, you can often acquire single-serve sachets of instant coffee from the courtesy trolley.)

Cooked Meats

Boiled ham, cold roast beef or chicken will keep longer than fresh, raw meat but not much. Make sure you keep cooked meat carefully wrapped, away from any raw meat. Keep it as cool as you can and eat within two days, less in warm weather.

Corn

Corn on the Cob Very nice for a campfire cookout, and pretty robust in transportation too, but a large part of the weight is inedible core. Cob cores take forever to decay, so they scarcely qualify as biodegradable waste – they have to be burned or carried back out.

Sweetcorn Delicious enough to eat cold straight from the tin, but equally good in salads or heated as a side vegetable, or added to stews, curries, pasta dishes, etc.

Popping Corn One of the best camp snacks, freshly popped corn is warm and moreish, low in fat, high in carbs. The kernels are cheap, and easy to transport and cook.

Cornflour

Cornflour is used mostly as a thickening ingredient in sauces and stews. It tastes of nothing much on its own, but can turn plain stock into gravy, or watery stew into a much heartier experience. Not to be confused with cornmeal.

EXPLOSIVE POWDERS

Loose powders such as flour and milk powder can be explosive, so be careful with them around naked flames.

Cornmeal (Polenta)

Another easily carried starchy food, cornmeal is a staple in parts of Asia and Central America, and the Italians cook it as polenta. You'll find it in the foreign foods aisle of the supermarket. Don't confuse it with cornflour (which the Americans call cornstarch) – cornflour is white, cornmeal is yellow.

Courgettes

Courgettes (or zucchini) are very useful for bulking out meals. Quick and easy to cook, they readily absorb other flavours, and when baked, sautéed or scorched they have a sweetness of their own. They're relatively easy to carry slid down the side of a rucksack, but try not to squash or bruise them or they'll start to rot. They go soft after a day or two exposed to the air, so keep them wrapped in plastic. Home-made storage boxes made from recycled plastic squash or fabric conditioner bottles are ideal for transporting courgettes (see *Recycled Packaging*, Chapter 6).

Couscous

A bad experience with couscous can put people off trying it again for a very long time, which is a shame. The thing about couscous is that it needs a bit of precision and practice to get right. It's much better in a pan where you can stir it properly than in a bag where it tends to clump in the corners. Done well, it can be brilliant, and weight for weight is about the most nutritious food you can get. This makes it very popular with mountain marathoners and adventure racers, and we use it a lot when we're travelling really light.

Crackers

Crisprolls, those little three-inch torpedo things dried to concrete hardness, are virtually indestructible, but delicious with cheese or pâté. They come in bags rather than rolls or stacks, so they take up more room than other types of crackers. Oatcakes, Ryvita, Dr Kargs flatbreads, and the 'biscuits brown' from army ration packs are also very robust. A roll of crackers is fairly resilient as long as the contents stay neatly stacked. A length of Scotch tape (the stuff that looks opaque, then disappears when you press it down) stuck on the pack before you leave can be used repeatedly to stick down the folded top.

Custard Powder

We use the instant stuff a lot – for breakfast, as dessert, or just a sweet, warming snack. Some people make it weak and drink it! You can buy it in portioned sachets, but it's cheaper to buy a tub or jarful and bag it yourself. Don't confuse it with ordinary custard powder, which is made up with milk and sugar and takes much longer to cook.

Cured Meats

Bacon One of the good things in life! Bacon is cured by smoking or salting and will keep two or three days unrefrigerated, ideally in a hanging larder or cool bag. Lean

bacon keeps better than streaky. For convenience we often buy lardons or pancetta –
chopped bacon bits. You can get them in
most decent supermarkets or ask a butcher to
chop them for you. Pre-chopping means you
have to handle the meat less in camp, which
makes good hygiene sense. Be very careful to
keep cooked meat apart from raw, and wash
utensils and boards used for raw meat before
allowing them to touch anything cooked.

Sausages German salami, Spanish chorizo
and Italian pepperoni were all invented as a
means of making meat last before the days of
refrigeration. As such they are an absolutely perfect camp food. For the purposes of
packing you're much better off with a whole sausage than with slices. Wrap the
whole thing in plastic or greaseproof paper and slice off just what you need each
day.

Prosciutto Also known as Parma ham, prosciutto is expensive, but a little goes a long
way and it keeps and travels well. It's best bought from a deli where the packaging is
minimal.

See also Tinned Meat, Fresh Meat, Dried Meat.

Dried Fruit

As well as making a good snack, dried fruits can be used in cooking. If you want to
use them as a substitute for fresh fruit you need to soak them first, ideally for several
hours or overnight. Then they can be added where a recipe calls for fruit, or just
stewed up to make a fruit compote or sauce. Most fruits dry well in a home dehydrator (see Dehydrating at Home, below), and if used soon afterwards they retain an
amazing amount of flavour.

See also Apples, Bananas, Berries, Sultanas and Raisins.

> Dried fruit is concentrated stuff. Remember that each scrummy bite-sized
> apricot piece is equivalent to a whole fruit. This is great for avoiding constipation,
> but eat too much and you'll know about it.

Dried Meat

Dried meat in the form of beef jerky or biltong is a popular trekking snack, especially in other parts of the world. It's taken a while to catch on in the UK, but you can now buy it in most big supermarkets and some outdoor shops. If you have a home dehydrator (see Dehydrating at Home, below) you can make your own jerky by drying marinated strips of beef.

Dried Vegetables

Most supermarkets sell dried onions, mushrooms and tomatoes, and some also sell dried peppers (capsicums). We use all of these a lot. Many also stock dried peas, but these require overnight soaking and long boiling so they're not camp friendly. Other dried vegetables can take a bit more searching out (try health food shops). If you invest in a dehydrator (see Dehydrating at Home, below) there's really no limit to your vegetable options. As with fruit, larger vegetables like carrot chunks and beans need soaking before you cook them. Small flakes of onion and pepper can be pretty much used from the pack.

See also Onions, Mushrooms, Peppers, Tomatoes.

Eggs

Carrying fresh eggs isn't quite the hassle it sounds. Carry them in their cardboard egg box (cut to size if you're not taking all six), with a bit of extra tissue paper to wedge them, then put the egg box in a rigid tub and pack it round with newspaper balls to stop it rattling about. Old-fashioned powdered egg seems to be a thing of the past in mainstream retail, largely because of concerns over *Salmonella*, which grows well in powdered egg given half a chance. To buy it you need to go directly to a specialist supplier – we use www.expeditionfoods.com. They sell the powder in packs equivalent to 20 eggs. The safest way to store this if you're not planning on using it all at once is to divide it up into one- or two-egg portions, seal them in little ziplock plastic bags (left) and put them in the freezer.

Energy Bars

Energy bars are an easy and convenient way to eat on the go, and lots of walkers, runners and bikers take them in preference to a packed lunch. There's a wide variety of specially formulated energy bars on the market, most of which are high in carbs and very low in fat, but unfortunately they're also expensive and make pretty dull eating. They also tend to be rather dense and hard to chew (especially in cold weather).

We normally carry a couple as emergency rations, because to us they're unappetizing enough not to provide temptation! For bars we actually intend to eat, we make our own flapjacks, bread pudding or fruit slice (see *Baked Sweets*, p272) or turn to mainstream cereal bars. The downside with most of these is a higher fat content, so check the nutritional info on the packs to see what you're actually getting. We especially like Jordan's Luxury bars, whose delicious natural fruit and nut flavours are much more enjoyable than any sports bar we've ever tried. We also like Cadbury's Brunch bars – just chocolatey enough to hit the spot without being too rich.

Energy Gels

For a quick boost late in a long day, gels are very convenient, but if you're considering using them in a race or event, try them first in training. Some people find them almost impossibly difficult to get down, and others claim gels just make them feel sick. The trick is to make sure you take in a little at a time – a small blob of gel followed by a mouthful of water. Don't try to take them neat, or to swallow the whole sachet in one go!

Gels come in a variety of brands and flavours. Some manufacturers make caffeinated gels – used sensibly, these are rocket fuel. The caffeine hit is actually quite small, no more than a cup of tea, but the effect on flagging muscles can be quite dramatic, if temporary. We wouldn't recommend using more than a couple of gels in a day.

Falafel Mix

Dry falafel mix is a really useful base for burgers, nut roasts and the like. It contains ground fava beans and chickpeas, flavouring and seasoning, and usually just needs cold water. The instructions usually recommend deep frying, but we find it's perfectly good shallow fried or baked, and served with a sauce or moist accompaniment such as salad or baked beans.

Fish

Fish cooks quickly and easily, and oily species in particular are extraordinarily good for you. Some recent reports suggested that farmed fish, in particular Scottish salmon, contain 'high' levels of toxins such as PCBs and dioxins. The reports advised consumers that North American salmon was safer (coincidentally, the reports were American!). The official line of the UK Foods Standards Agency is that Scottish salmon is perfectly safe to eat regularly. Any small risk is more than offset by the other benefits of eating oily fish.

Fresh It's great to be able to take advantage of fresh local fish on a camping trip, but unless you have access to a fridge its essential to eat on the day of purchase/catching.

Tinned Brilliant – a fabulous source of protein and good fats, really tasty too. The fish can be eaten cold, straight from the tin if need be. Fish tins are smaller than most and the flat rectangular ones are very easy to pack. Most have ring-pulls or an integral key for twisting off the lid – so no can opener is required but the sharp edges of opened tins are often responsible for severe cuts, so be careful. One small tin of mackerel, salmon, tuna or sardines will impart ample flavour to a pasta or rice meal for two people. Look for varieties packed in interesting sauces.

Smoked Delicious smoked fish such as kippers, salmon or haddock will keep a day in your pack. They can be eaten with no further preparation, or used to impart flavour to other dishes. A little can go a long way.

Pouches You can buy tuna in foil or plastic pouches, which look a bit like cat food, but make a very convenient alternative to tins.

Flour (Wheat)
An essential ingredient in bread, cakes and pancakes, flour is also used in various sauces. We tend to use self-raising flour for everything, as you can use it in recipes that call for plain flour, but not the other way round. It's important to keep flour dry – we normally pack it in a wide-necked plastic jar or a ziplock bag.

Fresh Meat
Eat on the day of purchase unless you have proper refrigeration facilities. If you buy meat from a butcher, ask for it to be cut the way you want it and save yourself a bit of time and effort.

Garlic
Fresh garlic keeps well in a pack, but the smell may contaminate other food and kit, so wrap it carefully.

Granules, purée or powder are easier to manage – just keep them dry. We use granules, carried in a tiny Nalgene bottle. These do lose their flavour over time, so try and use them within the best-before date on the original pack. Garlic has a host of supposed health benefits (and in large quantities it's reputed to deter midges, mozzies and vampires, which is always good to know).

Gels
See Energy Gels.

Ginger
Fresh root ginger travels well in a pack for a week or two, and adds an authentic tang to noodle dishes and curries. Dry crystallised ginger gives scroggan mixes a bit of pep. Ground ginger is delicious in curries and sponge cakes.

Gravy Powder
A useful ingredient for stews, curries, chillies and savoury sauces, adding flavour and thickening, pots of easily dissolved granules are available in beef, chicken and vegetable flavours from most supermarkets.

Herbs
Fresh herbs are wonderful, but not backpack friendly, so for all but car camping we're usually talking dried herbs. Freeze-dried varieties usually have the best flavour – look for the jars with very green-looking contents. Flavouring your food with herbs will mean you use less salt, something most of us eat too much of.

Instant Soup
A few sachets of instant soup go on almost all of our trips. They're good for a warming drink or to whet the appetite while waiting for a main meal, but they're also a brilliant corner-cutting ingredient in lots of camp recipes. We often use them as a base for improvised sauces or to season and flavour more substantial dishes.

Jerky
See Dried Meats.

Kumara
See Sweet Potato.

Leeks
Leeks bring a wonderful mild onion flavour, with a bit of green leafiness besides. They're also pretty robust – they slip easily into the sides of a rucksack and don't suffer too badly from bruising, even if you bash them around a little bit. Chop off and discard the rough dark-green stuff from the top before you leave home. Leeks keep unrefrigerated for several days.

Lentils
An excellent source of protein and carbohydrate, nutritionally lentils are pretty much a meal in themselves, though they need some accompaniment to make them interesting. For camp meals, make sure you buy the quick-cooking variety – red lentils and Puy lentils boil in 20–30 minutes, which is fine, but green and yellow varieties need soaking overnight, as well as long boiling, so give them a miss.

Maltloaf
Yes, it's squashy, it keeps well and, regardless of what shape it emerges from your pack, it'll taste good. Packed with fruit and carbs, its great trekking food in any season.

Margarine
See Butter, Margarines and Spreads.

Milk
Fresh We use skimmed milk at home, so if we're taking fresh milk on a trip, this is what we normally carry. It has the added advantage that it keeps much better unrefrigerated than the full-fat stuff. It's good in tea and coffee, porridge and cereals, pancakes and the like but you can't make butter with it and some creamy dishes such as rice pudding are nicer with full-fat milk.

Long-life Ultra-heat-treated (UHT) milk is convenient if you're not going to be in range of a fresh milk supplier. Cartons are easy to transport, especially in the car, and if you don't use them they'll keep until next time. The disadvantage of course is that once open, they can't be resealed. We usually take a mixture of fresh and long-life milk. A one-pint plastic bottle of fresh does the first one or two nights, then when it's gone, we wash the bottle and use it to store the long-life once that's been opened. Again, with long-life it's better to use the skimmed stuff – the taste is almost indistinguishable from fresh skimmed milk (the fat in UHT semi-skimmed and full-fat milk makes them taste odd).

Powder Powdered milk is one of the basics that goes on virtually every trip. We use it in hot drinks, porridge, pancakes and other milky recipes. You can buy full-fat or skimmed – we usually use the former. In dried form the fat doesn't have much of an effect on the longevity of the product and adds richness to recipes. If you're making up milk from powder, it's better to add powder to water rather than the other way around, and if you can leave it to stand for a few minutes before using, it will taste a bit better. On its own it's never going to taste as good as the real thing, but you can make a very passable milkshake by adding powdered flavouring such as Nesquik.

Mushrooms

Fresh mushrooms are a bit of a luxury if you're backpacking, but they add substance and flavour to a variety of dishes. Dried mushrooms aren't so great on the substance front, but flavour wise they're superb – in many cases at least as good as the fresh version, if not better. (You can buy tinned mushrooms, but we've never bothered with them.) If you're picking your own (see Chapter 8), make sure your identification skills are up to the job, or it might be the last meal you ever cook.

Noodles

Noodles are a great quick-cooking alternative to conventional pasta or rice. You can buy them made of wheat or rice (egg noodles are wheat-based).

Nutmeg

As unappetising as a small kernel of nutmeg looks, there is magic inside that can bring porridge, rice pudding, custard, crumble and mashed potato to life. Our tiny grater came free with a jar of kernels in France. Keep nutmeg dry by wrapping it in cling film.

Nuts

Packed with protein, carbs and fat, nuts punch well above their weight in nutritional terms. Nuts of all kinds are great for snacking, and make an interesting addition to many sweet and savoury recipes. For some reason, nuts (especially peanuts) are one of the foods most likely to cause the severe allergic reaction known as anaphylaxis (see Allergies, Intolerances and Aversions in Chapter 2). If one of your party is allergic to nuts, the whole team should avoid them for the duration of the trip (the nuts, not the person).

Oats

Oats are superb camp food – lightweight, compact, versatile, and packing a moderately low GI carb punch that will keep your engines revving for hours. Have them as porridge, oatcakes or crumble for breakfast, or in flapjacks as a snack on the go (see p274). Use them to thicken, bulk out or add starch to a variety of meaty dishes, and in crumble for dessert. We use oat bran in some recipes, but it's rolled oats that get taken on virtually every trip we make.

There are plenty of branded varieties of quick-cook porridge oats that come pre-sweetened or flavoured in single-serve sachets. They're convenient, but expensive for what you get, and most people we know will eat two or even three servings for a decent breakfast. Much better and cheaper is to buy a big bag of unbranded rolled or porridge oats, which you can mix up with sugar and milk powder for your own 'just add water' version. Check the cook times on the pack – ideally you want something that cooks in less than five minutes.

Oils

Oils are fats that are liquid at room temperature. They are extremely useful, but inherently rather messy and difficult to carry. For us the solution is a small, sturdy, screwtop bottle – most camp shops sell these pretty cheaply. If you're going to keep oil in a bottle for a long time (for example between trips), keep it in a dark cupboard to prevent deterioration. Oils do not need refrigeration. Sunflower oil is a good general-purpose cooking oil. It has no strong flavour of its own, so it's just as good in sweet or savoury dishes. Olive oil is healthier, and delicious in its own right for dipping bread or dressing salad, but it's not as good for recipes where you need really hot oil (such as popcorn or stir-fries), and its strong flavour can spoil delicately sweet things such as pancakes or sponge cakes.

Onion

Fresh onions keep well, but they're heavy. Dried ones (right) make life really easy – a long shelf-life, no chopping (hence no onion tears) and the flavour is excellent. Spring onions (scallions) are good for providing a bit of colour and fresh flavour, but will only keep a couple of days.

Oranges, Satsumas, Clementines

Oranges make a lovely refreshing snack, but they can be messy to peel – a penknife helps. Satsumas have looser skins and are thus easier to manage. All citruses are relatively robust and keep well, but their skins take years to degrade. You can burn them if you have a campfire, but otherwise you need to treat them like other non-biodegradable rubbish and carry them out.

Pasta

A perennial favourite of campers because it's relatively lightweight and many varieties travel well. In the backpacking context, some shapes are better than others. Bows (farfalle), straight tubes (penne) and twists (fusilli) are all pretty robust. Spaghetti, linguine, tagliatelle or lasagne sheets are all well and good for car camping, but a bit fragile for backpacking. Shells (conchiglie) are annoying because they collect water and don't drain properly. Any other speciality shapes are usually more expensive, so not really worth bothering with. Fresh pasta, especially the stuffed varieties such as ravioli or tortellini, is great if weight isn't an issue – really quick and easy to cook.

When cooking pasta, use a large pan at least half (preferably two-thirds) full with water. If you can't fit in the amount of pasta you want to cook along with this much water, the pan is too small. A large pinch of salt and a spoonful of oil added to the water beforehand will give the pasta a better flavour and stop it sticking together. Bring the water to a fast boil before adding the pasta, and then *keep it boiling*. Dry pasta expands to twice its size when cooked. Realising too late you don't have enough water and adding more cold is a cardinal sin, resulting in soggy clods of pasta stuck to the bottom of the pan.

Pepper

We always have a few sachets of ground pepper in our rations. When car camping we take a grinder – freshly milled pepper has a far better kick, but it's a luxury we wouldn't bother with when backpacking. If you really want a gourmet experience from a light pack, you could grind fresh pepper into a twist of paper or cling film before leaving home, or carry peppercorns and crush them between two spoons or clean pebbles.

Peppers (Capsicums)

When going lightweight, we often use mixed dried peppers (left) – they're very cheap, weigh next to nothing, hydrate quickly and have a good flavour. Camping from the car, we use fresh peppers, stored in a plastic bag. Red peppers are riper and thus sweeter than green ones (orange and yellow are different varieties of intermediate sweetness).

Pesto

A ready-made sauce for pasta, shop-bought pesto is usually made of pulverised basil, pine nuts and olive oil. For camping, the stuff sold in tubes is much better than that in jars, but it can take some tracking down. For some reason, in supermarkets it is often shelved alongside the tubes of tomato purée, rather than next to the pesto jars.

Pine Nuts

We use pine nuts in most pasta and couscous dishes, and in moreish seeds (see p196). They're highly nutritious and absolutely delicious when lightly scorched in a dry pan.

Polenta
See Cornmeal.

Popcorn
See Corn.

Porridge
See Oats.

Potatoes
Fresh Potatoes were first cultivated by the Incas about 5000 years ago. The starchy tubers were prized not only because they are highly nutritious, but also because they keep well and are easy to transport – they could be slung in a basket or sack and carried for weeks. There's no reason you shouldn't do the same. Try and keep them near the top of your pack though, and in hot weather they're better off in a cloth bag than a plastic one.

Dried Purists turn away now… the next bit is about the marvels of instant mash – we think it's fabulous stuff. Not only can it make a perfectly acceptable alternative to fresh potatoes, it can also be used as a versatile general ingredient for thickening stews and soups, or just giving other thin, sloppy, one-pot meals a bit more 'oomph'. (In fact dried potato isn't a newfangled invention at all. Those ancient Peruvians used to make their own version, called *chunu*, which was prepared by repeated freezing at night and pulverisation underfoot during the day.)

The recipe for Smash, probably the best-known brand, was recently changed from granules to flakes. Powders and flakes are more versatile and easier to mix than granules, and they take up less pack space. For lump-free results, add the flakes to the hot water rather than the other way around.

You can add any seasoning to instant potato, or flavour it with dried parmesan, Marmite, dried onion or garlic salt, or mix in an instant soup powder for one of the fastest possible camp meals. Soupy 'Smash' hash (see p248) is two minutes quicker than instant noodles. Used perfectly plain, instant mash makes a really good stomach-settling recovery food if you've had a bout of illness and can't face anything more flavoursome.

Gnocchi Gnocchi are potato dumplings. Shop-bought ones are very quick and easy to cook, and they are good simply buttered and seasoned as a side dish or starter. You can use them as a substitute for new potatoes in the jumble recipes (see p237) or if you have a bit more time you can make you own (see p205).

Raisins and Sultanas

A raisin is a dried grape; a sultana is a variety of raisin. The average raisin contains about 60% sugar, making it a great source of energy. Raisins are perfect for snacking on the go, or for adding sweetness to porridge, puddings and savoury dishes (especially curries and couscous). Add them to cakes, for a bit of gooey moistness.

Rice

Human beings have been cultivating rice for over 9000 years, and rice remains the world's most widely eaten cereal. The variety of rice available on an average supermarket shelf can be overwhelming, so here's a very quick guide.

American/Long Grain Slightly fatter than basmati and less fragrant, but probably the best general-purpose rice. You can buy white and brown and easy-cook versions. Cook time: c. 11–15 minutes for polished white; c. 25–30 minutes for brown; c. 9–14 minutes for easy cook.

Arborio/Italian A medium-grain rice, perfect for risottos because it soaks up lots of flavour. Cook time: c. 20–25 minutes

Basmati Long, skinny-grained and fragrant Indian rice. Often sold pre-flavoured as pilau rice. Cook time: c. 9–12 minutes.

Boil-in-the-bag This comes into its own in camp – no need to perform that awkward juggle with a pan lid to drain it, although you don't get much control of portion size. Boil-in-the-bag rice is usually a long-grain variety. Cook time: c. 8–12 minutes.

Long grain, arborio and easy-cook basmati rice

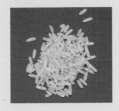

Brown, ground and wild rice

Brown Has had its outer husk removed, but the thin inner husk, called the bran, is left on. This makes it much the healthiest rice, but it takes a long time to cook. Cook time: c. 25–30 minutes.

Easy-cook Several varieties come as easy/quick-cook versions. These have been parboiled (boiled very briefly) before removing the bran, which allows the grains to soak up some of the goodness from the bran. It also removes the starchiness from the outside of the grains, so they don't stick together. Cook time: c. 11–15 minutes.

Flaked The grains are squashed flat (like little white cornflakes) to speed cooking while retaining some texture. Ideal for rice pudding. Cook time: c. 6 minutes.

Ground Great as a quick-cook rice pudding or a thickener. Cook time: c. 5 minutes.

Instant Pre-cooked and sold in sachets for the ultimate in convenience. Sometimes it's worth the extra weight and expense for simple ease and fuel efficiency, but relatively speaking pre-cooked rice is very expensive and there's no need to use it routinely. Cook time: 2 minutes.

Jasmine/Thai A long-grained variety used extensively in Thai cooking. Lightly fragrant, very sticky, and delicious with sweet, creamy curries. Cook time: c. 10–12 minutes.

Pudding Rice Short fat grains that swell and partially disintegrate when cooked. Cook time: c. 40–45 minutes.

White The outer husk is removed and the bran layer has been polished off. Cook time: c. 11–20 minutes.

Wild Not actually rice at all, but a kind of aquatic grass. The long, thin, brownish-black grains are tasty mixed sparingly with regular rice, but you wouldn't want to eat them on their own. Cook time: c. 45 minutes. (Partially pre-cooked varieties are included in some mixed-rice packs.)

Packs of flavoured rice make a quick and easy meal. If you read the ingredients you'll see it's pretty easy to mimic and improve on them yourself without using various artificial flavourings or preservatives. However, it's difficult to do so more cheaply unless you're making large quantities.

For most camp meals, an easy-cook long-grain rice is the easiest option. It's worth getting Arborio for a decent risotto, though not essential. Flaked or ground rice is the best choice for quick and easy puddings. Rice can be boiled, but much more efficient is the absorption method. Add the grains to three times their volume of boiling water, then cover and set to one side for anything from five to 20 minutes. Some rice will cook fully like this, other varieties will need simmering for a few minutes at the end.

Salt

Salt is an essential component of a healthy diet, but because it's also used to enhance flavour, most of us eat too much of it. Under conditions where you're sweating a lot, a little extra salt can be beneficial. Use sparingly in cooking. Carry in small sachets, a small plastic bottle or in a miniature shaker, and keep dry.

Sesame Seeds (and Tahini)

Sesame seeds are light and take up very little room, so they're an efficient way of adding interest to a noodle dish or stir fry. They're rich in protein and unsaturated fats, including essential fatty acids, and they're also a good source of vitamins and minerals. Tahini is sesame paste. It keeps well and makes a good substitute for butter or margarine. The nutrients in sesame seeds are more easily absorbed in this form.

Soya Mince (TVP)

Soya mince (or textured vegetable protein) doesn't have a great reputation in gastronomic circles – after all it was invented as a meat substitute, yet has none of the flavour of meat and none of the fat that gives meat its richness and succulence. On its own, soya mince tastes pretty grim. But it's a great alternative source of protein, it's very cheap, it weighs practically nothing and keeps for months, and it will take on the flavour of pretty much anything you add to it. So as a lightweight backpacking food, it's brilliant. As you'll see from our recipes for lightweight chilli and spaghetti bolognese, it's all about adding strong flavours. You can also buy big bags of plain soya mince incredibly cheaply in the Asian food section of large supermarkets. You can buy ready-flavoured versions, such as Beanfeast, at several times the cost.

Spices

A pinch of mixed ground spice adds interest to sweet and savoury stews, cakes and porridge. Cloves and cinnamon are really good with stewed apples, and essential in mulled wine! We make a mild but delicious curry powder from a blend of ground coriander, ground cumin, garam masala, ground turmeric and hot chilli powder, in a ratio of approximately 2:2:2:1:1.

Another favourite blend is Moroccan *ras-en-hanout*. We couldn't tell you everything that's in it, but apparently it has a nickname that translates as 'bad housewife spice', or something like that, because it turns anyone into a great cook! It's only slightly hot.

See also Chilli, Ginger, Nutmeg.

Stock Cubes

Another staple of the camp basics box, we usually keep a selection of beef, chicken and vegetable stock cubes, and use them in many of our stews, soups and savoury saucy dishes.

Suet

Depending on the recipe, suet can make a reasonable alternative to oil or fat for cooking. This is probably the easiest form of fat to pack and carry, since it comes in the form of dry granules. Some people use melted suet for frying, but it does leave a rather unpleasant greasy residue on the lips and tongue. That said, it's a good addition to stews and sauces, where it adds a bit of richness and boosts the calorie count. And of course it's an essential ingredient in dumplings. We use the vegetable version.

Sugar

A basic ingredient in many recipes, sugar adds sweetness and calorific content. We usually carry sugar in a small screwtop plastic bottle or jar. Most baking recipes call for caster sugar, but regular granulated works almost as well (it doesn't dissolve quite as quickly, but the taste is the same). Brown sugar is better in porridge, but it's not really worth carrying two different varieties.

Sunflower Seeds

A nice lightweight snack food, especially when the sugary, high-carb stuff starts to pall. Sunflower seeds are good in sweet and savoury recipes, adding texture and flavour, especially if scorched for about a minute in a hot, dry pan.

Sweetcorn

See Corn.

Sweet Potato

Sweet potatoes (also known as kumara) are bulbous root vegetables that store and travel well wrapped in a piece of cloth. They cook more quickly than regular potatoes and taste wonderful. Good as mash, or in soups and risottos, they also bake well in the embers of a campfire.

Tea

We're both big tea drinkers, so it's just as well tea is about as convenient a hot drink as you can get. Going ultra-lightweight, we usually drink it black, or switch to herbal or fruit teas to save the need for milk. Keep teabags dry – they rot quickly if damp. A small ziplock bag is ideal for storing them in camp. (You *can* get instant tea powder – it's OK if you're desperate!)

Tinned/Potted Meat

Tinned meats such as ham, corned beef and spam are a convenient source of long-life protein. The cheaper varieties are made from the bits of animals you wouldn't normally eat, but they're pretty tasty, if rather salty, and they last years in storage. Heating a tin of mince, stew, casserole or curry is as easy as camp cooking gets –

and in terms of the quality of the meat, you tend to get what you pay for. Some premium varieties are really rather good. You can bulk these tins out by mixing in extra tins of vegetables. Meat pastes and some pâtés can be bought in tins or small jars.

Tinned Vegetables
With the possible exception of sweetcorn, tinned vegetables are never as tasty or nutritious as fresh, but they are convenient, especially if you're cooking out of a vehicle. They're also a good way of getting certain vegetables out of season.

Tomatoes
Fresh tomatoes are really the preserve of car camping and picnics – small ones are a bit easier to carry in a recycled box (see *Recycled Packaging*, Chapter 6), but don't expect ripe ones to last more than a day or two in your backpack. For most recipes, tinned or sundried tomatoes are more than adequate. We buy chopped tinned tomatoes for convenience, sometimes with herbs and garlic already mixed in – these are just a few easy steps from a basic pasta sauce. Sundried tomatoes have a much stronger flavour, and their leathery texture adds an almost meaty bite to pasta or couscous dishes. In the absence of any of these, a tube of purée goes a long way.

Tuna
See Fish.

Vegetable Oil
See Oils.

Zucchini
See Courgettes.

LONG-LIFE FOODS

Long-life foods come in two states – wet and dry. Which will best suit your needs depends on various factors, including the nature of your trip (car camping or backpacking), your budget, your fuel allowance, the likely weather conditions and your personal likes and dislikes.

Wet Rations

Wet rations, often referred to as MREs (meals ready to eat) are regularly used by armies because they can be eaten straight from the pack, cold if need be. Their main drawback is weight – **a 24-hour ration pack as used by the British Army weighs about 2kg**. This is acceptable for a combat-fit individual, but probably more than the average backpacker will want to lug around. However, supplementing lightweight foods with the odd tin or pouch of meat or fish can be the making of a really great meal, and you only have to carry the empty pack home.

Another advantage of wet rations is that they take less cooking, and as **less cooking means less fuel**, you will make weight savings there. In adverse weather conditions, carrying a little extra weight so that you can quickly heat wet rations, such as pre-cooked rice and tinned meat, is preferable to sitting in the rain for half an hour or more trying to coax dehydrated ingredients into life. Most long-life 'wet' foods are tinned, others come in cartons, tubes and plastic or foil pouches.

ARMY RAT PACKS

It's possible to buy 24-hour ration packs identical to those used by the British Army. These come in a small cardboard box weighing about 2kg, and contain three full meals for one person, plus an array of snacks and sweets, and the makings of several hot and cold drinks. The meals are fully hydrated and vacuum-sealed in foil pouches, so they only need warming through. All those we've tried have been pretty tasty. They come in several varieties for hot and cold climates, and include vegetarian and religious variants (halal and kosher), though these aren't as easy to get hold of as regular varieties.

Dehydrated Foods

Dehydrated (dried) foods have two enormous advantages for camping – they have increased **longevity** and are **very light**. The downside is a small deterioration in nutritional value, but it really is very slight, and provided a healthy balance of carbs, proteins, fats, vitamins and minerals is maintained, you can live very well on dried foods.

Commercially, foods are dehydrated in a variety of ways. Sun-drying is used for tomatoes and fruit leathers (strips of dried fruit now widely available in health food and outdoor shops), while herbs and chillies might be air dried out of direct sunlight to preserve their colour. Wetter foods may be oven-dried, freeze-dried or spray-dried. **Oven-drying** happens over several hours at temperatures under 80°C. In **freeze-drying**, frozen foods are thawed quickly in a vacuum so that the moisture content 'sublimates' – in other words it turns from ice directly into vapour. Freeze-dried products are usually easier to hydrate than air-dried foods because they keep an open, porous structure that water can seep into much more quickly. **Spray-drying** is usually used for liquids like milk or soup, which are converted into a fine mist that is exposed to a current of warm, dry air. The moisture evaporates and the solids remain as fine powder.

Dehydrating at Home

You can dehydrate your own foods at home using the oven or a purpose-built **domestic dehydrator**. These gadgets take up about the same space as a bread-maker. They comprise a stack of trays that sit over an electric heating unit and a fan. They cost between £60 and £200 to buy and are economical to run. You can use them to dry your own fruit and vegetables, or to dry cooked foods like stews, mince or sauces. To be honest, where foods are commercially available ready dried, as with onions, mushrooms, apricots and sultanas, it's not worth the hassle, but for more unusual vegetables, fruit and good old home cooking, a dehydrator has the potential to completely transform your camp diet.

Fruit and vegetables dried at home retain more flavour than shop-bought varieties, but for best results use them as soon as possible.

If you don't want to invest in a dehydrator, you can dry food using a conventional oven. Fan ovens are much more effective for this. You need to set the temperature as low as it will go, and wedge the door open just a crack. Drying time varies with food type, but is usually between four and 10 hours. The larger the individual pieces of food, the longer they take to dry, and the longer they take to rehydrate, so the smaller or thinner you make the chunks or slices, the more efficient both processes will be. Fatty meats are not suitable for dehydrating. Once completely dry, foods

Cooked in the convenience of a proper kitchen and dried in a cool oven, this spaghetti bolognese will require two to three hours soaking before being reheated for a taste of home cooking in camp.

should be sealed in airtight containers or bags, with as little air as possible, and labelled and frozen until you are ready to use them.

Some dehydrated foods can be eaten in their dry state, as with dried fruit, while others need reconstituting before they can be used. Often the cooking process is sufficient to restore foods, but in some cases you'll also need to pre-soak your dried ingredients. As a general rule, the longer you can soak for, the better – ideally several hours in the case of meats and stews, but for something like home-dried cooked mince, for example, half an hour or so before heating will do.

> The thick sauces of dehydrated stews or casseroles don't reconstitute very well. To avoid watery meals, you need to add an additional thickening ingredient to the dried food. A spoonful of cornflower per serving does the trick.

We have nothing against commercial ready meals, and have used them on numerous occasions for lightweight camping. If you don't have time to prepare a home-made version, or to shop for fresh alternatives, they'll serve you well for a meal or two.

Most dry ready meals are packaged sensibly – no unnecessary cardboard or cellophane, just a foil pouch in which the meal is cooked as well as carried, with the instructions printed on the outside. Make sure you read these before you leave home. For most meals it's a simple case of adding hot water, sealing up the pouch for a few minutes and eating direct from the pack.

However, there are some that require additional preparation, for example frying using a sachet of granular hydrogenated vegetable fat or suet. If the idea of a super-lightweight breakfast fry-up in a bag sounds too good to be true, that's because it is. Lightweight camping and fried food are not compatible. To fry things properly you need proper oil or animal fat, and a decent sized, preferably non-stick pan (super-light aluminium or titanium pans aren't up to the job). Better to stick with more traditional dehydrated foods and promise yourself a proper fry-up when you get home.

In their favour, ready meals are very easy, you can buy them in camp shops, there's no washing up, and because they are prepared and packed in a sterile environment, they keep a very long time. On the down side, their texture and flavour isn't a patch on fresh food, the variety is limited and they are expensive, especially as most commercial brands, such as Wayfarer, Raven and Travellunch, produce relatively small meals containing 350–420kcal per 100g (about 440–530kcal per pouch) for a main meal. We're not particularly big eaters, but after a long day we usually need at least one-and-a-half of these. The special expedition meals made by Expedition Foods (www.expeditionfoods.com) are developed with serious energy provision in mind, and several contain in excess of 600kcal per 100g (800kcal per pouch).

CHAPTER 6
Packing, Storage and Transportation

Packing for camping expeditions is about protecting your rations from crushing, spilling, leaking, bruising, drying out, getting damp or dirty, or being eaten, damaged or contaminated by pests. It's also about protecting the rest of your kit from getting covered in food. This chapter deals with the business of getting your food to camp in good condition and storing it safely.

There's been a bit of a revolution in commercial packaging in recent years. Vast numbers of products are criminally over-packaged, but stricter industry regulations should soon begin to reduce this. Meanwhile, many more products are available in resealable bags or 'convenience' packs. Individual foodstuffs often come in more than one type of pack, and for camping, some are better then others. You can often save yourself mess and hassle by choosing the right one and avoiding the need to decant or repack. **Resealable packaging** is very useful. **Tins are better if long shelf life is your priority.** Look for purées and pesto in **tubes instead of jars**, and tuna and fruit pulp in **pouches rather than tins**. These are relatively light and easily resealed. They don't all have the recyclability of old-fashioned packaging, but check individual packs for advice.

SHOP BY WEIGHT

If you're shopping for a particular menu, it's useful to be able to buy exactly the amount you need, and avoid the hassle of splitting, decanting and repacking. Markets and delis are good for this, and large towns often have at least one shop that sells dry goods by weight – you serve yourself from big bins. Prices tend to be cheaper than supermarkets because you're not paying for packaging or branding and you only have to buy what you need.

MINIMISE PACKAGING

For backpacking and other expeditions, minimising the weight and waste that you'll have to carry out is an important consideration. Many products have excess packaging – for example, instant soup sachets in cardboard boxes, baked potatoes in plastic trays. Supermarkets are the worst offenders when it comes to fruit and vegetables. It's a good idea to strip products of this excess before you pack it. **Make sure you first note down any important cooking instructions** given on the part you're getting rid of.

Once you're actually on your camping trip, you can discard any packaging you don't need at the checkout when you pay for your shopping. In 2006 the then environment minister Ben Bradshaw actually advised the public to do just this in supermarkets to protest at excessive packaging. This might cause a few raised eyebrows, but if you explain your reasons for leaving the excess behind and ask shop staff to dispose of it responsibly, most will do so. Alternatively if there are recycling facilities nearby you can offload it there.

Bottles and Jars

The cooking section of most camp shops will stock a variety of **screwtop bottles and jars**. These are useful for cooking oils and washing-up liquid, fruit-squash concentrates, and for a wee dram of whisky or brandy, but check first that the lids are watertight. Cheap seals can be unreliable. We also use them for powdered or flaky ingredients that need to be kept dry, such as flour, milk powder, salt and herbs.

All food jars and bottles should be made of **food-safe plastic**, but it's still not a good idea to keep oil, alcohol or acidic liquids like vinegar in them too long between trips, as these are more likely to react with the polymer. Some claim to be dishwasher-proof, but the little ones tend to just get tossed around by the water jets and rarely come out properly clean. It's better just to wash them by hand with a small bottle brush. When backpacking it's wise to wrap bottles individually in plastic just in case they leak. The market leader in food-safe bottles and jars is Nalgene.

Fluids like wine can be decanted into plastic water bottles for a day with no real harm done. (Wine buffs, please forgive our Philistine habits.) Small glass bottles and jars, like those used for meat paste or Tabasco sauce, are fairly robust, but do require careful packing and wrapping.

Tubs and Lunchboxes

Tupperware-type boxes are robust, but quite heavy. The aluminium lunchboxes made by Sigg are the last word in outdoor bling – but with a hefty price tag to match. See *Recycled Packaging*, below, for the ultimate environmentally friendly alternative.

Tubes

Some camp stores sell reusable tubes that are filled from the bottom, which is then folded or rolled and clipped. They have a wide nozzle suitable for things like jam and cream cheese. It's easy to remove unused content and clean the tube at the end of the trip by unclipping the bottom. For some inexplicable reason, these are currently much easier to get hold of overseas than in the UK.

Cloth Bags

Cotton shopping bags are extremely useful. They fold up small and weigh very little. You can use them to wrap foods that like to 'breathe', such as potatoes, to store in camp (they hang easily), and of course for shopping if you don't want to take your pack to the shops, and don't need a bundle of plastic carrier bags. Remember to wash them from time to time.

DISPOSABLE PACKAGING

For short camping trips, especially if you are aiming to travel very light, it's convenient to be able to pack small quantities of ingredients in very light consumable packaging. This way you only carry what you need.

Cling Film

Cling film is extremely useful. It's very light, but difficult to carry in any form other than on the roll. Some films are chemically unsuitable for wrapping high-fat foods such as meat and cheese, so check the manufacturer's guidelines on the pack. Cling film should never be allowed to touch very hot food. A further drawback with cling film is that it doesn't degrade and can't be recycled, so try and use it sparingly and only where reusable alternatives are not an option. On the plus side you can use cling film in first aid to cover burns and scalds and thereby substantially reduce the risk of infection.

Plastic Bags

These come in a variety of sizes and styles, from **sandwich bags** with folding tops, **freezer bags** with tie handles or twist ties, plain tops or sticky tops, and the ingenious **ziplocks**. Squeeze out the air to help keep the contents fresh for longer. Reuse any plastic bag when possible.

ZIPLOCK BAGS

Ziplock bags are probably the single most useful form of consumable packaging. They are available in a huge range of sizes – the smallest are suitable for a weekend stash of herbs or condiments, while the largest might contain your entire food ration for a week-long trek in one neat, waterproof parcel. Medium to large ziplocks also make great map covers and water-storage bags. As with tie-top bags, try and squash as much air out of the bag as you can before you seal it. Supermarkets offer a rather limited range of these useful products, but you can find a great selection online – we use www.captainbags.com.

VACUUM PACKING

For longer trips and expeditions, a vacuum packer is a handy bit of kit, allowing you to seal dry foods such as pre-mixed porridge and dehydrated mince in meal-size packets that take up no more space than the food itself. The packer uses heat to weld the plastic of the special packs. We used a small vacuum packer borrowed from a local catering company to pack team meals for a two-week trekking holiday. Bought new, it would have cost about £200. You also need to budget for the special sealable bags.

LABELLING

Clear labelling of food packs is important, especially if someone other than you is going to be using the ingredients you've packed. Remember to note down any special cooking instructions too. You can write on bags with a spirit-based marker pen, but some of these tend to rub off. For dry ingredients such as milk powder and flour, a really foolproof alternative is to write on a scrap of paper in pencil and put it in the bag.

RECYCLED PACKAGING

Packing and storage can be achieved using all sorts of containers that might otherwise be thrown away. Reuse is much better for the environment than recycling, and in camp it doesn't matter what things look like as long as they work, so your camp box is the perfect place to give old packaging a new lease of life. These are some of the things we keep and reuse.

Items like these salvaged from the recycling bin can be reused for storing and transporting food.

Plastic bread bags are a good shape for carrying bread and sandwiches (obviously), but also for other bulkier food items or meal-packs. The long shape means they're easier to tie off than regular bags.

The little **plastic slit tags** sometimes used for closing bakery and fruit bags are useful because they are smaller and lighter than pegs or clips.

After seeing home-made **sandwich boxes made out of plastic milk bottles** by some outdoorsy friends in New Zealand, we copied their design to create a range of very lightweight boxes ideal for transporting sandwiches, vegetables, eggs, cakes and other crushable foods. Fruit juice cartons also make perfect sandwich boxes, providing you use a small loaf.

Plastic tubs of all shapes and sizes are useful for carrying loose, crushable foods such as tabouleh, rice and pasta salads. They can double up as bowls, but test them at home to make sure that they don't go floppy when you pour in anything hot.

The **plastic screwtop jars** used to sell some fruits are ideal for carrying pre-cooked home-made stews and salads.

Mini jam jars are pretty robust and make useful containers for things like butter or more jam, but make sure they're wrapped and packed carefully to reduce the risk of leaks and breakage.

If you dismantle a **cardboard wine box** carefully, the foil bag inside can make a great lightweight camp water-carrier, provided it has the right kind of tap or valve. This needs to come apart to allow refilling. Make sure you wash out the bag thoroughly first, and dry it by leaving it in a warm spot hanging on a stick or a bit of coat-hanger wire, as you would a hydration bladder.

Plastic soft-drinks and mineral water bottles usually have pretty good screwtops, and can make perfectly serviceable water bottles for a short hike. If you need to carry more, the bottles used for squashes and cordials are usually a bit more robust than those used for mineral water.

The **paper bags** you get from a traditional greengrocer are handy for wrapping firm fruit and vegetables.

You don't need us to tell you how to use **carrier bags** for packing. We always carry a few spare to use as rubbish bags, and on the overnight camps of mountain races you'll see most competitors wearing them between fresh socks and soggy shoes to keep their feet dry. (If you want to try this make sure you choose bags without holes.) Fold them neatly for transportation so they take up less space and don't get damaged.

Lighter than any purpose-bought lunch box, containers made from old milk bottles or juice cartons provide perfect protection for butties, cakes or delicate fruit and vegetables. To seal, slide one half inside the other.

PACKING FOOD IN YOUR RUCKSACK

Food is heavy. **Most backpacking guides advise you to pack heavy items near the top**, and we'd go along with this for large trekking packs. However, if you're travelling light, with a pack of 35l or less, for example, it's worth experimenting with different packing systems. Heavy items near the top can be a nuisance if you're running – **we tend to stow them in the middle**. Light packs have less padding, and it takes a bit of trial and error to work out what is comfy for you.

Wherever you pack it, it's much easier if everything you need for cooking is bundled together in one big packet, rather than shoved in at random. A **large ziplock bag** is ideal for keeping everything neat, secure and accessible. Keep your overnight food separate from the stuff you want to get at during the day, so you don't have to keep rummaging to find what you want. We usually pack snacks and lunches in the top and side pockets of our rucksacks rather than in the main compartment, so they can be reached at any time without stopping, let alone without major unpacking. Make sure liquid stove fuels are packed well away from food – the vapours of white gas, petrol and meths will taint food horribly.

STORING FOOD IN CAMP

When **car camping**, large stackable **plastic crates** (preferably with lids) make ideal larders for your non-perishable and semi-perishable ingredients. In all but very small one- or two-person tents there will normally be room for one of these in the porch, but don't overlook that great big metal storage box on wheels parked next to your tent. Keeping your food box in the car means your tent area is uncluttered, and packing up after each meal means you're more likely to keep things tidy and organised.

Rigid crates are clearly not an option for **backpacking**, so you need alternative means of keeping your larder in order. **Large ziplock or carrier bags** will keep the contents dry and clean, and keep most insect pests, such as ants, at bay, but they don't provide much protection from nibbling, gnawing or pecking by larger animals. If you are leaving food stored in camp when you go out for the day, you need to take a few extra precautions to ensure it's still there, unspoiled, when you get back. The best way to protect your food is by hanging it from a tree, preferably well away from the trunk. If there are no trees, a rocky overhang or large boulder will do – anything that will make it difficult for rats, mice, foxes and squirrels to get at your food.

If you have to leave things in your tent, make sure individual packets are sealed. Use pans and bowls to store packets of dry ingredients that might appeal to rodents. **Store rubbish in sealed, heavy-duty bags or tubs**, and don't leave it right outside the tent where it will attract animals. Clip bags together to prevent them being dragged away.

In places such as North America, where visits from wildlife can be a more serious threat, the precaution of a hanging larder well away from your tent site is a vital one. Official camp grounds in bear country often have large metal boxes for storing food. Use them.

Keeping Food Cool

Refrigeration is the best way to prolong the shelf life of a wide range of perishable foods. If you often camp out of the back of a vehicle, you might want to invest in a **portable fridge**. These run off the car battery, chilling food as you drive. They stop working actively when you turn off the ignition, but effective insulation means they keep food cool for hours even without power. We have used a car fridge extensively on summer trips to the Alps. When outside temperatures hover around 30°C, the fridge means we can keep milk, cheese, meat and salads fresh for several days and not have to shop daily.

A slightly cheaper option is a **cool box** with an integral fan, which also runs off the car battery. There's no active chiller unit, but moving air does keep the contents several degrees below ambient temperatures.

If you don't have any kind of power supply, a standard insulated cool box or bag works well in the short term. Larger campsites will usually freeze ice

packs for you – it's a good idea to label yours clearly with an indelible marker, so they don't get collected by someone else. If you take two sets, you can always have one set in use and one set chilling, and you can keep perishables reasonably cool around the clock. Before leaving home on a long journey, we often **freeze** plastic bottles of milk and blocks of cheese – with decent insulation these will keep other foods cool for at least 24 hours.

A basic cool bag will protect food from the worst ambient heat, but for active cooling you'll need to replace the ice blocks inside regularly.

> The insulation provided by cool boxes and bags is as effective at keeping food hot as keeping it cold. Use one to keep a dish warm enough for second helpings, or to transport your hot supper to a nearby scenic lookout (making sure pots are sealed inside).

You can make a **wet fridge** using a large drybag or a bucket. Just fill it with cool water, place your bottles or sealed food containers inside, seal it up and leave it in the shade. Replace the water once or twice a day.

Another alternative is an **evaporation cooler**. This uses less water and provides more active cooling, especially if there is a slight breeze. You'll need a shallow tray or pan, with an inch or two of water in the bottom. Put the items to be cooled in the water and drape them with a cloth (a tea towel, cotton shopping bag or clean t-shirt will do), making sure the edges of the cloth trail in the water. Water wicks up the cloth and evaporates. The cooling can be surprisingly effective – similar to that which you feel when you take off your rucksack and feel the breeze on your sweaty back.

Running water makes a very effective coolant, because any heat drawn from the food or drink is immediately carried away. Securing sealed (watertight!) containers in a shallow pool or stream is a great refrigeration option. However, you should take precautions against waterborne diseases. We often use this method on Alpine summer trips. Many of the rivers are fed by snowmelt and so they stay lovely and cold all year round.

Check upstream to make sure that there isn't a putrefying carcass just around the corner, always rinse off any silt or muck that accumulates, and carefully dry the bottle or container before you open it. Be careful where you put glass bottles, avoiding fast-moving water where breakages are more likely, and put them in a bag so that if they do break you can remove all the bits. A safer option for your wine is to transfer it to a plastic bottle for chilling. A loose-weave cloth or mesh bag will let some water flow through, and is thus less likely to be dislodged by the current than a plastic carrier.

In hot climates the kit in a large pack can provide surprisingly effective insulation. Pack perishable goods in rigid containers in the middle of your rucksack. ▶

CHAPTER 7
The Camp Kitchen

Whether you're preparing for a long-term base camp or a simple overnighter, it's worth spending a bit of time planning and setting up an organised cooking area – your 'camp kitchen'.

SETTING UP

For convenience sake, the best place for the kitchen is usually adjacent to your tent. When choosing a campsite, you're looking for an area flat enough to sleep on, and an adjacent area for cooking, with enough space for the tent to be accessed without the need to step over the cooking area. Consider the direction of the prevailing wind – you might be able to gain some shelter from the lie of the land, or if not, the tent will make a pretty good windshield. Note that there are circumstances in which cooking next to the tent is not a good idea, for example if you are trying to deter wildlife from visiting your tent, or planning an open fire. Many backpacking tents have a large porch area, which with care can serve as your kitchen in bad weather (see *Cooking in Bad Weather*, below). You need an area flat enough to keep your stove stable.

Wherever possible, **set your stove on bare ground** where it can't do any damage. If there is none, look for a flat rock to mount the stove on. It will be non-flammable, and by raising the stove off the ground you'll make it easier to use and easier to see, and thus less likely to get knocked over. Alternatively, a heap of sand or insulating non-flammable mat will protect short grass. Failing all of that, if the site has long grass or other ground vegetation, try to reduce the severity of the scorching you'll cause by cropping or trampling a small area nice and flat – the plants will recover better from this treatment than from being burned.

This said, a stove placed directly on the ground will inevitably cause some damage. Even if you don't actually burn the vegetation, the heat will dry out the soil and there will be some die-off, which may not be apparent for several days. This isn't necessarily a serious problem on permitted sites, as grass is resilient stuff, and the yellow circle where your stove sat will recover, but if you want to practice leave-no-trace wild camping – something we should all aspire to – you need to protect the ground.

Guy lines and tent pegs are a perennial campsite hazard, and nowhere more so than around your cooking area. If possible keep the area around where you are cooking free of potential trip lines. Some tents come with reflective guys that show up in torchlight – if yours doesn't have them you can always add a few reflective tags. This will reduce the risk of size 11 shoes in your pasta, and be good for camp harmony in

◀ *A plastic sheet is very useful for creating a clean food preparation area, but don't be tempted to stand the stove or hot pans directly on it.*

Where possible, place stoves on a non-flammable surface such as a flat rock or pile of sand.

general – few things lead to a more rapid sense-of-humour failure than repeated tripping, or a flattened tent on a wet evening.

If you're setting up in the middle of a busy camp it's worth **delineating your kitchen area** in some way – perhaps with a circle of stones or logs. Ask your companions to walk round it rather than through it, especially when you're cooking.

NUISANCE WILDLIFE

Sharing the environment with wild things is part of the pleasure of camping, but it can also be a source of major hassle and irritation. Insects, particularly midges and mosquitoes, usually top the list of unwelcome guests, but at various times we've been plagued by everything from grasshoppers to chickens, mice, seagulls, domestic cats and even birds of prey.

To avoid insects, chose your destination carefully, as most insects have distinct seasons and habitat preferences. In midge season you may be forced to use breezy, exposed sites rather than sheltered ones near water, or to spend your trip slicked in whatever repellent you find works best for you. Long trousers and sleeves make life a little more bearable, and you'll want a tent with insect mesh. Some formal campsites have installed gadgets called Midge Magnets, which used carbon dioxide to lure countless hordes of insects to their doom, leaving campers in relative peace.

The antics of birds and animals visiting your camp can be entertaining, but you may lose your sense of humour when a feathered or furry bandit eats your breakfast and casually poos in what was going to be your supper. To avoid problems with scavenging animals, **avoid leaving food or rubbish scattered outside your tent**. Always pack away after each meal, and if you have to leave food in the tent, wrap it well. Stand packets in pans and bury them under any other kit you're leaving behind, to minimise releasing tempting aromas and make it difficult for small animals to get access. If camping overseas in bear country, you must maintain a strict differentiation between your cooking and sleeping area – standard advice is 50m, but we'd go further! Official campsites in bear country usually provide heavy-duty bear boxes for food storage.

Encourage your fellow campers to **wear shoes around the kitchen area** – indeed around the camp in general. Many camp stoves are inherently unstable, and if something spills, chances are it will be feet that get spattered. Roy still bears the scars of an accident 20 years ago involving bare feet and a Trangia pan of boiling water – his entire foot became one giant blister and he was unable to walk without crutches for six weeks. There are easier ways to learn the lesson, take his word for it.

HYGIENE AND WASHING UP

Hygiene is a matter of habit. Away from the hot running water, dishwashers and antibacterial sprays of a domestic kitchen, keeping your hands and cooking equipment clean takes a bit of thought. Most people habitually wash their hands after using the toilet at home, but it's easier to overlook this basic practice in camp where you might not have access to running water. **Keep a bottle of antibacterial hand gel with the toilet roll** as a reminder. We also keep one in the utensils box.

Gulls are bold and tenacious thieves, especially where they are habituated to campers. Water pistols make good deterrents!

In camp your range of utensils is likely to be more limited than at home, and it's not as easy to just reach for a clean knife or spoon. Try not to put lids, spoons or anything else down on the ground. If you do have to put a lid down, place it upside down, so that any grass or dirt that adheres isn't transferred to your food when you replace the lid. Keep in mind what each item has been used for and try to **avoid cross-contamination between tasks**. This is especially important where you are dealing with raw meat. Knives and chopping boards used for raw meat should not be allowed to come into contact with anything cooked.

Antibacterial hand wash will help you avoid unpleasant tummy upsets. Use before eating or preparing food.

Because chopping boards are never quite large enough, it's useful to have a **clean plastic sheet** to use as a preparation area. If need be you can mark it in some way so that it only gets used for food preparation, and always on the same side.
For wild camping, we rarely use detergent for washing up. Warm water and fingers are enough to get metal pans clean enough to pack. We wash up in a pan and usually let everything drain then air dry. If the pans are going to be used again, they can be sterilised by heating, and are then washed properly when we get home. For longer trips a sponge

scourer and a little screwtop bottle of biodegradable detergent might be useful. Tea towels are only appropriate if strict discipline is observed about keeping them clean and letting them dry out between uses. The trouble is, they often get picked up and used for other things, like wiping surfaces or holding hot pans. **A damp, dirty tea towel left in a warm tent for 24 hours is a perfect germ incubator.**

If you have room for a bit more kit, it's great to have a bucket or a bowl for washing up – you can get collapsible versions of both made from tough, plasticised canvas. These work well enough, but beware chucking in a sharp knife and piercing the bottom or sides. If you're in a car or van, a regular rigid washing-up bowl is handy, as you can use it to pack stuff in. In some ways a bucket is even better, especially if you're going to be carrying

Where washing up facilities are provided it makes sense to use them, but try to avoid blocking drains with waste food.

MOVEABLE FEASTS

everything to and from a campsite dishwashing station to clean up. **Try and let your scourer dry out between uses** – left damp in your tent or pack it will provide great conditions for bacteria to multiply. Wash and dry it thoroughly after every trip.

Don't wash up under the camp tap, or directly in a stream. Carry a pan or bucketful of water some distance away, and dispose of the waste responsibly – the water can go down a drain or into the ground somewhere where it won't create a mudbath; any solids should go with your rubbish.

Just because you're outside doesn't mean you don't have to clean up after yourself. To reduce spillages, keep other people from hanging about in your cooking area. Wherever possible, pour, drain or transfer liquids outside and away from tents and equipment. Small backpacking tents and poor weather increase the likelihood of spillages and make cleaning up difficult. Have something other than your mate's sleeping bag handy to mop up with.

RUBBISH DISPOSAL

If you're on an official campsite, use their rubbish-disposal facilities, and try not to accumulate rubbish next to your tent, as it will attract vermin. If you're camping wild, **carry your rubbish out**, ideally sealed in a large ziplock or tightly knotted carrier bag. (Keep some folded carrier bags in your basics box.) **Some rubbish can be burned** if it is safe and permissible to do so (see *Open Fires*, below).

COOKING IN THE DARK

Some kind of light source is essential while you're cooking. Even if you're planning to be in camp long before nightfall, you should always carry a torch. While a hand-held torch is OK for moving about, you're usually much better off with something that leaves your hands free, and this is especially so when cooking. Ideally your camp setup should include a lantern that will cast a pool of light big enough for you to work in, but for lightweight backpacking a head torch will do nicely.

COOKING IN BAD WEATHER

Cooking inside a large canvas tent is fine, but we're talking big, stand-up-and-walk-around mess tents here, not backpacking tents. Most large canvas tents have a porch area, which you can cook in with great care if the weather is really too cold, wet or windy outside.

Cooking in the porch or tent doorway is a one-person job – or at least something to take turns at. Other spare bodies are better off tucked out of the way at the back of the tent. Get as much preparation as you can done in advance, as once the stove is lit you want to give it your full

attention, and not be chopping or unpacking or fiddling with packets. Ask your tent mates to go for comfort breaks before you start, then get everyone to stay put once you're busy with the stove.

Set the stove as far away as possible, in all directions, from any tent fabric, including above the flame. Keep the porch as open as possible for ventilation or escape if need be. If your tent is pitched so that it opens downwind, there is usually enough shelter to cook with the porch wide open. If you do have to shut the outer door, leave as big a ventilation gap at the top as possible to let out the steam – otherwise it will condense inside the tent and you could be as soggy by morning as if you'd cooked in the rain.

Consider what you could do to escape if your tent caught fire. With very small tents, the answer is probably not much, but with larger tents you may have a chance to exit through another door, or by cutting your way out – keep a knife handy for this purpose.

Cooking safely in the porch requires discipline. Make sure everything is organised and everyone is settled before you light the stove.

When to Give In…

Don't be tempted to try and cook in the inner section of a small tent. We can't think of any occasions when this would be necessary. If the weather is too bad to use the porch (or you have no porch), eat your food cold or wait until conditions improve – **you won't starve in one night**. You might be hungry and miserable, but you won't be risking your life, and if you're camping near civilisation it should be a no-brainer. Go and enjoy a pub meal or fish-and chip supper. Tent fires are over in seconds, but the effects can be utterly horrific – victims usually suffer extensive burns to much of the body, but especially the face, hands and respiratory tract as a result of breathing in hot fumes.

COOKING AT ALTITUDE

The most important difference between cooking at altitude and cooking at sea level is **air pressure**. This decreases as altitude increases and the air gets 'thinner'. This has implications for human physiology, in that the air contains less oxygen, so we have to breathe harder. After a few days, the body responds by increasing the proportion of red blood cells, making our blood more efficient at picking up and transporting oxygen.

In terms of cooking, the effect of thinner air is a reduction in the boiling temperature of water, a phenomenon explained by Boyle's Law (and no there's no pun intended, it's named after the physicist Robert Boyle). Boyle's Law says that 'For a fixed mass of ideal gas at fixed temperature, the product of pressure and volume is a constant.' What this means in practice is that **while water boils at 100°C at sea level, for every 165m of altitude the boiling point drops by 1°C**. If you're cooking at 1000m, your water will boil at 94°C; at 2000m it will boil at just 88°C.

Most foods will take much longer to cook at these low boiling temperatures, and some (dried beans or lentils for example) will boil for hours and never cook properly. Apart from being unpleasant to eat, uncooked pulses can create all kinds of digestive problems, and some raw or inadequately cooked beans, especially kidney beans, are toxic. Tinned kidney beans are fine, but raw ones are best avoided in camp cooking even at sea level, and certainly in the mountains.

Mountain guides rustle up a feast in the high Atlas. Water from a nearby stream had to be boiled for five minutes to make it safe to drink.

Boyle's Law is especially important if you are using boiling to purify water – at high altitude you need to boil water for much longer to ensure that harmful bacteria, protozoan parasites and viruses have been killed (see *Water Treatments* in Chapter 4 for more on water purification).

SHELTERS FOR COOKING

Overseas campsites often have purpose-built cooking shelters, but for various reasons these are not common in the UK. If you want to cook in comfort, you must either resign yourself to being a fair-weather camper or build your own shelter. This can either be a large mess tent or an improvised structure.

First, **decide what type of shelter is required**. If it's just to protect your cooking area (and the cook) from the elements, which is more important – a roof (protection from rain and strong sun), or a windbreak? If it's also going to be a social space, you need a much bigger area, and bear in mind that social areas take a lot of foot traffic – wear and tear on the grass or other surface will be relatively severe. You have to decide whether this is appropriate in any given location.

Make sure you have a sufficiently large tarpaulin (or tarp). A 2m x 2m tarp is only big enough for two people – the black tarp in the photos below was about 5m x 5m. You will also need plenty of rope or cordage (you'll almost always use more than you expect).

Lay the tarp out on the ground in moreorless the position you want to erect it and look around for suitable high anchor points. If the site doesn't offer natural supports, such as trees, boulders or fence posts, you'll need to improvise. Car roof racks, trekking poles and kayak paddles can all make good supports. **Never** attach a tarp to a drystone wall – you will damage the wall, and maybe yourself, in the process.

BALL CORNERS

If your tarp lacks eyelets you can create alternative attachment points using smooth pebbles or firm balls of clay. Place these about 20cm in from the corners of the tarp and bunch the fabric around them, sealing with a slip knot. Note that this method will reduce the effective area of your tarp substantially.

Make sure you have enough rope by running lengths out to your high anchor points. If your tarp has eyelets, use them to attach the cords. If not, you can improvise using pebbles or balls of firm soil or clay (see box below left). Raise the tarp and begin making the fine adjustments necessary to get it into the most useful position.

OPEN FIRES

Open-fire cooking is camp cooking in its purest form – an art in itself. A campfire is not only a means to cook, it also offers heat, light and comfort, drives away insects and deters other wildlife, and provides a fabulous focal point for a sociable evening. But get it wrong and a campfire can be the cause of anything from disgruntled locals, to pain, distress and landscape devastation. **Even an entirely safe fire has a cost to the local environment** if you are collecting wood or other fuel. The rotting of dead wood is an important part of natural regeneration – if you collect and burn too much, the ecosystem will be the poorer for your visit.

Open-air fires are prohibited in many parts of Britain, and in other countries you may need a permit to light one, so check out the local situation. Don't light a campfire in a drought zone or other ecologically stressed environment. In fact the only places we'd recommend lighting a fire are in specially designated areas, such as you find at some campsites or outdoor recreation areas, or on beaches below the high-water mark. Elsewhere, pay attention to local regulations and the wishes of landowners.

Above all, **make sure that the fire you start stays fully under control**. If a cooking fire becomes a sociable campfire, there is always a tendency for it to grow larger than originally intended, especially if those enjoying it have had a drink or two. Someone has to take responsibility for keeping the fire small, and ensuring that it is not only put out by morning, but completely dismantled. By the time you leave, there should be no sign that it ever existed.

Open-fire cooking is camp cooking in its purest form – but make sure that the fire you start stays fully under control.

Preparing the Ground

Locate the fire well away from your tent, preferably **downwind** – tiny sparks will pepper most textiles with holes.

You should only **start a fire on ground that will not burn** – this means sand or rock. Stony or sandy beaches by the sea or rivers are perfect, especially as the next high tide or flood will remove any trace you leave. When setting a fire on a beach, make sure you know what the tides are doing. Ideally, set your fire below the water mark, so that all trace of it will be washed away, but **don't risk getting caught by the tide** coming in faster than you expect. Likewise, some rivers have inviting beaches, but make sure you know what is upstream. Many larger rivers in mountainous areas have hydroelectric stations – water may be released suddenly from dams upstream, causing levels to rise several metres in a matter of seconds. Usually there are signs warning you of the danger – don't ignore them.

If you must lay a fire on **grassy ground**, you should remove an area of turf large enough for no grass to be scorched by the fire. You'll need an area at least twice the diameter of your intended fire bed (see box).

REMOVING AND REPLACING TURF

1. Choose a flat, open area not overhung by vegetation.

2. Mark out an area at least twice as wide in both dimensions as your intended fire bed and use a spade to cut clean edges, deep enough to remove the grass root-mat and a layer of topsoil.

3. Roll the turf or cut into squares and carefully lift out. Beware: turf is heavy. Remove to a safe distance where it won't be sat or trodden on.

4. Treat the turves carefully. Stack them in the same order they are cut, so you will know which piece goes back where later. Water the turf stack twice a day for the duration of your stay.

5. If the bottom of the pit is organic topsoil, dig out a further 10cm layer. Lift the soil onto a polythene sheet, so it can be dragged cleanly away (don't heap soil onto the surrounding grass, as it will create a mud bath). Ideally, you should dig down to rock or mineral soil, but this can be difficult in the UK. You can protect organic soils by piercing them with a sharp stick and watering generously before setting your fire, or by lining your fire pit with stones or bricks.

6. The area around the fire pit will get heavily trampled. If you can protect it in some way, for example with a groundsheet, then do so.

7. **After your fire**, remove all unburned material. Rake out the fire bed, which should feel completely cold to the touch. Douse well with water,

8. Begin replacing the stored topsoil. Distribute it evenly over the pit and stamp it down well.

9. Replace each turf carefully in its original position, pushing it down well. Try not to trample it too much – it has been abused enough already!

10. Water the area well. The pit should be undetectable within a week or two.

NB The fire pit shown is a big one. It contained two group cooking fires, feeding 14 people.

In a **woodland setting**, you need to go a step further than just removing the surface vegetation and leaf litter. Woodland soils contain a large proportion of organic material, which can burn for days with a long, slow smoulder. In a setting like this it's all too easy to do a superficial job of putting out a fire, only to have it reignite hours or even days later, with disastrous consequences. For a safe fire you should **dig a pit** (you should have a spade or at least a trowel in your kit for toilet pits anyway) and **line it with rocks**. Alternatively, use a heavy-duty tarp, then replace the soil and build the fire on top. The next morning, when the fire is doused, you can remove the rocks or lift the tarp and all the hot soil from the pit, spread it out and make sure there is nothing still smouldering. It's all a bit of a faff, but at least you walk away with no nagging doubts.

Open fires on **moorland** carry the same risk. Certainly **never light a fire on peaty soil** – peat burns so well that in many areas it is cut and dried as fuel. Either look for sandy or stony areas and keep the fire small, or preferably, in these environments, don't bother. Use a conventional stove, carefully, and wait for another trip to have your fire.

If there are fire pits or hearths already in place, use them to limit your fire – keep the burning inside the circle, ideally not touching the stones. A fire about 50cm across should be more than big enough for all cooking needs – anything bigger will waste fuel, and can become difficult to control. In a wild camp, don't collect hearth stones. You'll only blacken and spoil them.

In the absence of fine tinder, use a sturdy knife to shave a larger piece of kindling into a feather stick that will ignite easily.

It takes time to make a good cooking fire, so aim to get it going half an hour or so before you want to cook. You want a heart of glowing embers, not a smoky, flaming inferno.

Keep a bucket of water or sand on hand to douse runaway flames.

Collecting Fuel

Some campsites with permitted fire areas will sell you firewood, in which case use this rather than trying to collect your own. **If you do need to collect firewood, try and do it over a wide area**, and not immediately next to the camp. Sites that are used often become denuded of dead wood, and this is bad news for wildlife and the environment in general. Driftwood, however, is fair game. Just give it a shake to make sure it's not harbouring any beasties. For cooking you need small sticks, not big logs.

Lighting a Fire

Lighting a fire isn't difficult as long as you **start with very small, very dry tinder** – shredded paper, dry leaves, sawdust, or the parchment-like bark of silver birch. But relying on entirely natural tinder can make life more difficult if conditions are anything less than very dry, and it will help enormously to have something a little more flammable to hand. Firelighters do work but they're greasy and nasty to carry, and you don't want to buy a whole box for one fire, so here are some alternatives.

Once your tinder or feather stick is alight, add small sticks a few at a time.

Pocket fluff makes great tinder – have a whip-round for all those dry, disintegrated tissues and strands of cotton.

Many outdoor suppliers sell **Maya Dust** – a fine, pine sawdust. The resin in the wood makes it burn hot and long, and it ignites easily from a flint spark, so no matches or lighter are required.

Old **bicycle inner tubes** work very well. When they've passed their useful life on your bike, cut them up into one-inch sections and keep a handful as firelighters – they burn brilliantly, even when wet.

MOVEABLE FEASTS

Tending a Fire

Once you've got your tinder burning, start adding small twigs, and when they've caught, add bigger ones. Don't add too much at a time – let each addition catch before adding more. **Sticks make better cooking fires than logs**, and don't need chopping. Bigger logs need cutting up, otherwise they take too long to burn, and the charred leftovers will be an unsightly sign that you were there.

For a cooking fire cut logs into sections no thicker than your wrist. Three or four of these will be plenty for a full meal.

Dousing a Fire

You should let your fire burn down to nothing but ash. Before you leave, rake the fire apart, spread the ashes out, douse them thoroughly with water, then scatter them. The ground you leave should feel cool. If you cleared leaf litter or turf to make the fire, put it back to cover the site. If you used stones to delimit the hearth, put them back where you found them – leaving a hearth intact in a wild place will encourage others to light fires, and they might not do so as carefully as you have.

Campfire Cooking Techniques

Grills and Pan Stands

There are any number of ways of supporting a pan on a fire (see left). Pan supports can also be made from logs or stones – three or four evenly sized ones will do the job well on their own, but if you add a wire grill (a cake cooling rack will do) you can use it for grilling as well as heating pans.

You can also buy campfire grills with folding legs, which is a good idea if you're intending to use an open fire a lot.

Camp Oven

A traditional camp oven sits directly in the fire with a heap of hot coals on its lid. If you're cooking stews this way, make them directly in the pan. For dry roasts and baking, you'll need a rack inside the oven to prevent food touching the sides and burning.

Pot roasts, where a joint of meat or whole chicken cooks in stock along with some roughly chopped vegetables, are particularly good in a camp oven, producing succulent meat and a rich gravy.

Spit Roasting

Spit roasting can take a long time, during which the fire and the meat need fairly constant attention to maintain even heat and prevent burning. In days gone by, when spit roasting was still done in the kitchens of great houses, a small urchin was paid a pittance to sit for hours in a massive fireplace, turning the spit. Scorched flesh and singed eyebrows were an occupational hazard. On a small campfire the job is less onerous (which is just as well, as the availability of urchins isn't what it was, and you'll be doing it yourself).

Metal roasting spits for campfire use are available from some outdoor or camp stockists, or you can buy them online. Alternatively, you can buy battery operated 'camp rotisseries' to do the job for you. But if this isn't something you intend doing regularly, you may as well construct your own spit using a sturdy steel poker and a couple of forked sticks.

Cooking on the Embers

If you want to be a purist, you can cook some food directly in the fire with no pots, no pans, no foil packaging, and no more than a decent knife.

Fish cook well wrapped in wet newspaper. The fish should be gutted, but with the skin still on. Use five or six sheets of newspaper, soaked well in water, per fish. Wrap securely and bake in hot embers, turning occasionally, and sprinkling on more water every so often to stop the paper drying out. Once the fish is cooked the paper can be burned along with the other waste.

Large potatoes can be baked directly in glowing embers. Turn them regularly to ensure even cooking. You'll only be able to eat the insides – the skin will be charcoal. You can cook a steak by laying it on hot coals. Scrape off the ash when it's cooked, and although it might be a bit gritty, provided the meat is fresh, it will be perfectly OK to eat.

There are hundreds of other surprising ways to cook on a fire. If you felt inclined you might try such unlikely wonders as eggs in orange skins, sausages in banana skins, or bacon in a suspended paper bag. But frankly most of these are camp novelties   we wouldn't rely on them to make good eating!

Cast iron cookware comes into its own on an open fire. Slow-cooked stews are wonderful cooked this way.

CHAPTER 8
Wild, Local and Seasonal Food

Some of the best meals we've had in the outdoors have been when our planned menu was served with a few opportunistic extras or seasoned with a dash of serendipity. There's something special about eating food that has come from the countryside around you.

WILD FOODS

The idea of foraging for supper seems to be inherently popular, but while lots of people claim to want to know how, very few actually go out and practise it alongside their other outdoor pursuits. Living exclusively off the land is really hard work. It's a hobby in its own right, and in reality we're no more likely to whip up a spread from the bounty of the land than the next people. We're not survival or bushcraft experts, we've never caught a rabbit, and when it comes to all but a few fungi, our identification skills are so limited that discretion remains the better part of valour. What's more, we like to know that there's a full and satisfying meal ahead of us, without spending the whole day searching for it or devising ways to catch it.

However, like most people, we agree that there is something gleeful and satisfying about a free handful of nuts or berries, a bucket of beachcombed seafood, or a salad pepped up with some freshly plucked dandelion or watercress leaves. So while none of our recipes comprise exclusively wild food, several of them can make use of wild ingredients if you're lucky enough to come across them (see *Collecting Wild Plant Foods* below).

When it comes to preparing animal foods, we're happy enough dealing with simple seafood and gutting fish, but the plucking, skinning and butchery required for birds and mammals is really more trouble than it's worth in our view. (Besides, as a biologist Amy would only end up turning the exercise into a dissection and anatomy demonstration, which tends to impair appetites all round.)

BUYING LOCAL

We're strong advocates of using local produce. While this might not be quite the same as hunting and gathering, it lends an additional pleasure knowing the food on your plate was grown or reared nearby. Usually local food is fresh food, so it will taste better, and fewer food miles is good news for the planet in general.

Britain has an amazing food culture, and the best places to try regional delicacies are in the regions where they are made. Each part of the

◀ Who doesn't relish the opportunity to sample fresh foods straight from the land as nature intended?

Buying from markets is a great way to sample local produce and you only need to buy the small quantity you will use that night.

country has its own specialities, and you can find differences not only from county to county, but sometimes between one valley and the next.

One of the advantages of popular tourist areas such as our national parks is that local producers take the opportunity to sell direct to the visiting public. Do them and yourself a favour and visit a **market** (especially a farmers' market). These are great places to shop and sample. If you've missed market day, most small towns have a **deli** or speciality grocer that stocks local goods. From a camping perspective, another great thing about delis and markets is that you shop by weight, only buying what you need, so there's no excess to carry around and no waste.

Roadside stalls selling seasonal farm produce are common in many parts of the country, and buying a few ingredients can inspire a whole menu. Usually you pay into an honesty box, so it's useful to carry loose change if you're planning to shop this way. Don't be shy about knocking on doors where you see roadside signs advertising eggs, honey, fruit or vegetables, which are often produced in back gardens or allotments.

Co-op supermarkets make a point of stocking locally produced foods, as do Booths supermarkets in the north of England. Good for them!

If you're on the coast, check out the availability of fresh fish and seafood, or, in Scotland in particular, visit a **smokehouse** for a delectable selection of treats. If you're travelling and camping overseas, take the opportunity to try local produce, and relish the cheapness of 'exotics' such as oranges, avocados, bananas, seafood and spices which don't grow at home.

There's something wonderful about roadside stalls like this one. The honesty box system, non-existent food mileage and the freshness of the produce create an unbeatable feelgood factor.

BUYING SEASONAL

Buying local usually means buying seasonal too. The farm and garden produce you see for sale on roadsides will be seasonal by definition – people usually offer for sale excess produce that is being harvested at the time.

Even if all your shopping happens in a supermarket, you can save money and food miles by buying seasonal fruit and vegetables. The availability of imported fruit, vegetables and other produce in most stores is so boosted by foreign imports, it's easy to have a completely skewed perception of which fruits are in season when. We're not saying it's wrong to use imported foods. Indeed we'd both be sorry to go without bananas, satsumas and avocados. But fresh, seasonal UK produce will save you a stack of money, and being guided by nature is as good a way as any of deciding what to cook.

	Jan	Feb	Mar	Apr	May

● In season ◆ Stored fresh produce may still be available

	Jan	Feb	Mar	Apr	May
Apples	◆	◆	◆	◆	◆
Asparagus					●
Aubergine					●
Beans, broad					●
Beans, runner					
Beans, French					●
Blackberries					
Blueberries					
Bilberries					
Broccoli	●	●	●		
Brussels sprouts	●	●			
Cabbage	●	●	●		
Carrots	●	●	●	●	●
Celery				●	●
Cherries					●
Chestnuts	◆				
Corn (cobs)					
Courgettes					
Elderberries					
Gooseberries					
Hazelnuts					
Lamb		●	●	●	●
Leeks	●	●			
Mackerel (at their best)					●

Jun	Jul	Aug	Sept	Oct	Nov	Dec
◆	◆	●	●	●	●	●
●						
●	●	●	●			
●	●	●	●			
	●	●	●	●	●	
●						
		●	●	●		
	●	●				
	●	●				
		●	●	●	●	●
					●	●
●	●	●	●	●	●	●
●	●	●	●	●	●	●
●	●					
●	●					
			●	●	◆	◆
			●	●		
●	●	●	●			
				●		
●	●	●				
		●	●	◆	◆	◆
●						
			●	●	●	●
●	●					

continued on pages 150–1

WHEN TO FIND UK FOODS IN SEASON

	Jan	Feb	Mar	Apr	May
● In season ◆ Stored fresh produce may still be available					
Morels				●	
Mushrooms (field)					
Mussels	●	●	●		
Onions	●	●	●	◆	◆
Oysters	●	●	●		
Peas (including sugarsnap/ mangetout)					
Pears	◆	◆	◆		
Plums					
Potatoes (new)					●
Potatoes (main crop)	●	●	●	●	◆
Pumpkin					
Raspberries					
Rhubarb	●	●	●	●	●
Salmon (wild)		●	●	●	●
Samphire					●
Spinach				●	●
Strawberries					
Swede	●	●			
Tomatoes				●	●
Trout (rainbow)	●	●	●	●	●
Venison					
Watercress			●	●	●

Venison: **M** male and **F** female deer have different seasons

Jun	Jul	Aug	Sept	Oct	Nov	Dec
			●	●	●	
				●	●	●
♦	●	●	●	●	●	●
			●	●	●	●
●	●	●				
			●	●	♦	♦
		●	●	●		
●	●	●	●			
♦	●	●	●	●	●	●
		●	●	●	♦	♦
	●	●				
●	●	●	●			
●	●	●				
●	●	●				
●	●	●	●	●		
●	●	●	●			
		●	●	●	●	●
●	●	●	●	●		
●	●	●	●	●	●	●
M	M	MF	F	F	F	F
●	●	●	●	●	●	

FRESH FISH

Fish is one of nature's convenience foods. It cooks extremely quickly, and even with no accompaniment whatsoever can be utterly delicious. Some of the best are also some of the easiest to come by. Trout, whether caught yourself or purchased from a fishmonger, or mackerel if you're by the sea, typically come in convenient one-person serving sizes. They just need cleaning, gutting and cooking, either in a pan, or wrapped in foil, wet newspaper, seaweed or moss on a fire. Ten minutes later, dinner is served. (Some fish can be eaten raw, but we wouldn't recommend this for anything other than the freshest of fresh fish, and not all species are suitable. The preparation of raw fish is usually best left to experts.)

FISH BUYING GUIDE

Look: Whole fish should not look bashed around. Their eyes should be clear and not sunken or concave, and fillets should be evenly coloured.

Touch: A whole fish body should feel firm and springy, like well-toned muscle (which is what it is). Filleted fish should also be firm. A bit of flakiness is OK as long as it's not dry, but there should be no mushy bits.

Smell: Sea fish should smell faintly of the sea; oily fish like trout should smell slightly oily. No fresh fish should smell strongly fishy, or strongly of anything else for that matter.

If you're concerned about the sustainability of wild fish stocks, look for a Marine Stewardship Council accreditation label or check out the *Pocket Good Fish Guide* produced by the Marine Conservation Society, which you can download free from www.fishonline.org.

Gutting a Fish

Baked trout (p225) is about as simple as campfire cooking gets.

If you're buying fish, you can usually get it gutted for you, if not fully filleted. Fishmongers do it all the time, and they'll make a much neater and quicker job of it than the average camper nervously wielding a penknife. If you've caught your own fish, you don't have much choice. Processing fish is quite simple, but it can be messy, so it's best done away from your camp. This is especially the case if you happen to be camping in parts of the world where scavenging or predatory animals are resident – rats, foxes, or even bears, wolves and big cats will all be attracted by the smell.

First **clean the fish** with water to get rid of the coating of slime. If it's a scaly species you'll need to remove the scales by scraping 'against the grain' (from tail to head). You can skip this messy step with types of fish that have very fine scales or no scales at all, such as trout, eel or mackerel.

If you've caught your own fish it's only fair to dispatch it as quickly and efficiently as possible. Hold the fish firmly by the tail, and swing it forcefully against a hard surface such as a rock, tree stump, jetty or step. Aim to bash it where the neck would be if it had one. You might need more than one go, but once you've started you owe it to the hapless creature to persevere.

Gutting can be done easily enough with a penknife. Lie the fish belly up in your hand or on a relatively clean surface. Find the cloaca, the small opening two-thirds of the way from the head to the tail. Using a sharp knife, make a long cut from this opening to just between the gill covers. Don't stab the blade in deeply – you want to avoid puncturing any of the internal organs, and once you've made the cut it will be relatively easy to lift out the guts and other organs.

If you can bear it, the best tools for **loosening the innards** are your fingers – being blunt they're less likely to pierce any organs. However, you'll need your knife again to make two further cuts at the throat and the anus to sever the oesophagus and cloaca. You'll be left with a neat, clean cavity, with a dark vein running alongside the backbone – scrape this out with your fingernail or a spoon.

SHELLFISH

Seafood isn't to everyone's liking, and a bad experience can stay with you a very long time. If done right, however, the delicate flavours and succulent meatiness of various molluscs and crustaceans found around British shores make a meal to remember. Seafood doesn't travel very well, so overseas trips are a great opportunity to sample more exotic varieties the way they should be – fresh out of the sea.

Buying and Collecting Shellfish

In the UK (and the rest of the temperate northern hemisphere) there is an old saying **'Only eat seafood when there's an "r" in the month'** – September to April. This avoids the spawning season, when the flesh is in poor condition, and reduces the chances of eating moribund shellfish that have been sitting round in the warm for too long. It's best not to collect mussels, cockles, scallops or other shellfish during the summer months, but you may be able to buy some cultivated varieties year round. You should **discard any bivalves that don't close up when you remove them from the water** – they might be dead or dying.

Garlic mussels (p218) and a splendid crayfish – a very special seafood treat.

The biggest danger with collecting your own seafood isn't from poisoning, it's from becoming so engrossed in the hunt that you get caught by the tide. On shallow coasts the tide can race in faster than you can run; on rocky coasts there is the added danger of slipping and hurting yourself. Always **check the tide times**, be aware how far you've walked, and ideally tell someone where you're going and when you expect to be back.

Shellfish poisoning is caused by certain algae that are taken in by bivalve molluscs, such as mussels, scallops and cockles. The algae, known as dinoflagellates, occasionally appear in large 'blooms'. The algae produce toxins, which accumulate in the shellfish and cause conditions with unnervingly descriptive names such as diarrheic shellfish poisoning, paralytic shellfish poisoning and amnesic shellfish poisoning (DSP, PSP, ASP). In the UK there is very close monitoring of shellfish stocks, and outbreaks of poisoning from commercial shellfish are extremely rare, but if you're collecting your own seafood you don't get the same guarantee. It's always worth asking a bit of local advice – the locals might not tell you the very best spots (why would they?), but they will almost certainly let you know of any problems.

COLLECTING WILD PLANT FOODS

The **Countryside Code** asks that you always 'protect plants and animals', and it's difficult to see how you can pick a wild plant or collect a wild animal and eat it while keeping its best interests at heart. Fortunately the code is open to a little interpretation where wild foods are concerned. By 'plants and animals' it doesn't mean each and every shoot and shell. With most of the species listed here, you can pluck a few fruits or stems or collect a handful without doing any serious harm to the species as a whole or the local population. There's no law against considerate harvesting, provided the foods don't already belong to someone and the species is not protected. The **Theft Act** (1968) and the **Wildlife and Countryside Act** (1981), forbid the digging up and removal of wild plants (including fungi) without permission of the landowner. The collection of most wild foods from public land for personal consumption is legal, but amassing wild fruits, nuts, flowers or fungi for personal commercial gain is not. Note that the **Wild Birds Protection Act** (1954) forbids collecting the eggs of most wild birds.

Take ultimate revenge on stinging nettles by picking a few for the pot. See green soup, p198.

To many farmers and proud gardeners (and potentially some campsite owners) lots of edible plants are weeds, so don't collect them from places where they may have been sprayed with weed-killer (or any other chemical for that matter). In areas that are frequented by dog walkers, don't collect anything from below leg-cocking height!

Blackberries and apples are conveniently ripe at the same time of year and make a classic combination for crumbles (p261) and compotes (p264).

Roadside verges are often particularly well stocked with edible plants, but if the road is busy they'll probably have been liberally coated with dust, grit, salt and vehicle emissions. Quiet country lanes are a better bet, but even then you should be trying to collect from the back of the verge, as far from the roadside as possible. Watch for traffic and don't get run over.

Wash berries and leaves in slightly salty water to bring out any maggots and other unwanted beasties.

Fruits and Nuts

Bilberries/Blueberries
Found carpeting large areas of UK uplands, especially in Scotland. Not usually as sweet as blueberries you might buy, but very rich in vitamin C, and great cooked in cakes, crumbles and fruit compotes. Peak fruiting season is in high summer.

Blackberries
Pick them when they're black and plump and leave some for the next passers-by. Eat fresh or cook them in a pie or crumble (see p261).

Bullaces
Smaller, firmer, sharper-tasting versions of plums. Cook with plenty of sugar.

Chestnuts (sweet)
Best harvested in October. The nuts have a definite point at one end, and grow inside very spiky cases, like little green hedgehogs. Don't confuse them with inedible horse chestnuts (conkers), which are smoothly

Sweet chestnuts are great to nibble on their own or used to flavour savoury dishes.

rounded and whose cases have fewer, tougher spines (more like Second World War sea mines than hedgehogs). Can be eaten raw, but much better roasted on a hot griddle or dry pan for between five and 10 minutes. Peel as soon as they're cool enough to touch. You can eat them as they are, with a sprinkling of salt, or add them to recipes like nut roast (see p241). Also good chopped and used like pine nuts with pasta.

Crab apples
Tiny wild ancestors of eating apples, with a mouth-puckering, eye-watering sharp taste. To eat they need cooking – with lots of sugar.

Elderberries
Easy-to-recognise clusters of glossy red–black berries that ripen in late summer. Check the leaves to avoid confusion with similar inedible or poisonous fruits – elder leaflets grow in groups of five or seven on one stem, and each leaflet is pointed with a roughly serrated edge. Berries need cooking, and are good added to stewed apple or crumble, with plenty of sugar.

Too tart to eat fresh, a handful of elderberries makes a good addition to a cake, crumble or compote. Use lots of sugar!

Hazelnuts (cobnuts)

Trees have smooth grey bark and broad leaves with a pointed tip and saw-toothed edges. The nuts have a little jaggedy edged ruff, and ripen from green to reddish or golden brown in late summer and autumn. They can be eaten straight from the shell, or used in any nutty dish. You'll need nutcrackers or a couple of clean hammer stones to get in.

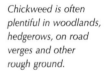

Raspberries

Wild raspberries grow on prickly scrambling canes in woodlands and are usually ripe a bit ahead of blackberries.

Sloes

Another member of the plum family. No immediate usefulness, but good for making sloe gin. This takes a long time, but the result, sipped on a chilly night in camp is very acceptable indeed! Sloes ripen in autumn and can't be picked until after the first frost.

Wild strawberries

Tiny, super-sweet versions of the garden variety, best enjoyed straight from the plant. Leaves can be steeped in boiling water for five minutes to make tea – serve with a half teaspoon of honey or sugar per cup.

Vegetables and Salads

Chickweed is often plentiful in woodlands, hedgerows, on road verges and other rough ground.

Chickweed

Very common scrambling weed. Young shoots can be eaten raw in salads or chopped and mashed with pine nuts and olive oil to make a pesto. Boil or steam older shoots like any other leafy green vegetable.

Dandelion

Leaves are best enjoyed in early spring, before the flowers or seed heads appear. Wash young leaves and use in salad. Older leaves can be boiled or steamed and used like spinach in omelettes or pasta sauces. Taste the leaves before you add them to a dish. If they are still bitter, change the water and cook a little longer.

Dandelion leaves are best eaten raw as salad in spring when the leaves are tender. Later in the year, treat them like spinach.

Japanese knotweed

We were delighted to discover that this obnoxious and invasive weed can be eaten. Collect only very young shoots, no more than 20cm tall. Cook like asparagus and serve as a side vegetable.

Samphire (glasswort/sea asparagus)

A coastal plant that looks a bit like segmented asparagus, samphire is available from specialist grocers and fishmongers, or on tidal flats in mid summer. Collect only the top 10cm of the stems. Cook for a minute or two in boiling water and serve with melted butter and/or olive oil, black pepper and a squeeze of lemon. Don't add sal. It has plenty already.

Stinging nettles

Wear gloves to collect the tender young leaves. A loosely packed carrier bagful makes green soup for four people (see p198).

Watercress

Belongs to the cabbage and mustard family, and has the same peppery zing. Avoid gut parasites and other waterborne nasties by taking the same precautions as for collecting stream water (see Springs, Streams and Rivers in Chapter 4). Wash leaves very carefully in treated water and eat fresh in salad, or chop and add to scrambled eggs, cheese sauce or chicken soup. Cooks very quickly, like spinach.

Samphire is a seasonal delicacy that people will pay a lot for in restaurants. On beaches around the UK coast, it's free.

Fungi

Wild mushrooms can be delicious. **They can also be deadly.** Some are both. (Apparently those who eat the aptly named death cap say it is absolutely delicious… but these are just about the last words they ever get to utter.)

Foraging for fungi is no joke, and we're not even going to attempt to describe the safe ones here, because we're not experts, and many species have inedible or poisonous lookalikes. If you're interested in learning to identify wild mushrooms, go on a course and buy a couple of field guides. Be aware that most species show a bit of variability, and an expert will use a combination of different features, including general appearance, habitat, season, smell and spore colour to identify a good eating fungus with confidence.

As a general rule, fresh mushrooms are best – fungi are often just as popular with insects as they are with people, and older ones will be riddled with holes and may well be maggoty inside.

There is a specific **code of conduct** for collecting fungi. You should respect the rights of landowners, never collect more than you need, avoid collecting anything that is rare, and avoid causing damage to the habitat or other wildlife.

CHAPTER 9
Camping à la Carte

People camp for so many different reasons, and in many different ways. At opposite ends of the spectrum the experiences can be completely different – the only common factor being the lack of solid walls. The way you cook and eat on a trip varies just as much, so it's difficult to provide a set of guidelines that will apply to everyone. In this chapter we've focused on a few special situations. If you're relatively new to any of them, we hope you'll find some ideas here that will help you plan effectively.

There are pros and cons of planning. One of the pros is that things are less likely to go wrong. One of the cons is that if they do go wrong there's a good chance everybody will blame the planner. Usually it makes sense for one person to be in charge of food, but this doesn't mean they have to do all the work, nor does it mean that nobody else gets a say. Decisions on food and cooking, including budget, menus and kit, should be made in consultation with all members of the group, and jobs such as shopping and packing can be delegated. But it's the planner who needs to make the lists of ingredients and equipment and keep track of who does what.

When catering for a trip, be it an overnight jolly or a month-long expedition, you need answers to the questions below before you start out.

How many people? This has a direct bearing on how much food you'll need and on how much help you can expect preparing it. If you need assistants, notify or recruit them sooner rather than later.

How many days? This determines the amount of food you need, and the kinds of food you can plan on cooking. There's no point planning menus from perishable ingredients five days into a trek. On very long trips you'll probably need to factor in opportunities to restock your supplies.

How many meals? Will you be preparing all your food in camp or will you be having lunches in pubs or cafés?

What is the budget? Set a food budget and try to stick to it, to avoid leaving anyone out of pocket. Make sure everyone on the trip knows what is included in the food budget and what is not (for example lunches, snacks, drinks).

Down on the Mediterranean, a lightweight bivvy allows you to escape the crowds even in busy tourist areas. ▸

What is 'team kit'? What kit will you need as a group, who is providing it, and who is transporting it? Are people bringing their own personal kit, such as plates, cutlery, mugs?

Are there any special dietary requirements? Do any of your camp-fellows have allergies, intolerances, aversions? Are there any vegetarians or vegans? Do any of them avoid certain foods on religious grounds?

What activities will be taking place? This will influence appetites and make some foods more appropriate than others. Give winter hill walkers cottage cheese and cucumber sandwiches for lunch and they might not speak to you for a week. Give them hot noodly soup or lentil kedgeree and flapjacks and they may propose marriage.

Where are you camping? Wild camping offers big rewards, but also carries big responsibilities. Don't forget you'll have to carry your rubbish back out – pack trash bags to wrap it securely. Do you have a bad weather contingency, such as a cooking shelter, or does your tent have a big enough porch area for safe cooking? If you're planning to use an official campsite, remember that these vary profoundly in terms of the facilities provided. Some offer fully equipped kitchens complete with water boilers and fresh tea towels. Others have one leaky outdoor tap and a composting toilet with no door. Most are somewhere inbetween, but it's worth doing a bit of research in advance.

Who is doing the cooking? It doesn't always have to be the same person. Different people have different ideas and levels of experience, and most won't thank you for presenting them with ingredients they don't recognise while demanding culinary miracles. Make sure the cooks know which ingredients are for which meals.

What will you be cooking on? A lightweight gas stove will cope with boiling water and heating one-pot wonders, but is likely to burn stews. Small burners aren't great for frying over either. A petrol stove will cook pan meals efficiently, but it may be unsuitable for some stove-top ovens, so no fancy baking. A campfire can be as versatile as you like, but do you have permission to light one? What about fuel? Are you taking it with you or buying it on your trip? If your trip is overseas, check the availability of fuel at your destination. Have a look at *Stoves* and *Fuels* in Chapter 3 for more information.

What can you carry? If you're camping from a vehicle, weight shouldn't be a problem, within reason. If you're backpacking, you'll need to consider the overall weight and packability of kit and food (shared between the group) more carefully (see the suggested kit lists in Chapter 3).

Where is your water going to come from? If it's likely to be from an unreliable source, you'll need to decide how to treat it, and remember to pack the puritabs/iodine/Steripen/filter, or whatever else you'll need. Boiling isn't necessarily the cheap option it sounds, because you'll be burning a lot of fuel, especially if you're camping at altitude. (See Chapter 4 for more on treating water.)

DUKE OF EDINBURGH'S AWARD EXPEDITIONS

The Duke of Edinburgh's Award Scheme (known to most participants as the D of E) was launched in 1956 in order to give young people (initially just boys – a girls' award was started two years later) experience and confidence in a wide range of situations. Half a century later thousands of youngsters still find the experience challenging, enlightening, inspiring and, above all, great fun. We have both spent several years instructing and assessing the expedition section of the award, and got even more enjoyment and satisfaction out of that.

Depending which level of award you are working towards, you'll be planning a two-, three- or four-day expedition. In order to complete the expedition section of the award successfully, most participants need to demonstrate their competence and understanding in a number of key areas, including planning and preparation, awareness of health and safety issues, first aid and navigation. You'll also be expected to get to grips with aspects of camp craft, equipment and hygiene, and food and cooking.

Earlier sections of this book should give you a good head start on all of this. For example, at bronze level you must be able to choose suitable camping gear and know how to use and care for it (see Chapter 3); know how to pack a rucksack (Chapter 6); choose a suitable campsite, make arrangements for water, cooking and sanitation, and refuse disposal and fire precautions (Chapter 7); understand cooking and the use of stoves, including the safety procedures and precautions that must be observed when using stoves and handling fuels (Chapter 3); and be able to cook simple meals under camp conditions.

The skills acquired on Duke of Edinburgh's Award expeditions can last a lifetime, so get into good habits from the start.

At silver and gold levels the requirements are much the same, except you are expected to produce more substantial camp meals entirely from the contents of your pack. Several of the lightweight recipes in this book would be suitable for use on an expedition. As with any new skill, cooking is something that takes practice, and we'd always recommend trying recipes at home or on a practice cook-out before relying on them in a real camp.

When planning an expedition menu, it's wise to **keep things simple**, but this doesn't necessarily mean going for the easiest option. You want to be sure the food you carry earns its place in your pack by being nutritious, energy giving, and above all tasty! Dehydrated foods vary enormously in quality, so it pays to shop around a little and try new things.

We know plenty of people who started their outdoor careers with the award scheme, cooking packets of pasta and sauce followed by cake and instant custard for every meal. There's nothing wrong with this, but some of them are still doing the

'Pasta Milanese coming up...'

SUGGESTED EXPEDITION MENU	
Day One	
Lunch	Home-made sandwiches, banana, chocolate brownies*
Evening meal	Pasta Milanese*, pears in chocolate sauce*
Day Two	
Breakfast	Breakfast crumble*
Lunch	Crackers and pâté, apple, flapjack*
Evening meal	Spicy sausage couscous*, lemon cheesecake* (keep back a little condensed milk for breakfast)
Day Three	
Breakfast	Oatcakes* with jam and condensed milk
Lunch	Crisprolls, Primula cheese, maltloaf
Evening meal	Home-made instant chilli (mixed at home before you leave), Squirty fruit crumble and custard*
Day Four	
Breakfast	Porridge* with dried fruit and jam
Lunch	Energy bars and scroggan* as you push to the finish!

Supplement your meals with snack bars, dried fruit, nuts, instant noodles, instant soups and plenty of hot and cold drinks. The * denotes a recipe from this book.

same thing 10 or 20 years later – for them this is all there is to 'camping food'. Next time you're in the supermarket, steer your trolley down a few other aisles – have a look at dried foods, whole foods, Asian foods, the baking section. You'll find the makings of some brilliant dehydrated menus, often at a fraction of the price of ready meals, but including really interesting ingredients such as sundried tomatoes and mushrooms, exotic sauce mixes and fancy cured meats.

ADVENTURE RACING, MOUNTAIN MARATHONS AND OTHER ENDURANCE EVENTS

A marathon is no longer the jaw-dropping feat of endurance it once was. These days most reasonably fit and active people consider a half marathon as at least achievable – with some training there's no reason most people shouldn't manage one. When we mention mountain marathons, however, people start to look at us strangely. Elaborate a bit on the pleasures of leaping through thigh-deep bogs, or hauling up hillsides in driving rain, hail or impenetrable fog, and camping with minimal kit in freezing conditions, and some folk begin to infer that we might be not quite right in the head.

A mountain marathon is basically a long fell race – usually run over a weekend with a compulsory overnight camp. Runners typically compete in teams of two, carrying all they need to camp and sustain themselves. There is a minimum kit list designed to ensure all participants are as safe as possible in the hills.

Competitors in the now famous Original Mountain Marathon (formerly the KIMM) can expect to burn around 5000 calories in a day.

Many of the competitors in these events are supremely, astoundingly fit. We're not, but for two days' hard effort we still need food that is **quick and easy to cook, energising** and **light**. When kit is pared down to the minimum, your team kitchen comprises no more than a stove, fuel, lighters, a small billy, two mugs and two spoons. The total weight of all this can be as little as 640g, shared between two people. Food on the other hand, is heavy. There's a lot you can do to lighten the load, but even using dehydrated foods and compact energy bars for lunch, you'll find it hard to manage with less than 1kg, and water is more again.

On day one of a mountain marathon, it's food that weighs you down. Despite this, most people pack a few 'treats', which increases the weight but brings a little cheer when needed most. Everyone has

These are menus we used on the OMM (Original Mountain Marathon) in 2006 and 2007, and how they were eaten. They reflect our different tastes and physiologies. Roy likes everything very simple and regular – he sets his watch to beep on the half hour to remind him to eat on the run. Amy finds it difficult to eat on the move, so her intake of 'proper food' (as opposed to sweets and gels) is weighted to the mornings and evenings. Everyone is different, and we'd recommend experimenting with different foods before the event. We drink as much water as possible throughout the weekend. Amy carries two 500ml bottles; Roy carries one and refills more often from streams during the day (drinking untreated water is a calculated risk weighed against the benefits of carrying less).

ROY'S MENU

Food	Weight (g)	Usage
Porridge*	–	Breakfast Day One
3 bananas	–	Breakfast Day One
12 Jordans Luxury Bars (6 Cranberry & Almond and 6 Absolute Nut)	672	4 while moving Day One; 2 for breakfast Day Two; 4 while moving Day Two; 2 spare (emergency rations)
2 slices bread pudding*	c. 150	1 while moving Day One; 1 after evening meal Day One
1 pack jumbo raisins	131	After evening meal Day One
4 slices flapjack*	c. 200	2 while moving Day One
Green & Black's dark chocolate	35	After evening meal
Fruit teabags	c. 50	4 cups during evening Day One; 2 cups for breakfast Day Two
Racing snake couscous*	150	Eaten as evening meal
1 bowl Wilf's famous veggie chilli *	–	In refreshment tent after finish
Total food weight carried	c. 1388	

AMY'S MENU

Food	Weight (g)	Usage
Porridge*	–	Breakfast before the start on Day One
2 bananas	–	1 for breakfast Day One; 1 walking to the start Day One
4 Jordans Luxury Bars (Cranberry & Almond)	224	2 while moving Day One; 1 while moving Day Two; 1 uneaten
4 Cadbury's Brunch Bars	140	2 while moving Day One; 1 while moving Day Two; 1 immediately after finish in download queue

MOUNTAIN MARATHON MENUS

Food	Weight (g)	Usage
2 small bags scroggan*	200	1 during Day One, (including evening); 1 while moving Day Two
3 caffeinated energy gels	82	2 used while moving Day Two; 1 spare
1 round Marmite fingers*	300	Evening of Day One
Noodly soup*	70	Immediately after pitching camp Day One
Fruit teabags	c. 50	4 cups during evening Day One; 2 cups for breakfast Day Two
1 sachet hot chocolate	50	Before bed Day One
1.5 x 400-calorie meal packs	225	1 about 6pm Day One; 1 shared with team mate about 8pm Day One
Porridge*	60	Breakfast Day Two
Go-Bar	65	Emergency rations, not eaten
2 bowls Wilf's famous veggie chilli*	–	In refreshment tent after finish
Total food weight carried	c. 1466	

The * denotes a recipe from this book.

their own idea of what makes a treat – for our friend PK it's always a little bar of dark chocolate, while Roy's team buddy Ian is more likely to go for a miniature of whisky. Amy always finds room for Marmite fingers, but her team mate Orna prefers peanut butter – with extra butter! Another all-female team, Helen and Sarah, go for salted cashews or Moreish Seeds (p196). If you haven't done an event like this before, you might be surprised to learn that sweet treats aren't all that welcome – **after a day chugging energy gels, syrupy flapjacks and Jelly Babies, most people are craving savoury, salty or bitter flavours.**

During an event, **more than half your food is likely to be eaten on the go.** Some people pack sandwiches, but most opt for chewy grain bars, trail mixes, dried fruit, and energy gels, bars and drinks. We've tried most things and have our own ideas about what works best for us. Roy will eat flapjack, maltloaf and cereal bars until they come out of his ears, and detests energy gels. Amy likes fruity snacks and scroggan and thinks gels are brilliant. We both enjoy bread pudding (see p277) as an alternative to flapjack. Being moist it needs less chewing, and it's easier to swallow when you're breathing hard, although it's relatively heavy and needs more careful wrapping.

We both drink water rather than energy drinks. In theory an isotonic drink goes in quicker, and we'd certainly use them for something like a road marathon. But on a mountain marathon you're drinking the stuff all day and water is about the only drink you won't be heartily sick of by the end. If you fill a rucksack bladder with energy drink, but then stop drinking it because you can't bear another sickly mouthful, you're in danger of dehydrating.

We recently supported our friends Ian and Lyndon on the infamous Devizes to Westminster canoe race. This is a 125-mile paddle with 77 portages, which competitors aim to complete in 24 hours. The 2008 event was marked by driving sleet and snow during the day and freezing conditions at night. Under such circumstances it's virtually impossible to take in enough food to sustain high-level performance, especially as the boys couldn't afford to stop paddling for more than a few minutes at a time. Again, a mixture of sweet and savoury foods was important, along with a steady intake of fluids and electrolytes to ward off dehydration and cramp. Refilling drinks bottles with warm drinks helped during the coldest part of the night.

A typically chilly and dreary overnight camp on the OMM 2007. Most competitors are tucked up in bed by 8pm.

The evening meal on a mountain marathon is about two things – packing in the nutrition and making you happy. The chances are that it will have been a hard day – for some people one of the toughest they've ever had. If you're cold, tired, stiff and famished, the food needs to be hot, easy and fast. We aim to have two meals.

Start with a noodly soup or a hot drink and cereal bar as soon as the tent is up, then boil water to either reconstitute a dehydrated meal pack, or a home-made version such as instant chilli and bulgar, instant spaghetti bolognese, soupy 'Smash' hash or racing snake couscous (see *Recipes* for all these), then have another main course a bit later on. We used to carry puddings as well, but found that we were usually happy with a bit of chocolate. At least as important as the food is drink. You'll probably be dehydrated from the day's exertions, and you have to do it all again tomorrow. Drink water or weak tea (fruit or herbal options are easier as you won't need milk), until your pee is close to colourless.

Racing snake couscous (p243) is easy and lightweight, an ideal racing food.

The 3-4 day Kepler Track in New Zealand can be achieved with a 35l day sack if food is chosen carefully.

LONGER EXPEDITIONS

It's a truth of living on a small island that camping trips in the UK are unlikely to take you far from civilisation for more than a few days. Even if you're undertaking a long-distance footpath in the UK – a journey that may take a month or more – you'll probably pass through a town or village at least every couple of days and thus have a chance to restock. In mainland Europe, there are usually plenty of wild camping opportunities in wilderness areas, but again, you're rarely more than a day or two from some form of civilisation. Many European national parks are dotted with huts. These sometimes have cooking facilities, and some will sell you basic supplies, but you will have to pay inflated prices to cover their carriage costs.

Long-term wilderness camping is something you're more likely to do elsewhere in the world. The Americans, Canadians, Australians and New Zealanders are all pretty keen on the outdoors, and in all these places books are published with ideas and advice devoted to their particular style of camping. There are hundreds of websites dedicated to the subject too. In Australia, long camping trips are as likely to be by vehicle, with heavy-duty swags for bedding and a cast-iron camp oven to sling in the back of the 4 x 4. In North and South America, Asia and New Zealand they'll very likely involve long-distance trail walking, trekking or tramping. Depending on the venue, you may be accompanied by a guide and/or porters, in which case you might not have so much input into the cooking.

On longer trips it becomes more efficient to carry **raw ingredients** rather than pre-assembled meals. Even if you have porters, horses or mules, considerations of weight will usually mean you're using mostly dried foodstuffs, so you need to know how to turn these into decent meals. A bag of flour is the basis of bread, pancakes, dumplings and cakes. Rice can be used for risottos, stews or puddings. Potato flakes serve as thickeners for soups and sauces as well as mash. Carrying the basics gives you the opportunity to cook a variety of different meals and to take advantage of other ingredients you are able to come by. Been fishing? Great – grilled fish with rice. Collected some mushrooms? Splendid –

HUNGRY IN THE HIMALAYAS?

Our friend, te expedition kayaker Daz Clarkson and two companions made a 14-day descent of the renowned Dudh Koshi, the river that drains the southern flanks of Everest. Their total food rations for the entire trip comprised two bags of mixed nuts, one pack of salted peanuts, one pack of apricots and a sachet of powdered fruit drink. This laid-back approach to catering comes as no surprise to anyone who has met Daz, who is one of life's characters. In fact the nuts were really only for emergencies, and they were a good choice – rich in fat, protein and carbs, with plenty of salt to replace that lost through sweating. There is a limit to the amount of food that can be carried in a kayak, and most expeditions of this nature rely on finding hospitable locals from whom meals can be bought.

mushroom stroganoff it is. Farm-fresh eggs? Hurray, it's pancakes again! Chestnut season? Stuffing balls or nut roast coming up.

With the best will in the world, it can be difficult to ensure a good balance of foods every day. This is one circumstance where a **pack of vitamin and mineral supplements can be useful**, especially vitamin C, B vitamins and iron, if you're not getting much fresh fruit, vegetables or meat, or if you're relying on tinned produce.

Remember that on long expeditions you will almost certainly need to treat water – there's more information on this in Chapter 4. This can be a time-consuming chore, so share it.

CAMPING WITH CHILDREN

We believe that every child should go camping. It's active, educational, character building and great for firing the imagination and developing an understanding of nature and our place in the world. Most importantly, it's damn good fun!

It seems rather sad to us that some people live well into adult life without ever having spent a night under canvas. We'll grudgingly admit that camping might not be for everyone, but believe that every child deserves the right to find out for themselves, before they turn into a committed 'campophobe' (doomed to a life of staying at home or spending a fortune in bed-and-breakfast land, never watching the sun rise from a sleeping bag, mug of hot tea in hand... a cruel fate indeed).

It's never too young to start camping but be careful whom you put in charge of guiding you to the site...

The very best people to introduce children to the joys of living outdoors are parents, uncles, aunts and grandparents, because they can begin the 'indoctrination' at a much earlier age than youth leaders and teachers (who nevertheless do a great job with older kids). The following is our advice for camping with, and cooking for, youngsters you know well.

It's never too early to start kids camping. Our nephew Zack had done it before he was a year old, and our nieces Izzy and Milly are veteran campers at the ages of six and four. Youngsters are very receptive to new ideas, and most will accept that things are sometimes done a little differently when camping. The important thing is to make sure that you are comfortable with the situation and alert to any potential problems.

Like a home kitchen, the camp kitchen is a potentially dangerous place, especially if you're cooking on the ground. As a result, you may well be tempted to set the children up with an activity well away from your cooking area, and to get a meal prepared without them really being aware that you're doing it. However, it's a good idea to give your youngsters a tour of the cooking area and equipment when you first set up. This will demystify it and give you a chance to explain the dangers of stoves, fuel bottles, sharp knives and the like. **Designate a no-go zone for running and games.** Keep sharp or breakable items (knives, glass, opened tins, bottles, skewers) out of harm's way, ideally in a sturdy box with a lid.

When it comes to eating meals, **camping chairs and a table** to sit at will save a few spillages – children can be clumsy (bless them!), and it's even more likely that things will get knocked over if you're sitting on the ground. Most children love having their own miniature version of grown-up stuff, and mini camping chairs and tables are available cheaply in most camping shops.

Comfort foods such as toad-in-the-hole (p259) and cowboy feast (p238) go down well with kids young and old.

Youngsters are willing workers, so **give them a 'very important job'**, such as mixing, crushing, spreading or mashing for the little ones, or a bit of chopping or pot stirring for the older ones. Be prepared for a bit of mess. A large, clean plastic sheet or plasticised tablecloth spread on the ground will mean that minor spillages can be recovered – as long as it's clear that the sheet is like a table and not for walking on.

Quite aside from the fact that the best way to learn is to do, it is also quite remarkable how the vegetables that may normally be shunned suddenly become tasty to children who have scrubbed and chopped them themselves. Even washing up has novelty value to kids used to dishwashers. With a bit of clever manipulation by their parents, our nieces adopt the superhero personas 'Captain Teatowel and the Wonderwasher' for the task – complete with tea towel capes and magic scrubbers.

Involve children in the decision-making processes and planning. Ask them what they think the group should eat. If you're out walking or biking during the day, ask them where they'd like to stop for lunch – at the top of the hill, or next to the stream on the other side – or maybe in that cave marked on the map?

Children can be difficult to feed at the best of times, with likes and dislikes that seem to vary wildly from day to day, even hour to hour. This can be particularly tricky in a camp situation, because you're less likely to have the means to produce alternatives on request.

Fortunately, hearty 'fresh air' appetites and the novelty of food cooked outdoors are often enough to make all sorts of things go down well, and because camp foods tend to be relatively simple they are often popular with kids. Treats are very definitely an essential part of the menu, and preparing them is all part of the fun.

CHILD-FRIENDLY WEEKEND MENU

Friday	
Evening meal	Cowboy feast*
	Strawberry cheesecake*
Saturday	
Breakfast	Banana and blueberry pancakes* with maple syrup
	(make extra batter for evening meal)
Lunch	Bannock* or chapattis* with leek and potato soup*
Evening meal	Toad-in-the-hole* with fresh or tinned vegetables or,
	if you don't have a camp oven, pasta tonno*
	Rocky road*
Sunday	
Breakfast	Breakfast crumble*
Lunch	Falafel* sandwiches with lots of relish and salads

If snacks are required (they will be), have some dried fruit, popcorn*, flapjack* or a bag of scroggan* at the ready. And don't forget a few toasted marshmallows before bed – heaven. If you're really adventurous, producing proper bread* and hand-churned butter* will occupy most of a summer afternoon. The * denotes a recipe from this book.

LARGE GROUPS

You might think nothing of cooking dinner for six at home, but in a camp context this is a lot of people. To provide meals for six or more, you really need at the very least a **larger burner stove**, and preferably more than one – multi-burner gas hobs are ideal. Alternatively, a campfire will do a great job too. A large group means a larger food budget, and you can often take advantage of economies of scale by buying some foods in bulk. (It's easy to get carried away with the idea of a bargain. Don't be tempted to buy more than you need.)

BUNGS

The 'bung' was developed by our friends at York Canoe Club in the 1990s. At this time venues for weekend trips tended to be camping barns with limited kitchen facilities. Everyone was invited to bring a contribution to the main evening meal, which would be cooked in a single giant pan. The theory was that if everyone brought a volume of food to satisfy their own appetite, there would be enough to go round. All sorts of unlikely contributions went into the bung, which would be heated and stirred and eyed nervously for a while until someone took the plunge. Bowls were loaded, noses were held and bellies were filled. Dubious as it sounds, the bung idea can work surprisingly well, so long as someone takes charge, assesses the various offerings, and polices the addition of more weird and wonderful ingredients.

Mass catering in camp needn't be more difficult than cooking for a small group, but it does take longer. There are economies of scale in terms of shopping and preparation time, but they're not necessarily as great as you might think. A small, lidded pan of water over a gas stove might boil in five or six minutes; a 2–3l pan, even if it's lidded aluminium, might take 20 minutes or more to come to a full boil on the same stove. Big pans are essential for mass catering (see Chapter 3, *Cookware*), but the contents can take much longer to cook, especially outside, where a fresh breeze might be cooling the top of the pan as fast as you heat the bottom. You can improve things greatly by setting up a decent windbreak, but you still need to **allow lots of time**.

Recruit help for tasks such as chopping. It's worth doubling up on some basic equipment in order to speed things along – an extra board and spare sharp knife can halve your prep time. When delegating tasks like this, make sure your volunteer knows exactly what you want. Explaining at the start is much better than complaining later that it's not been done right.

Some people do mornings better than others and everyone has their own routine, so you can't expect everyone to sit down together for breakfast the way they might to an evening meal. **DIY breakfasts are much the simplest option.** Leave out bread and jam or cereals so people can help themselves. Alternatively, a big pan of porridge (see p187) will stay warm over a very low heat for up to an hour – keep an eye on it and stir regularly, or it will stick or burn. Add water or milk as it thickens, but leave out sugar and other flavourings so people can add their own to taste. If people want a full cooked breakfast, bacon and egg scramble (see p191), made

using lardons, is about the quickest and easiest option. Pancakes (see p189) are great if you have plenty of time. Make up the batter, turn out the first few pancakes, then get people to take turns cooking their own. With more than five or six people, you'll need two pans on the go.

A self-service breakfast in Nepal keeps things simple before a day on the river.

Like breakfasts, packed lunches are best arranged in a DIY fashion. Set up a table with bread, sandwich fillings, cake and fruit or bags of scroggan, and get everyone to make their own butties and pack their own mid-day meal and snacks. Ideally everyone will have a lunchbox, but if not, you'll also need to provide bags for wrapping. If you're cooking lunch in camp, much the same guidelines apply as for evening meals, but you'll probably want smaller meals, such as tabouleh, roasted vegetable butties, falafels (see *Recipes* for all these) or hot dogs from a barbecue.

Some recipes lend themselves to mass catering much better than others. Most of the pasta recipes in this book are winners in this respect – carbonara usually goes down well, especially as many people have only ever had it ready made, and find the real thing far more delicious. The ingredients are easy to come by, even in very small village shops. Quick soya curry (see *Recipes*) is another easy option if you have some assistance with the chopping, and the bigger the group, the more you can go to town on salads, sprinkles and side dishes. Cheese fondue (see p226 and Mars Bar fondue (see p263). In good weather, **a self-service barbecue works well**. Make sure the barbecue is big enough, and that you have plenty of fuel – and if there are veggies in the team, make sure everyone knows which part of the grill is for non-meaty stuff.

CHAPTER 10
Saving the Day: Mistakes, Mishaps and Misfortunes

All sorts of things can go wrong on a camping trip, and some are related to food or food preparation. Nutritional condition has an impact on well-being and performance, and if you fail to feed yourself well, other problems are more likely to occur. A silly mistake like failing to treat water, wash hands or pack the can opener can ruin your whole trip. And the camp kitchen itself is fraught with potential dangers – sharp tools, hot stoves and unchilled food storage. In this chapter we'll suggest how to avoid some of these situations and also how to tackle commmon culinary mishaps and oversights.

ILLNESSES
Prevention being better than cure, here are a few tips on how to avoid falling ill on your trip.

Food poisoning
What it feels like: Nausea, vomiting, diarrhoea, cramps, faintness, dehydration.
Why it happens: Usually food or water contaminated by an organism or toxic chemicals.
How to avoid it: Treat water, strict hygiene, appropriate storage of food.

Dehydration
What it feels like: Thirst, cramps, vomiting, nausea.
Why it happens: Inadequate fluid intake for conditions.
How to avoid it: Adequate fluid intake (see Chapter 4).

Diarrhoea
What it feels like: Repeated and sometimes uncontrolled loose-to-liquid bowel movements, stomach cramps, dehydration, weakness.
Why it happens: Usually a reaction to toxins produced by microorganisms ingested with food or contaminated water.
How to avoid it: Scrupulous hygiene and water treatment.

Anaphylaxis
What it feels like: Sudden swelling, especially of face, lips and tongue, rash, wheezing, sometimes nausea, cramps, diarrhoea, unconsciousness.
Why it happens: Exposure to a particular allergen eg nuts, or stings, seafood, or penicillin.
How to avoid it: Tell companions about allergies. If medication is carried, make sure they know how to administer it.

Diabetic hypoglycaemia
What it feels like: Confusion, dizziness, lack of coordination, appearance of drunkenness.
Why it happens: Low blood glucose, often exacerbated by exercise or lack of food.
How to avoid it: Eating regularly and appropriately and/or taking prescribed drugs. Tell companions how to recognise problems and administer medication.

Other preventable conditions
Heat exhaustion and **heat stroke** can both be avoided by wearing appropriate clothing, avoiding extremely hot conditions and taking on adequate levels of fluid before and during exercise. **Exhaustion** as a result of over-exertion, particularly in very cold conditions, can also be avoided to a large extent by eating the right food and drinking enough water. **Hypothermia** is caused by exposure to cold, and is more likely to happen in people who have failed to eat enough.

ACCIDENTS
Basic rules of camp and kitchen safety should prevent you needing to treat any **cuts**, **burns** or **scalds**. However, accidents do happen. Cuts should be cleared, cleaned and dressed and burns or scalds cooled for at least 10 minutes in cold running water and then dressed – with cling film if necessary.

Always have a basic **first aid kit** in camp. We have several, packed for different activities. The smallest, used for lightweight backpacking and racing, contains a couple of sterile wipes and dressings, a crepe bandage, a roll of micropore tape, a few sticking plasters and some painkillers. The mid-weight kits contain latex gloves, blister kits, a much more comprehensive range of dressings, bandages, plasters, various forms of tape, antiseptic wipes, painkillers, antihistamines, a re-hydration spoon and medicines for diarrhoea, constipation, colds and flu.

Chemists and outdoor shops stock a range of pre-packed first aid kits, some of them tailored to different kinds of activity. If you buy one, it's important to familiarise yourself with the contents of the kit and check that they match the risks of your activity. It's often better and usually cheaper to make up your own kit. Make sure that it is readily available and easily recognised – someone else may be looking for it for you – and that it is 'environment-proof'. If you have to open it in rain and wind, will the contents be protected? Can things be got out easily with wet and cold hands?

In cases of mild hypothermia the restorative effects of shelter or a bothy bag and a warming drink can be miraculous. However, the casualty may become ill again rapidly when re-exposed to the elements.

There is no substitute for going on a proper first aid course – we can't recommend it highly enough. If you get the chance, take it! A good pocket first aid manual is Jim Duff and Peter Gormly's *First Aid and Wilderness Medicine* (Cicerone Press 2007).

CULINARY MISHAPS

Burned Food and Pans

Basically, once food is burned, you can't 'un-burn' it. Chopping away the worst bits helps, as does disguising the taste with sauces or strong flavours.

If you've properly burned something like a stew, sauce or soup to the bottom of the pan, **don't scrape it off** and mix it with the unburned food – you'll taint the whole dish. Either remove the unburned food to another pan and start again, or finish cooking slowly with the burned food in place – it will protect the food above to some extent.

Something not to your liking?

To clean burned food from a pan, remove what you can by scraping gently with a spatula or spoon, then immediately half fill the pan with water and a squirt of washing-up liquid, if you have it, and return it to the stove. Keep scraping as the water heats up. Don't bother with a scourer until all soft food remains have been removed. If your scourer isn't up to the job, try dipping it in sand to give it more abrasiveness. If the burned material can't be shifted, you might just have to leave it there. As long as any moist food is cleaned away it will be sterile. However, once you've burned a pan, food is much more likely to stick to it and burn again in future.

Some burned pans come up shiny and clean if you **cook something acidic** like rhubarb in them. (But don't eat rhubarb that has been cooked in an aluminium pan as it will have absorbed more metal than is good for you.)

That's better...

Too Much Chilli?

If you've made your food too spicy, you can tone it down by **adding cream or yoghurt**, or dilute the effects by adding more of any of the other ingredients. Potato is good for bulking things out and absorbing flavour. Alternatively, you can try to counteract the heat by **adding sweetness** – sugar, jam or chocolate will all do this – and the result can be surprisingly tasty! Best of all is to go easy with the spicy stuff in the first place. For camping we always buy mild chilli powder and mild Tabasco (made with jalapenos and sold in a green bottle rather than the traditional red). Cater to the person with the mildest taste – the others can always add spice.

Lumpy Sauces

If your white sauce or custard is full of lumps, tip out the runnier stuff into a spare bowl or pan and use a sturdy spoon to beat the lumpy part into a paste. Then add the thinner stuff a little at a time, making sure it's all mixed in before adding more.

Too Greasy?

Some dehydrated meals include hydrogenated fats or suet, which can be unpleasantly greasy. Adding a squeeze of lemon juice or a couple of spoons of vinegar (you can get small sachets of this from some chip shops and cafeterias) will help break this down. Decide for yourself which is more appropriate in terms of flavour for the dish you are cooking.

Forgotten Utensils

Can Opener

Sooner or later we all do it, and the advent of easy-open ring-pull cans somehow makes it even easier to be caught out. If it happens to you, begin by searching for a purpose-built alternative. Often there are can openers on other pieces of equipment, such as multitools and key rings. If not, using a hand-held stone as a hammer to repeatedly puncture the lid with a sharp stout knife, chisel, flat-head screwdriver or even a tent peg can work. These are rather desperate measures, however, and **almost all improvised means of getting into a tin will involve substantial risk of injury**. The cut or torn edges of food cans are viciously sharp, and it is all too easy when exerting pressure on them to slip and lacerate your hands or wrists. Consider the consequences carefully before attempting emergency tin opening and, if the contents of the tin aren't essential, you might be better off going without.

The best camp recipes are hard to get wrong, as long as cooking receives your full attention.

Corkscrew

Screwtop wine bottles make life rather easier, but if you find yourself stuck with a bottle that has a cork, don't despair. It's much easier to get into a wine bottle without a corkscrew than it is into a can without a can opener. It's usually pretty easy to push the cork in using a sturdy stick or a tent peg. Wrap the bottle in something (there is a small chance it will break and this will stop glass going everywhere), put it on the ground, and use your improvised tool to push the cork slowly in. Lean sideways so that you don't stab yourself in the neck or chest if you slip. The main problem with this method is that you won't be able to reseal the bottle, so you'll either have to let it go to waste, or drink it all. (Shame!)

Cutlery

If you forget cutlery and your food is too wet or sloppy to be eaten with fingers, serve it in bowls, mugs or billies, so it can be slurped, or make chapattis and used them to shovel food.

Pot Grab/Pan Handle

You can pick up a pan using a tea towel or t-shirt to protect your hands, but be careful not to trail the cloth into the stove flame. Alternatively, for pans with a pronounced lip, you can improvise a loop handle using a length of string. Measure the string around the pan, and make pairs of knots at intervals of a quarter the circumference of the pan. Tie two lengths of string about one-and-a-quarter times the diameter of the pan between the first and third and the second and fourth pairs of knots. Tie the knotted string tightly just under the lip of the pan, so that the two cross strings intercept in the middle. Where the two cross strings meet, make a loop big enough to pass a stick or utensil through, so you can lift the pan without scalding your hands in the steam. Test it with the pan full of water before heating it. This method is only suitable when using a stove to heat the bottom of the pan. Don't use it on a campfire or a stove that licks flame up the side of the pan.

Equipment Repairs

Damage to equipment may be inconvenient or life-threatening, depending on the state of the weather, the state of your group, and the long-term consequences of the failure of the item in question.

You could take a repair kit that to cover many eventualities when camping. Useful items to go in the kit might be gaffer tape, a penknife or multi-tool, ripstop nylon patches, a few zip ties, waterproof patches for water-carriers/hydration bladders, spare straps and cordage, spare tent pegs, safety pins, a sewing kit, a knife sharpener and a stove maintenance kit (see also *Useful Ancillaries* in Chapter 3).

Part Two

WEIGHTS AND MEASURES

The quantities given are designed to feed hungry campers. In most cases portions will be fairly large – we'd hate you to go hungry. Few campers have the means to measure or weigh things accurately, so our ingredients are quantified in other ways. Inevitably this will mean some variation, but it shouldn't ever be disastrous. Likewise, if you can't buy ingredients in exactly the quantities suggested, in many cases it won't matter. You can supplement our directions with those on packets and sachets.

Where we talk about a mugful, we mean a mug like this. It's an insulated camp mug that holds about 400ml. We fill it *without* tamping down the contents or encouraging them to settle.

When we talk about a spoonful, we mean a spoon like this. It's a 7.5ml Lexan camp spoon, and when we talk about dry ingredients, spoonfuls are heaped unless otherwise stated.

A small handful of dried ingredients is one like this. Fingers should be more or less closed. Obviously if you have big hands it will be more, but chances are you'll have a bigger appetite too.

A large handful is one like this. Basically, it's as much as you can pick up with one hand.

A double handful is like this – as much as you can scoop up with two hands held together.

WATER

Where water is used as part of a dish, rather than a means of cooking, it is listed as an ingredient. Water used as an ingredient should be treated if it comes from a less than reliable source (see Chapter 4).

WEIGHTS AND MEASURES OF COMMON INGREDIENTS						
Ingredients	Spoonful (heaped)	Mugful	Small handful	Large handful	Double handful	Notes
Flour	10g	200g	•	•	•	
Cornflour	10g	•	•	•	•	
Egg powder	7g	•	•	•	•	2 spoonfuls (15g) makes up one egg
Milk powder	7g	•	•	•	•	6 spoonfuls (40g) makes one mugful
Quick-cook oats	•	160g	20g	•	•	¼ mug (40g) makes one portion
Dried potato flakes	•	150g	•	•	•	
Rice	•	300g	•	•	•	⅓ mugful (100g) makes one portion
Cornmeal	•	180g	•	•	•	
Bulgar wheat	•	300g	•	•	•	⅓ mugful (100g) makes one portion
Pasta twists	•	120g	•	60g	160g	120g makes one portion
Couscous	•	270g	•	•	•	60g makes one portion
Lentils	•	260g	•	•	•	
Sugar	10g	300g	•	•	•	
Leafy veg (spinach)	•	•	100g	•		1 small handful is one portion – it shrinks a lot when cooked
Dried veg (onion)	•	•	5g	•	•	1 small handful is about a medium-sized onion
Liquids	7ml	400ml	•	•	•	

INDEX OF RECIPES

* Quick (less than 10 minutes to prepare); At home (suitable for preparing in advance)

HOT BREAKFASTS

Breakfast Crumble

Kick-start the day with this warming, energy-packed and scrummy plateful. It makes a great dessert too, but the calorie count is pretty stratospheric, so it's better to enjoy the decadence then go out and burn it off with a big day out. For a slimmed-down version you can leave out the butter, but be prepared for your crunchy crumble to become a rather soggy mulch (still tasty, though).

Serves 2

Pans: 1 or 2

Stoves: 1

Other equipment: plate, spoon

Cook time: 5-10 minutes

Pack weight: about 180g per person

Prep time: 5–10 minutes

Vegetarian

• *1 golfball-sized knob (25g) butter or margarine* • *6 digestive biscuits* • *2 handfuls porridge oats* • *2 handfuls mixed dried fruit (raisins, sultanas, cranberries, papaya, pineapple, mango)* • *5 spoonfuls instant custard powder water* • *optional: a handful of cornflakes for extra crunch, 1 teaspoon mixed spice or ground ginger, small handful chopped mixed nuts, fresh chopped banana*

Crush the digestive biscuits in a plastic bag, or on a plate or board with the back of a spoon. Melt the butter in a pan over a low heat. Add the crushed biscuits and oats to the butter and stir well to form a crumbly mixture. If you have only one pan, set the mixture to one side in a mug, bowl or bag if you have one.

Bring half a mugful (200ml) of water to the boil and use it to make up the custard (stir carefully to avoid lumps). Add the dried fruit and any other ingredients you're using to the crumble mix and serve immediately with the hot custard.

Hint: *serve the crumble on top of the custard rather than the other way round – this way it keeps its crunch!*

Porridge

Serves 2

Pans: 1

Stoves: 1

Campfire: yes

Other equipment: spoon for stirring

Prep time: 10 minutes

Pack weight: about 80g per person for basic recipe; optional
   extras increase weight

Fuel efficiency: very good

Vegetarian

> A million grandmas can't be wrong – porridge is the breakfast of champions. If you want to be a purist and make it with water and salt, be our guest, but if it's a multi-carb-packing delicious breakfast you're after, try it sweet and milky!

• ½ mug (75g) porridge oats • 6 heaped spoonfuls (40g) milk powder • water (treated if from suspect source) • pinch of salt (not essential) • sugar/honey/golden or maple syrup to taste • optional: fresh fruit (berries and bananas are very good), dried fruit (sultanas, cranberries, chopped apricots, dates) or chocolate chips

Put the oats and milk powder (and salt if using) into a pan with 1¾ mugfuls (700ml) of water and heat gently. Try to avoid actually boiling the mixture, and keep stirring until it thickens. Bear in mind that the porridge will continue to thicken in your bowl, so serve it slightly sloppier than you want to eat it. Add your sweetener, and any optional extras, and serve.

Hint: you can reduce cooking time and fuel consumption by mixing up the porridge and leaving it to soak for a while before you start heating it.

Hint: as soon as you've finished with the pan, fill it with water. Do the same with any bowls – porridge dries like cement, so keep it soaking and wash up quickly.

Porridge with summer berries and brown sugar

Alternative
No-washing-up Porridge (honestly)
If you hate washing up, or you're going lightweight and don't want to bother with anything but a kettle or water billy, quick-cook oats can be cooked in a plastic cooking bag (see Cookware in Chapter 3) or old foil packs from dehydrated ready meals. This means your billy stays perfectly clean. Varieties we've tried that cooked fine this way include Mornflake Breakfast Oats, Flanahans Quick Oats and Quaker Oats-So-Simple. Measure out your oats/sugar/milk-powder mix into the bag before you leave home. To cook, add boiling water, give it a squidge to make sure it's mixed, then tie the bag top securely and leave it somewhere warm for five minutes to absorb the water.

Pancakes

Serves 2

Pans: 1 frying pan (non-stick will make life easier)

Stoves: 1

Campfire: yes

Other equipment: bowl or pan for mixing batter; a small spatula is useful

Prep time: 10 minutes

Pack weight: about 80g per person (using milk powder), not including fillings

Fuel efficiency: good

Vegetarian

• ½ mug (100g) flour • 1 egg or 2 spoonfuls (15g) whole egg powder • ¾ mug (300ml) milk, or 4 heaped spoonfuls milk powder and ¾ mug water • pinch of salt (optional) • ½ spoonful bicarbonate of soda (this makes your pancakes nice and fluffy, but it's not essential) • 2 spoonfuls (15ml) oil (you can leave this out, but it helps stop pancakes sticking)

Serve with anything you like – here are some suggestions:
• *the classic – lemon juice and sugar* • *syrup (golden or maple)* • *chopped fruit – bananas, strawberries, blueberries or blackberries are all great* • *butter and jam* • *chocolate spread* • *savoury fillings such as cheese sauce with ham and mushrooms*

Put the dry ingredients into a bowl or pan. Crack in the egg if using a fresh one. Add a splash of milk (or water if using powdered milk) and mix vigorously to create a smooth paste. Add the rest of the milk or water little by little, each time whisking until smooth. Your batter should be pourable but not runny – you might not need quite all the liquid.

Heat the oil or fat in the frying pan over a moderate heat for a couple of minutes before trying the first pancake. Pour a small amount of batter into the pan and let it spread naturally. If you've used bicarb you'll soon see bubbles forming in the batter. When the whole surface is riddled with bubbles, a bit like a crumpet, lift the pancake and flip it. The other side will cook much more quickly. Without the bicarb you might not get bubbles, but you can lift an edge of the pancake to see when it's ready to turn.

This recipe is for thick American- or Scottish-style pancakes. For thin, continental-style crêpes, use more milk, but bear in mind that they are more fiddly to cook.

Hint: if you're using fruit, chop it into the batter and cook it as part of the pancake. Blueberries or finely chopped banana are great this way. The cooking not only makes them deliciously gooey, they are much easier to eat bound into the pancake, rather than sliding around on top.

Pancakes with stewed apple and bacon – a delicious combination.

Oatcakes

Serves 2 (large portions)

Pans: 1 frying pan or griddle (non-stick makes life easier)

Stoves: 1

Campfire: yes

Other equipment: bowl or pan for mixing batter; a small spatula is helpful but not essential

Prep time: 10 minutes

Pack weight: about 60g per person, not including toppings

Fuel efficiency: good

Vegetarian

As well as being recommended by Simon, this recipe is also inexpensive, lightweight, the basic ingredients don't spoil in heat or cold, and – unlike pancakes – no eggs are used, so there is no danger of 'eggcidents'. As if that weren't enough, it blends low-GI oats with high-GI flour, so it should keep your energy levels up for hours.

• *1 mug (150g) porridge oats* • *¼ mug (50g) flour (plain or self-raising)* • *¼ mug (50g) milk powder* • *water (you can replace the milk powder and water with fresh milk if you have it)* • *4 spoonfuls (25ml) vegetable oil – groundnut or sunflower is ideal, but any type will do* • *toppings – serve spread with something sweet. Simon's favourite is* dulce de leche *– a kind of caramel gloop from South America made from condensed milk and sugar. In Europe it's often sold as* confiture du lait *– look in delis and supermarkets, either among the jams and spreads, or among dessert sauces near the ice-cream chiller. Alternatively, use honey, jam, chocolate spread or condensed milk from a tube – it's all good.*

Mix the dry ingredients into a batter with a slurp of oil and a dribble of water. Add the water gradually so as not to over-shoot – a batter about the consistency of wet cement seems to work well. Heat a pan or griddle and fry dollops of batter gently until they're golden on both sides. This takes about a minute.

Bacon and Egg Scramble

Serves as many as you like

Pans: 1 – the largest you have

Stoves: 1

Campfire: yes

Other equipment: bowl or spare pan, fork for whisking, wooden/
*   plastic spoon or spatula*

Prep time: 10 minutes

Pack weight: 100g per person with fresh eggs, 80g with
*   powdered*

Fuel efficiency: good

Vegetarian options

A great cooked breakfast without the hassle, this is particularly suitable for larger groups, where turning individual rashers of bacon and keeping things hot becomes difficult. Most mid-size supermarkets now sell packs of lardons (chopped bacon), or a butcher will chop bacon for you, or you can just chop up two or three regular rashers per person.

• *2–3 eggs per person, or 6 spoonfuls (45g) whole egg powder and 8 spoonfuls (60ml) water* • *1 small handful (about 50g) bacon lardons per person* • *dash of milk – about 4 spoonfuls (25ml) per person* • *oil or fat for frying* • *salt and pepper*

Heat a drop of oil or fat in the pan and throw in the lardons. Let them cook for five minutes, stirring occasionally. Mix up egg powder and water if using, or crack the eggs into a bowl or pan and give them a brief whisk to break the yolks. Add the milk and remaining oil, season well with salt and pepper and tip the whole lot in with the bacon. Stir the mixture slowly but continuously, making sure you scrape up the layer of cooked egg as it forms on the bottom of the pan.

Turn off the heat when there is still a tiny bit of runny egg in amongst the cooked stuff – it will continue to cook in its own heat for another minute or two. Serve alone, or with flatbreads or potato patties. Get the people who like soft eggs to help themselves first – you can always turn the heat back on and firm things up for those who prefer their eggs well cooked.

Vegetarian alternative
For a vegetarian version, replace the lardons with chopped mushrooms.

Scrambled Eggs in a Bag

To make this work properly you need to use proper cooking bags (see Cookware in Chapter 3). Regular food bags sometimes work, but as they are not meant to be heated, more often than not they split. This recipe works well with fresh eggs, but not powdered.

Serves 2

Pans: 1 – the largest you have

Stoves: 1

Campfire: yes

Other equipment: cooking bag, wire bag tie

Prep time: 10 minutes

Pack weight: 60–80g per person

Fuel efficiency: good

Vegetarian

• *2–3 eggs per person* • *splash (25ml) of milk, fresh or reconstituted* • *1 spoonful oil* • *salt and pepper* • *optional: small handful grated cheese*

Boil two mugfuls of water in a large pan. Put the oil in the bag and squish it around to coat the inside. Crack the eggs into the bag, add a splash of milk, and season. Seal the bag top with the wire tie, expelling most of the air as you do so. Give the bag a good massage so that the eggs are well mixed. Lower the bag into the boiling water and allow to cook, leaving the top un-submerged for easy retrieval.

After about a minute, lift the bag out and jiggle the contents a little (beware – it will be hot). Replace and continue to cook until most of the liquid egg has gone. Open the bag, add and mix in the grated cheese if using, and serve. Use the hot water to make tea or coffee to go with the eggs.

Eggy Bread/French Toast

Serves 2

Pans: 1 frying pan

Stoves: 1

Campfire: yes

Other equipment: bowl or spare pan for mixing, fork for whisking,
   spatula

Prep time: 20 minutes

Pack weight: about 150g per person with fresh ingredients, 120g
   using dried

Fuel efficiency: good

Vegetarian

This popular breakfast dish can be made either sweet or savoury, or for a bit of both, serve American-style with bacon and maple syrup.

• 2 fresh eggs or 4 heaped spoonfuls (30g) whole egg powder and
8 spoonfuls (40ml) water • splash (50ml) of milk or 2 heaped
spoonfuls milk powder and 50ml water • 4 slices bread • salt and
pepper or a spoonful of sugar and a pinch of ground nutmeg •
a little oil or fat for frying

Suggested toppings:
• tomato ketchup/brown sauce • chopped fresh or tinned fruit
• baked beans • bacon and maple syrup

Make up the egg and milk if using powdered. Lightly whisk the egg
and milk in a pan, and add the salt and pepper or sugar and spice.
Heat a little fat in the frying pan, and one by one dip the bread slices
in the eggy mixture. Allow them to soak for a few seconds, then transfer them to the pan. Fry until golden brown on both sides, and serve.

Snacks, Soups, Side Dishes and Starters

Scroggan

This isn't so much a recipe as a collation job. You can buy all kinds of trail mixes – health food shops usually have a good selection, as do some supermarkets – but do you often find there's a bit too much of one thing and not enough of the ones you really like? Much the best option is to make your own.

Makes about a 1 litre jarful

Equipment: bag or bowl for mixing

Prep time: 5 minutes

Pack weight: 1 mugful (200g) provides ample snacking for one person on a big day out

Vegetarian (except for Jelly Babies)

Scroggan's name comes from the original list of suggested ingredients:

S – sultanas

C – chocolate

R – raisins

O – orange peel (candied)

G – ginger (crystallised)

G – glucose

A – anything else you fancy

N – nuts

Below is a list of suitable ingredients – aim for a ratio of about 2:2:1 of fruit:nuts/seeds:sweets. This will mean the overall mix is carb-rich, but not too sweet. Take your pick of ingredients from the list in the box opposite and then just mix 'em and bag 'em!

• unsalted peanuts • brazil nuts • hazelnuts • almonds • cashew nuts • coconut chips • sunflower seeds • pumpkin seeds • banana chips • sultanas and raisins • dried cranberries • dried apricots • chopped dried papaya • chopped dried mango • dried, pitted cherries • dried, pitted dates • dried, pitted prunes • crystallised ginger (the dry, sugar-coated type, not the sticky syrupy version) • Jelly Babies/Dolly Mixtures • Smarties/M&Ms • chocolate chips/buttons (dark ones are less sweet) • fudge, chopped small (fudge fingers are better for this than the crumbly stuff, which tends to just disintegrate when mixed with everything else) • granola clusters (these go soft after a day, so add them at the last minute or leave out if you want the scroggan to keep) • honey loops or Cheerios (ditto)

…plus anything else you fancy, although it's best to avoid really sticky or crumbly items, as they just make a mess of everything else.

Moreish Seeds

Makes about a 1 litre jarful

Equipment: home oven heated to 180°C/gas mark 5, oven-proof dish or roasting tin, 1 small and 1 large mixing bowl

Prep time: 60 minutes at home

Pack weight: a handful for sprinkling on savoury dishes weighs about 30g; bring a bit more for general snacking

Vegetarian

These seeds are great as a snack on the go, or as a bit of a pre-dinner nibble with a well-earned beer, but it's as a supplement to other dishes that they really come into their own. For very little extra weight, a handful of these morsels turns a plate of pasta, risotto, salad or couscous into something special.

You can buy mixed seeds from health food shops, but these mixes often don't include pine nuts, which you'll need to buy separately.

• 700g mixed seeds – we use sunflower, sesame and pumpkin, plus pine nuts • 20ml Worcester Sauce • 100ml dark soy sauce • optional: large pinch of chilli powder

Heat the oven. Mix the soy, Worcester Sauce – and chilli powder if using – in a small bowl. In a larger bowl, mix all the seeds and tip in half the blended sauce. Give the mixture a good stir so that all the seeds are coated. Tip them into a roasting tin and spread out evenly. Bake in the oven, removing every 10 minutes to give the seeds a good stir, and to break up any clusters that form. When all the original sauce has almost dried, add the rest and continue baking and stirring.

After about half an hour you will smell the seeds beginning to roast. When the second lot of sauce has completely dried, the seeds should be a rich conker-brown. Spread them onto a clean surface to cool. Store in an airtight container, and take a couple of handfuls in a plastic pot or bag when you go away.

Popcorn

Serves 4 as a snack
Pans: 1 large, must have a lid
Stoves: 1
Campfire: yes
Prep time: 5 minutes
Pack weight: about 30g per person
Fuel efficiency: excellent
Vegetarian

- *½ mug (100g) popping corn* • *6 spoonfuls (40ml) vegetable oil*
- *sugar or salt*

Heat the oil in a pan and tip in the corn. Jiggle the pan a little and place back on the heat with the lid on. After about 30 seconds you'll hear popping. Don't be tempted to take a peek until the popping slows to just one or two a second. Remove the pan from the heat, sprinkle in salt or sugar (we like it with both) and serve.

Quite how your local cinema gets away with charging as much as it does for a carton of popcorn when the raw ingredients cost a few pence is a mystery. Perhaps it's the delicious smell of warm corn that scrambles the senses and makes people willing to part with their cash.

Warning Hot oil is dangerous, and popping can be quite explosive. Keep the lid on the pan all the time.

Marmite Fingers

Serves 1 as a light lunch or snack
Equipment: chopping board or plate, knife
Prep time: 5 minutes
Pack weight: about 150–200g per person, depending on the bread
Vegetarian

Note If you're in the Marmite 'hate it' camp, use some other savoury filling such as Bovril, or pate with a little extra salt added.

- *4 slices white bread* • *butter* • *Marmite (or alternative)*

Butter the first slice of bread and spread it with Marmite. Put the next slice on top and spread that too. Continue until you have a four-slice, triple-filling stack. Squash it down really well, cut off the crusts and cut into fingers or bite-sized squares. Put the whole block in a ziplock bag, squeezing out as much air as possible before sealing. It doesn't matter how squashed it gets during the day, it'll taste just as good at the end.

Note A quick-fix snack like this should be followed, within an hour or so of stopping prolonged exercise, with a low-GI meal.

This is really just a recipe for Marmite sandwiches, but we swear by them as a snack on the go, or as an end-of-day treat on multi-day events such as a mountain marathon. They can be gobbled down in one go in that crucial first half hour after stopping, or savoured slowly over the evening. The high-GI white bread does a good job of replenishing blood sugar, the salt helps ward off cramp, and the savoury flavour is a blissful relief after a day of sweet and sickly energy drinks, gels and bars.

Green Soup

Serves 2

Pans: 2

Stoves: 1

Campfire: yes

Other equipment: plate or board and decent knife for chopping;
    gloves if using stinging nettles

Prep time: 15 minutes

Pack weight: 200–250g per person

Fuel efficiency: good

Vegetarian (depending on the stock you use)

This basic recipe works well for any number of leafy green vegetables – including spinach, kale, spring greens, watercress, chickweed and stinging nettles. They all have their own flavour – try a mixture. The secret of a good soup is to chop the greens very finely, as you won't be able to liquidise the finished soup as you might at home.

• 3 big handfuls washed leafy greens • 1 onion or a small handful dried onion • 2 cloves garlic or ¼ spoonful garlic powder • 1 golfball-sized knob (25g) butter or margarine, or 4 spoonfuls (25ml) oil • 2 heaped spoonfuls (25g) cornflour • 4 heaped spoonfuls (30g) milk powder • 2 stock cubes (we use chicken, but vegetable would be fine) • salt and pepper • 1½ mugfuls water • optional: sour cream or Greek yoghurt to serve

Bring the water to the boil, crumble and stir in the stock cubes and set to one side. Chop the onion and garlic clove if using fresh. Heat the fat or oil in a large pan, and fry the onion and garlic for three minutes, or until soft but not browning. Chop the greens into shreds (no need to remove the stalks, but make the chopping as fine as you can) and add them to the onion.

Cook until tender, then add the cornflour and milk powder. Add the warm stock a little at a time, stirring often. When all the stock is in and the soup is simmering, season with salt and pepper and serve – if possible with crusty bread and a dollop of sour cream or Greek yoghurt in each bowl or mug.

Green soup made with spinach and watercress

Leek and Potato Soup

Serves 2

Pans: 1

Stoves: 1

Campfire: yes

Other equipment: plate or board and knife for chopping

Prep time: 15 minutes

Pack weight: 140g per person (if using potato flakes)

Fuel efficiency: good

Vegetarian (depending on the stock you use)

• ½ mug (75g) dried potato flakes (or 2 large potatoes) • 1 leek
• 2 heaped spoonfuls (15g) milk powder • 4 spoonfuls (25ml) olive
oil or a golfball-sized knob (25g) butter or margarine • salt and
pepper • ¼ spoon garlic powder or 1 clove fresh garlic • 1 stock cube,
vegetable or chicken (for a non-veggie version) • 2 mugfuls water

There are two versions of this classic winter warmer. The purist version is made with fresh potatoes, which is fine if you're not carrying them too far and have plenty of time and fuel; the shortcut version uses dried potato flakes – good old Smash. They taste equally good, but the Smash version is much easier, so save yourself the hassle and make that.

Remove and discard the rough leaves of the leek, and wash out any grit. Slice the remainder once lengthways then chop it into slices about 5mm wide. Add the oil or fat to a large pan, heat it gently and add the leek and the garlic. Cook for three to four minutes until soft, but try not to let it brown.

Set the leek aside on a plate, bowl or clean plastic bag and use the pan to heat the water. When this is hot (no need to boil unless the water supply is suspect) crumble in the stock cube. Sprinkle in the potato flakes and milk powder, stirring as you go, then add the cooked leek. Season with salt and plenty of pepper and return to a low heat, simmering but not boiling for five to 10 minutes to let the flavours blend. This is good served with slabs of heavy, grainy brown bread and butter.

If you have the time and inclination to make this using fresh potatoes, prepare them in advance by peeling and chopping them into 2cm cubes. Put them in a pan of salted water, bring to the boil and simmer for 15 minutes. Drain and set aside. Make the recipe as above, but use half as much water, substitute the real potatoes for the instant ones, and mash them up a bit before you add the leek.

Not-Very-French Onion Soup

Serves 2

Pans: 1

Stoves: 1

Campfire: yes

Other equipment: spoon

Prep time: 15 minutes

Pack weight: 50g per person

Fuel efficiency: good

Vegetarian

You can buy sachets of instant French onion soup, but if you have a reasonable camp larder you can make it just as quickly with ingredients to hand. Good as a snack lunch or a starter.

- 1 small handful dried onion • 1 stock cube (chicken or vegetable) • 1 dollopy spoonful Marmite • ¼ spoonful garlic powder • 1 level spoonful dried parsley • ½ spoonful sugar • 3 heaped spoonfuls potato flakes • pepper • 1¼ mugfuls water

Put the onion, Marmite, crumbled stock cube, garlic, parsley and sugar into a pan with the water and heat. Bring to the boil, reduce the heat and simmer for five minutes. Remove from the heat and stir in the potato flakes to thicken the soup slightly. Serve with crusty bread and cheese if you have it. Alternatively, put the soup in your flask for a day out.

Noodly Soup

Serves 2

Pans: 1

Stoves: 1

Campfire: yes

BBQ: yes

Other equipment: spoon

Prep time: 5 minutes

Pack weight: about 60g per person

Fuel efficiency: good

Vegetarian, depending on choice of flavouring

This is intended as a starter, or a hot snack to take the edge off your hunger while you prepare a main meal. If it's going be your main meal you may want to increase the quantities.

Noodles with spicy beef and vegetable soup

• 2 packs instant soup • 1 portion instant noodles (wheat, rice or egg noodles are all fine, just make sure they are the type that cook very quickly) • 1½ mugfuls water • optional: dash of Tabasco or pinch of chilli powder

Boil the water and add the soup powder. When it has dissolved, crush the dry noodles and add them to the pan. Season with a few drops of Tabasco if using and cover. Leave to stand for three minutes and serve. Alternatively, make the soup up in the mugs and add the noodles. You need lids to keep the heat in while the noodles soften – a piece of foil folded round to make a seal, or a plate balanced on top, will do fine.

Sweet Potato Chowder

Serves 2
Pans: 1 or 2
Stoves: 1
Campfire: yes
Other equipment: fork or wooden spoon
BBQ: yes
Prep time: 20 minutes
Pack weight: about 300g per person
Fuel efficiency: moderate
Vegetarian

• 2 medium-sized sweet potatoes • 1 large onion, chopped very fine, or a small handful dried onion • 1 clove garlic or ⅛ spoonful garlic granules • 4 spoonfuls (25ml) oil or a golfball-sized knob (25g) butter or margarine • vegetable stock cube (or chicken for a non-veggie version) or one packet instant soup granules • ½ spoonful mixed spice • ¼ spoonful chilli powder • salt and pepper • 1½ mugfuls water • optional: small tub of sour cream or thick natural yoghurt

Soak the dried onion if using. Peel the sweet potatoes and chop into 2cm cubes. Add to salted water in a large pan, bring to the boil and cook for 10–15 minutes, or until tender. Drain and set to one side in the pan, or in a bowl or bag if you only have one pan. Heat the oil or fat in the pan and gently fry the onion and garlic for five minutes or until soft. Add the cooked sweet potato, and using a fork or wooden spoon beat everything to a coarse-textured mush.

Boil the water and make up the stock. Return the vegetable mush to the heat and gradually add the spices, seasoning and stock, stirring as you go. Let the whole thing simmer with a lid on for five minutes, stirring and squashing out the biggest lumps. Remove the lid and allow the soup to thicken to a hearty but pourable consistency. Stir in the cream or yoghurt, if using, just before serving.

Chowder is a thick, chunky, filling soup, traditionally containing seafood, but this vegetarian version is just as wholesome and heartening. This recipe can't help but turn out orange and lumpy, so be ready for inevitable comments about 'sweet potato chunder'. That said, we've yet to meet anyone who doesn't think it's delicious served with slabs of crusty bread or savoury biscuits. A good lunch, hefty starter or lightish evening meal.

Lentil Kedgeree in a Flask

Serves 4 as a hot snack, 2 as a full meal

Pans: 1 (in advance)

Stoves: 1 (in advance)

Other equipment: 1 litre vacuum flask, bag or tub for salad if using

Prep time: 5–10 minutes, plus 3+ hours standing time

Pack weight: 65/130g per person dry weight (315/630g in flask)

Fuel efficiency: excellent

Vegetarian

This recipe is based on an idea given to us by Dr Sugoto 'Soggy' Roy, a zoologist specialising in the eradication of non-native predators, such as mink and mongooses, from small islands where they play havoc with native wildlife. Soggy spends long periods of time in the field in remote areas where a limited store of food has to last him weeks. This means a lot of dry ingredients, supplemented with whatever he can source locally, which often isn't much.

Flask-cooked kedgeree is a wonderfully easy, efficient way to an instant hot and very healthy lunch, or even the ultimate hassle-free supper. You can make it up in camp or at home before a day out. We've used it for sea kayaking trips and on long mountain days.

You might be surprised to discover that this recipe does not contain fish. What most people think of as traditional breakfast kedgeree was in fact a British colonial modification of the traditional Indian dish *khichdi*, which is made with lentils, so this version harks back to the original.

Kedgeree

• ⅓ mug (100g) rice – the quick-cook mixtures including wild rice are really good in this recipe • ⅓ mug (100g) split red lentils and/or Puy lentils – make sure they are the kind that cook in 30 minutes or less, with no long soaking required • 1 small handful dried onion • 2 or 3 chicken or vegetable stock cubes • 1 heaped spoonful curry powder or ras-en-hanout – a traditional North African mixed spice – or use your own mixture of ground curry spices, such as cumin, turmeric, garam masala and mild chilli • 1 heaped spoonful brown sugar • salt and pepper • optional: finely chopped carrot, celery, green beans

Salad *(optional)*

• ½ cucumber • 4–6 tomatoes • 2–3 spring onions

In camp or at home, mix the dry ingredients in a bowl or plastic bag, then tip them into the flask. They should take up about a quarter of the volume. If you have a mug marked with a 250ml line you can measure the mix precisely to make sure you haven't overdone it – this is quite important, as the capacity of your flask limits the amount of water available for cooking. Think three to one: it takes 750ml water to slow-cook 250ml rice and lentils.

Boil a pan of water, and use it to fill the flask. Seal it up carefully. Adding any of the optional fresh vegetables will make a more interesting dish. Chop them finely and add them to the flask at the start of the day. For the salad, chop the fresh ingredients quite finely, and store them in a plastic bag or tub (see Chapter 6).

The kedgeree will be ready in about three hours and should keep hot all day. When you're ready to eat, tip it into small bowls or mugs and add the salad.

Alternative

For a quick-cook version to eat right away, just put all the ingredients in a pan and simmer gently for 25 minutes, with a lid on, until the rice and lentils have absorbed the water and become tender.

Hint: to maximise the efficiency of a stainless steel flask, pre-heat it with boiling water and let it stand for a few minutes, then refill with your hot food or drink immediately – this makes a huge difference. Maximise fuel efficiency by using the pre-heating water to make a hot drink.

Polenta

Polenta, or corn meal, is very bland on its own, but can be made tasty with the addition of various herbs and seasonings. Serve it as a side dish with barbecued meat or stews.

Serves 2

Pans: 1 (non-stick will make life easier)

Stoves: 1

Other equipment: chopping board or plate; sharp knife unless all ingredients are pre-prepared

Prep time: 10 minutes (plus 30 minutes standing time)

Pack weight: about 100g per person

Fuel efficiency: good

Vegetarian

• *½ mug (90g) polenta • 2 spoonfuls (15g) powdered milk • 1 small handful pine nuts • 4 spring onions • 4 large tomatoes • 1 large handful grated cheese • ¼ tube red or green pesto • 1 clove garlic or ¼ spoonful garlic granules • a large pinch of both salt and pepper • ½ spoonful mixed herbs*

Chop the onion, tomatoes and garlic and herbs. Toast the pine nuts in a large dry pan for between 30 and 60 seconds, then set them aside. Heat one mugful of water in the pan. When it begins to boil, remove it from the stove and add the milk powder and polenta to the water a little at a time, stirring well. Return to the heat for about a minute or two, stirring all the time to prevent lumps forming – the polenta will thicken to the consistency of creamy mash. Add all the other ingredients, stir and serve.

Alternative

You can make polenta cakes by using half the quantity of water, to make a thicker paste, and frying dollops of it in a little oil until golden brown on both sides.

Polenta cakes

Gnocchi

Serves 2 as a starter, snack or side dish; 1 as a main meal

Pans: 1

Stoves: 1

Campfire: yes

BBQ: yes

Other equipment: plate

Prep time: 15 minutes

Pack weight: about 75g per person as a side or starter, 150g as a
    main, 250g with salad

Fuel efficiency: very good

Vegetarian

Gnocchi are little Italian dumplings, traditionally made with potato flour. You can buy them ready-made as a faff-free alternative to potatoes, or, if you're feeling more adventurous, try making your own using these camp larder standbys.

• ½ mug (75g) dried potato flakes • ⅓ mug (75g) flour • 1 heaped
spoonful dried parmesan flakes • large pinch of salt • pepper
• optional: dried or fresh parsley, ground nutmeg

Garlic butter
• 1 golfball-sized knob (25g) butter • ½ spoonful garlic powder
• pinch of salt • optional: ½ spoonful dried parsley

Mix the dry ingredients in a bowl or pan and add half a mug of water
a little at a time, mixing to a stiff dough. Turn this out on a board or
plastic sheet and knead for five minutes or so until it becomes
stretchy. Cut up the dough into small pieces and roll into cherry-
sized balls. Boil a large pan of salted water and add the dough balls.
Cook on a fast boil for two minutes and drain. Serve with garlic butter as a starter or side dish, or with a stew for a main meal.

Alternative
Make a warm salad by tossing the cooked,
drained gnocchi with olives, tomatoes, finely
chopped red onion, torn basil leaves and
green beans (cooked for 2 minutes in
boiling water). Add a dressing of olive oil
and balsamic vinegar and sprinkle with
shavings of fresh parmesan.

Potato Cakes

Serves 2 as a starter, snack or side dish

Pans: 2 – one for boiling water and a frying pan (preferably non-stick)

Stoves: 1

Campfire: yes

Other equipment: spoon or fork for mixing/mashing; a small spatula is useful for flipping patties in the pan

Prep time: 15 minutes

Pack weight: about 240g per person if made with potato flakes

Fuel efficiency: good

Vegetarian

These make a good a starter, snack or side dish, or this is a good way to use up spare potato mix – you could make extra in the evening and keep it for a potato-cake breakfast. Potato cakes are better made with real potatoes if you have time.

• ½ mug (75g) dried potato flakes or 2 large potatoes • ½ small red or white onion or 3 spring onions or 1 spoonful dried onion • 4 spoonfuls olive oil (25ml) or 25g (golfball-sized knob) butter or margarine • 2 heaped spoonfuls (25g) flour • salt and pepper • optional: a handful of grated cheese, chopped olives or sun dried tomatoes, ¼ tube/jar of red or green pesto

Finely chop the onion if using fresh, or rehydrate dried onion by soaking in water for 10 minutes. Boil a third of a mugful (100ml) of water and use it to make up a thick potato mash. Mix in the flour, onion and seasoning, and the other ingredients if using. Heat a little oil or margarine in your frying pan and drop in dollops of the mixture. Press down with a spatula or the back of a spoon until they are about 1cm thick, and turn after one or two minutes. Cook until golden brown on both sides and serve.

If using fresh potatoes, chop into 2cm cubes, boil for 15 minutes, then drain and mash before stirring in other ingredients.

BREADS

Simple flatbreads can be made so easily that there is almost no point trying to carry bread into a wild camp. Not only do they provide a satisfying staple to bulk out a meal, they can also be used in place of cutlery for shovelling in other food.

Chapattis

Makes about 16 (serves four or five as a side dish)

Pans: 1 flat griddle or frying pan – non-stick will make life easier

Stoves: 1

Campfire: yes

Other equipment: bowl or pan for mixing, clean board
or clean plastic sheet for kneading

Prep time: 20 minutes

Pack weight: about 60g per person

Fuel efficiency: good

Vegetarian

Chapattis are the traditional accompaniment to spicy Asian dishes, including dhals and curries, but go just as well with western-style stews such ratatouille, chilli or chicken hot pot.

• *1 mug (200g) chapatti flour (ordinary plain flour works OK too)* • *pinch of salt* • *vegetable oil* • *warm water* • *optional: to add interest to plain chapattis you can add a handful of small seeds (sesame, poppy or similar) or herbs to the dough*

Tip most of the flour into a bowl or pan, keeping a little aside for rolling, and mix in a generous pinch of salt and a dash of oil. Add the warm water a splash at a time and work into the flour to make a dough. Knead the dough in the bowl or on a board or a clean plastic sheet, then cover it with a cloth and leave to sit for 10 minutes. Divide it up to make golfball-sized pieces, which can be rolled in flour and flattened in the palm of your hand to make thin rounds.

Heat up a pan, griddle, or a clean smooth rock, and cook the chapattis for about a minute on each side, or until bubbles start to appear. You can eat them like this, or finish them off by holding them briefly over a naked flame using tongs or a wire rack – this will make them puff up like pittas. Serve plain or with butter as a snack, or as an accompaniment to a savoury main dish.

Bannock

Makes 4

Pans: 1 flat griddle or frying pan, non-stick will make life easier

Stoves: 1

Campfire: yes

Other equipment: bowl or pan for mixing, clean board or clean plastic sheet for kneading

Prep time: 15 minutes

Pack weight: about 60g per person

Fuel efficiency: good

Vegetarian

Bannock is Scotland's version of flatbread, made with ordinary plain flour.

• *1 mug (250g) plain flour or half and half plain and wholemeal for a nuttier flavour* • *½ spoonful baking powder* • *pinch of salt* • *2 spoonfuls (15g) powdered milk* • *warm water* • *optional: sweet or savoury add-ins give interest to the bread – try seeds, herbs and finely chopped nuts, or a spoonful of sugar, some mixed ground spice and some dried fruit*

Mix the dry ingredients. Add water a tiny dribble at a time and mix to a malleable, very slightly sticky dough in the bowl or on a board or a clean plastic sheet. Divide into four balls. Knead each one briefly before flattening into a small loaf about 2cm thick.

Cook on a hot griddle or a frying pan for about five minutes each side. If the loaves are sticky, keep them moving for the first 30 seconds or so until the dough seals. Then continue cooking until a good brown crust has formed and the loaves sound hollow when you knock them. Serve plain or with butter as a snack or as an accompaniment to a main dish.

Damper

Serves 2

Campfire: yes

Equipment: bowl or pan for mixing dough, foil or wooden kebab skewers for cooking

Prep time: 15 minutes

Pack weight: about 50g per person

Vegetarian

This traditional camp speciality is a bit of a nostalgia trip for anyone who ever attended a Scout, Guide or school camp as a child. Often these early experiences are less than positive – leaving many of us with memories of gritty, charred artefacts with raw gooey innards, smothered in jam to make them edible. Done right, though, damper can be a very acceptable and versatile alternative to proper bread – it takes a fraction of the time to make and can be enhanced with all kinds of add-ins – you can improvise to your heart's content.

• ½ mug (100g) flour • small quantity water • optional: a knob of butter or dash of vegetable oil added to the mix will help make a smoother dough and give the finished damper a slightly better texture

Put the flour in a pan or bowl, add the butter or oil if using, and rub it in with your fingers or a utensil until it looks a bit like breadcrumbs. Add the water a little drizzle at a time, mixing and kneading until you have stretchy dough.

You can cook it whole in a camp oven, or make individual damper twists by forming long thin sausages of dough with your hands and winding them around wooden kebab skewers pre-soaked in water, or green sticks stripped of their bark. Hold these over hot embers until crusty on the outside and cooked through.

Variations: you can make your damper sweet or savoury by adding any of the following:

- dried fruit: raisins, sultanas, cranberries, chopped dates or apricots
- honey
- sugar and mixed spice
- chocolate chips

- seeds: sunflower, pumpkin, sesame, poppy, pine nuts
- chopped sundried tomatoes
- chopped garlic and herbs
- chopped salami or pepperoni
- grated cheese

Proper Bread

Serves 2–4, depending on appetites!
Pans: 1 lidded, or a camp oven
Stoves: 1
Campfire: yes
Other equipment: plate, board or plastic sheet for kneading
Prep time: 2 hours, including 1 hour rising time
Pack weight: about 250g in total
Fuel efficiency: low
Vegetarian

Some camp recipes are an entertainment in themselves, and a spot of baking is a great way to while away a summer afternoon. Undoubtedly, it's easier and probably cheaper to buy bread, but nothing beats the smell of the real thing emerging freshly baked. Turning out a loaf on a camp stove imparts a very special satisfaction that you have to experience first hand to understand! It's an ideal group activity following a strenuous morning, or on a rest day – if you're part of a large group, how about a baking competition?

Bear in mind that this is very much a summer recipe – not only does it take quite a long time, but you need warm temperatures to help promote the reaction by which yeast makes the bread dough rise.

1 mug (200g) flour • ½ spoonful sugar • ½ spoonful salt • 1 spoonful (5g) dried yeast or ½ spoonful fresh yeast (many bakeries, especially those in supermarkets, will give this away free if you ask) • 1 golfball-sized knob (25g) margarine or 3 spoonfuls (25ml) vegetable oil • ½ mug (200ml) warm water

Dissolve the yeast in about two-thirds of the warm water (no need to heat this specially – the contents of a water bottle left in the sun all day will be perfect), keeping some back to add later if the dough is too stiff. Set aside in a warm place. The yeast will gradually foam up as it begins to ferment.

After five minutes, tip the yeast into your mixing

bowl and stir in half the flour. After a couple of minutes you should have a smooth, elastic batter. Add the salt, oil/margarine and other remaining ingredients, then the spare water a little at a time to create a thick dough. Turn this out onto a clean, flat, floured surface (a chopping board, plate, or a clean, heavy-duty plastic bag like a rucksack liner). Knead the dough for five to 10 minutes, using a rocking motion of your hands and knuckles, folding it often until it becomes smooth and springy to the touch.

Push the dough into a well-greased or oiled pan, or a camp oven, which it should only half fill. You can improvise a camp oven using nesting pans, separated by a handful of fine gravel – make sure the dough goes in the smaller one! If you like you can mould it into rolls instead of a single loaf.

Set the pan aside in a warm place, and leave for about one hour to rise. Ideally it should more or less double in size, but not outgrow the pan. If this happens, you'll need to remove some. Place a lid on the pan (it's a good idea to grease the inside of the lid in case the loaf rises further when cooking).

To Bake

If you're using a stove-top camp oven, bake on a moderate heat for 20–25 minutes. If you're using an open fire or BBQ you want a loose, twiggy fire or glowing embers. Place the pan in the fire, making sure it's well surrounded, and place some hot coals on the lid to create good all-round heat.

Baking times vary, but check the loaf after about 20 minutes, then every 5–10 minutes thereafter. When cooked, it will be golden brown on the outside. Turn it out of the pan for the final test – it should make a hollow knocking sound when you rap it with your knuckles or the back of a spoon. If you get a dull thud, it means the dough is still damp in the middle and you need to bake it for a bit longer.

Leave the loaf to cool somewhere where the air can get all around it – support it off the ground on a grid or some clean stones. Five minutes will do – the smell will mean it will be almost impossible to resist any longer! Serve with your choice of sweet or savoury spreads or toppings (garlic butter is fantastic), or as an accompaniment to any meal.

Alternative

Even if you only have one pan, it's possible to bake bread on a stove using a single pan with a snug-fitting lid, as long as the lid is completely heatproof and doesn't have any wooden or plastic handles or knobs. You'll have to keep moving the pan around on the heat, with no more than a minute or two in any one position. After about 15 minutes, turn the pan upside down (holding the lid in place) and cook the top for the same time. (In New Zealand we heard that an aluminium disc a couple of millimetres thick, or even several thicknesses of foil, set beneath the pan will help disperse the heat and reduce the tendency to burn. It sounds plausible though we haven't tried it.)

Alternative

For an easier option, use one of the many 'just add water' bread mixes available from most supermarkets – you'll find them on the baking aisle next to the flour.

> **Warning** Loose flour is an explosion hazard: avoid pouring it – or allowing it to form clouds – anywhere near a naked flame.

Hint: when dealing with imprecise measurements, such as our 'mugs' and 'handfuls', it's always better to introduce plentiful ingredients like water gradually – you can always add a bit more if required, but taking some out if you overdo it is tricky!

Butter

*Equipment: airtight plastic container – a 1 litre soft drink bottle is
   ideal, but you'll have to cut it to get the butter out; alternatively,
   use a wide-necked Nalgene bottle*

Prep time: 1–2 hours

Pack weight: 300–500g

Vegetarian

This works best with rich milk or cream that has had a day or so out of the fridge to ripen slightly, so having it in your pack all day is no problem – it may even get the churning process started. (Butter is thought to have originated in Asia, when milk being transported by pack animals was accidentally churned by the constant motion.)

Churning your own butter is something different to do in camp – perhaps while the bread rises and bakes. It's a bit of a novelty really – great for kids who might never have considered how butter is made before – but be warned, it's a bit too tiring to be attempted solo. Tell your climbing mates it's good for strengthening their arms!

• *500ml full-fat milk or 300ml single cream, not chilled* • *salt* • *elbow grease – lots of it* • *optional: 1–2 cloves garlic or ¼ spoonful garlic salt*

Pour the milk or cream into the plastic bottle, screw on the lid firmly and start shaking it vigorously. When your arm gets tired, pass the bottle on to someone else who has nothing better to do. Depending on the richness of the milk/cream and the effectiveness of your churning technique, it will take between 15 and 30 minutes before butter starts to form and up to an hour to get a decent lump.

When you have a good lump that doesn't seem to be getting any bigger, open the bottle and drain off the liquid. If possible, chill the remaining solids by standing the bottle in a stream (wedge it securely!). The butter will set – how well depends on how much you can chill it and how well you shook. Cut the bottle open (if necessary) to remove the butter. Stir it to even the consistency and add salt (and garlic or herbs if making flavoured butter) to taste.

Braised Cabbage

Serves 4 as a side dish

Pans: 1

Stoves: yes, but it's very inefficient

Campfire: yes

Other equipment: sharp knife and cutting board, wooden spoon

Prep time: 50 minutes

Fuel efficiency: lousy, unless you're using a campfire!

Vegetarian

- ½ red cabbage • 2 cooking apples • 2 onions • 1 clove garlic
- ½ spoonful grated nutmeg • ½ spoonful mixed ground spice
- 6 spoonfuls (75g) brown sugar • 6 spoonfuls (50ml) wine vinegar
- 3 golfball-sized knobs (75g) butter • salt and pepper

Slice the cabbage, apples and onions and layer them in a heavy pan (preferably cast iron) with the spices and seasoning and sugar. Pour the vinegar over everything and dot the butter over the top. Cover and cook for 40 minutes (longer if you have time), stirring occasionally. Serve with barbecued meat, stews or burgers.

This is a lovely, slow-cooking campfire dish. We adapted it from one of Delia Smith's recipes. Her original recipe takes hours and hours to cook and is divine. This one is still very tasty, but it too improves with keeping, and tastes even better the following day.

Tabouleh

Tabouleh is the traditional dish to make using one of our favourite easy-to-cook ingredients – bulgar wheat. It's most appropriate as a summer recipe, but goes down well as either a side dish or a main meal, with lots of optional extras.

Serves 2 as a lunch or side dish, 1 as a main meal

Pans: 1

Stoves: 1

Campfire: yes

BBQ: yes

Other equipment: chopping board or plate, sharp knife unless all ingredients are pre-prepared

Prep time: 25 minutes

Pack weight: 200g per person

Fuel efficiency: very good

Vegetarian

* ½ mug (150g) bulgar wheat * tomato: if fresh, use 1 beefsteak size, or 3 regular salad size, or 8 cherry size; alternatively, use three sun-dried tomatoes and soak them in water for a few minutes beforehand * 1 fresh capsicum/pepper (any colour) * handful pine nuts * mint – handful fresh leaves or a heaped teaspoon dried parsley – handful fresh leaves or a heaped teaspoon dried * salt and pepper * optional extras: chopped spring onion, red onion, salted peanuts or cashew nuts, finely chopped or grated carrot, olives, sweetcorn, tinned chickpeas or tinned (pre-cooked) green lentils

Heat a pan and add the pine nuts. Jiggle them in the pan for about a minute, or until they are nicely browned, and set to one side for later. Add two mugfuls of lightly salted water to the pan and bring to the boil. Remove from the stove, add the bulgar wheat, cover and leave to stand for 15 minutes.

Meanwhile chop the tomato into 1cm chunks. If you're using dried tomatoes, chop them finely and add them to the wheat and water now. If using fresh, set them aside. Chop and de-seed the pepper. If you are using fresh herbs, remove any tough stems and roughly chop the rest.

Drain the bulgar wheat and stir in all the other ingredients. Season to taste with salt and pepper and serve either still warm or cold. Tabouleh will keep well for a day in a sealed tub.

Guacamole

Serves 2
Pans or bowls: 1
Prep time: 10 minutes
Pack weight: about 300g per person
Vegetarian

• *1 large ripe avocado (it should give slightly when you press the skin)* • *1 clove garlic or ¼ spoonful garlic powder* • *1 lemon or 3 spoonfuls lemon juice* • *1 small tub sour cream or Greek yoghurt* • *2 spoonfuls (15ml) olive oil* • *1 small red chilli* • *1 small onion* • *1 fresh tomato* • *pepper*

First de-seed and finely chop the chilli, roughly chop the tomato, finely chop the onion and crush and finely chop the garlic if using fresh. Put them all in a bowl or pan and squeeze in the lemon. Now cut the avocado in half and remove the stone. If it's really ripe you'll be able to just squeeze the skins and the flesh will pop out into the pan. If it's a bit firmer, use a spoon to scoop out the flesh. Mash it into the mixture. Add a dash of oil, the cream or yoghurt and a little pepper. Serve immediately or cover and keep cool until needed.

Using all the ingredients listed here will give you a full-on gourmet guacamole, but the great thing about this dish is that you can leave out any of the ingredients, except the avocado, and still produce something perfectly acceptable – even plain mashed avocado on toast is delicious. Serve with crusty bread, toast, crackers or tortilla chips as a light lunch, a starter, a side dish or an anytime snack.

Hint: *you can make a version that keeps better (for example so you can carry it for lunch) by leaving out the cream or yoghurt, making sure you use plenty of lemon juice, and storing in an airtight container. It will discolour slightly.*

Hint: *try not to touch your face or rub your eyes after chopping chillies. If you have some spare oil, rub a few drops into your hands before chopping the chilli – it will prevent the stinging juices soaking into your skin. Wash your hands afterwards.*

Garlic Mussels

A classic seafood recipe, very simple, and perfect to eat on the beach using freshly harvested mussels. See Chapter 8 for advice on collecting or buying shellfish.

Serves 2 as a starter

Pans: 1

Stoves: 1

Campfire: yes

Other equipment: sharp knife and cutting board, wooden spoon

Prep time: 10 minutes

Pack weight: about 700g per person

Fuel efficiency: good

• *about 30 regular edible mussels (or 1 dozen large green-lipped ones)* • *1 lemon* • *½ mug (200ml) white wine* • *4 spring onions or a small handful dried onion* • *2 cloves garlic or ½ spoonful garlic granules* • *2 golfball-sized knobs (50g) butter*

Wash the mussels and tear off any clusters of threads that might be attached (these are part of the animal – they were used to attach it to the sea floor). Chop the spring onions, if using, or soak dried ones in warm water for five minutes before draining. Melt the butter in a pan, then add the onion and garlic. Fry for a minute then add the wine. When the wine starts to simmer add the mussels and cover. Cook for about three minutes, jiggling and stirring occasionally. Discard any mussels that haven't opened up. Serve with wedges of lemon and crusty bread.

Hint: *use one pair of empty mussel shells like tweezers to pick the meat out of the others.*

MAIN MEALS

Fifteen-minute Soya Curry

Serves 2

Pans: 2 (or 1)

Stoves: 1

Campfire: yes

Other equipment: plate or board and knife for cutting additional
*   ingredients (if they haven't been pre-chopped)*

Prep time: 15 minutes

Pack weight: about 250g per person, including a selection of add-ins

Fuel efficiency: very good

Vegetarian

• ½ mug (150g) bulgar wheat or instant rice (1–2 packs, depending on appetites) • ½ mug (65g) plain soya mince granules • 1 small handful dried onion • 3 spoonfuls (20ml) oil (ideally groundnut or peanut, but any vegetable oil or even margarine will do) • ⅓ tube tomato purée • 2–3 spoonfuls curry powder or an equal mix of ground turmeric, ground cumin, garlic powder, garam masala, mild chilli powder • ¼ spoonful salt

Add-ins

Any or all of the following:

• handful sultanas • handful desiccated coconut • handful salted peanuts, cashews or pistachios • virtually any fresh vegetables you fancy or have to hand – carrot, spring onion or leek, cauliflower, courgette and green beans are all great • fresh fruit – a sliced banana, chopped apple, small tin pineapple chunks

In its simplest form, super-easy and super-lightweight, this recipe is filling, tasty and easily adapted to suit the ingredients you have to hand. It's a winner for backpacking, especially if you're cooking for a large group. The one thing you shouldn't skimp on is the spices – if you prefer you can use a pre-mixed curry powder in place of the individual varieties. We usually mix ours up at home and transport them in a Nalgene bottle or film canister. The quantities suggested below should give you a curry that is deliciously spicy but not hot. If you like heat, use more chilli, but if this is your only meal it would be a shame to ruin it – better to err on the side of caution.

Boil three mugfuls (1200ml) of water. Tip half into a second pan and add the wheat or rice. Cover and leave to soak while you cook the rest of the meal.

To the remaining hot water, add the soya mince, dried onion and any other dried fruit or vegetables you are using. Leave to soak for a couple of minutes while you finely chop any other vegetables you have. Drain the soya and onion and set aside so you can use the pan to gently heat the oil. Add the spices, vegetables and any

extra ingredients you're using to the hot oil. Sauté lightly for a couple of minutes. Add the soya and onion, a half mug of water and the tomato purée and cook together for a further three or four minutes. If using wheat, drain any remaining water and serve with the curry. If using instant rice, this will need heating for a minute or two before serving – see pack instructions.

Serving options

Good served with a chopped tomato and cucumber salad, and accompanied with pittas or chapattis (see previous section) for a real feast. If weight is no object, a dollop of thick Greek yoghurt on the side makes this already delicious meal even more of a treat.

Alternative

For a one-pan version, soak the wheat first then set to one side in a bowl/plate/mug/plastic bag. At the last minute stir it into the curry, and allow to heat through before serving.

Baked Baby Haggis/Beefburgers/Meatballs

Serves 2

Pans: 1

Stoves: 1

Campfire: yes

BBQ: yes

*Other equipment: chopping board or plate, sharp knife unless all
ingredients are pre-prepared, foil sheets if cooking on an open fire
or BBQ, 2 spoons for mixing and moulding*

Prep time: 30 minutes

Pack weight: about 300g per person

Fuel efficiency: moderate

Haggis and meatloaf usually take a long time to cook, but this recipe cuts down the cooking time by making individual-sized portions. You can serve them as part of a larger meal, but the recipe is almost a balanced meal in itself. Any leftovers can be eaten cold as part of a packed lunch next day.

• *2 big handfuls (200g) minced beef* • *½ mug (80g) oats* • *1 clove
garlic or ¼ spoonful garlic powder* • *1 egg or 2 spoonfuls (15g) egg
powder made up with 4 spoonfuls (30ml) water* • *1 onion*
• *30g gravy powder* • *salt and pepper* • *optional: 1 carrot, 1 stick
celery, dash Tabasco sauce*

Sauce for meatballs

• *1 tin chopped tomatoes* • *3 heaped spoonfuls beef gravy granules*
• *salt and pepper*

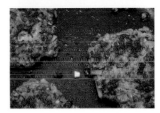

Chop the onion (and the carrot and celery if using) as finely as you
can and crush and chop the garlic if using fresh. Tip all the chopped
vegetables into a bowl or pan and add all the other ingredients.
Season really well, using *lots* of pepper, then mush the whole lot up
together with a spoon or clean hands.

To cook on a fire: use a smear of oil or butter to grease eight 20 x
20cm foil squares. Divide the mixture into eight and shape each portion into a round using a spoon. Wrap them in foil and bake on a
grill or in the embers for about 25 minutes, or until cooked through.
Alternatively, shape the meat into a long sausage about 4cm thick
and roll in foil. Cook the same way

The traditional accompaniment to haggis is 'neeps and tatties'.
For two people you'll need half a swede and two large spuds. Chop
them all into 2cm cubes and boil in salted water for about 15 minutes, or until tender. Drain, then roughly mash together with a dash
of oil and a pinch each of salt, pepper and ground nutmeg.
Alternatively, use instant potato flakes to make up the 'tatties' and
forego the 'neeps'.

To cook as burgers: flatten the balls into fat little burgers and cook in
a non-stick pan with a little oil for about five minutes each side.
Alternatively, grill on a BBQ.

To cook as meatballs: heat the tinned tomatoes, stir in the gravy granules and season. Add the meatballs. Cover and simmer for about 20
minutes. Serve with pasta.

Ornaburgers

Our friend Orna is a veggie, and she loves potatoes above all other foods. She didn't believe we'd name these after her, but since they were made for her benefit, why not? We first made them as a veggie alternative to the beefburgers we were preparing for a beach BBQ, substituting the beef with a spicy mixture of sweet and regular potatoes with some pine nuts and seeds for protein. You can try it using instant potato flakes, but the burgers will fall apart too easily to be barbecued.

Serves 2

Pans: 1 large, and one frying pan or griddle

Stoves: 1

Campfire: yes

BBQ: yes

Other equipment: spoon, sharp knife, fork for mashing, fish slice or spatula for flipping

Prep time: 25 minutes

Pack weight: about 400g per person

Fuel efficiency: moderate

Vegetarian

- *1 large potato • 1 large sweet potato • 2–3 spoonfuls (30g) flour*
- *1 large handful pine nuts • 1 handful sunflower seeds • 1 onion*
- *1 egg or 2 spoonfuls (15g) egg powder made up with 4 spoonfuls (30ml) water • dash of Tabasco or a large pinch chilli powder*
- *salt and pepper • a slurp of vegetable oil*

Peel and chop the potatoes into 2cm cubes, keeping the two types separate. Add the 'regular' potato to a pan of salted water and bring to the boil. After five minutes add the sweet potato (it cooks faster than the normal spud) and boil for a further five minutes before testing with a fork. When the cubes are soft, drain and mash with plenty of salt and pepper, and a little chilli or Tabasco. Set aside to cool a little.

Chop the onion as finely as you can. Add the chopped onion, nuts, seeds and flour to the potato mix. It should be rather stodgy and dry-looking compared to regular mash. When the mixture is no longer hot (warm is OK), add the egg and give it a final good stir. Mould the mixture into thick patties. If it's still too dry, add a little oil. You can use your hands for this if they're clean; if not, use a couple of spoons to make a ball, which you can flatten into a pattie in the pan. Cook in a frying pan or on a griddle until golden brown both sides.

MOVEABLE FEASTS

Spanish Omelette

Serves 2

Pans: 1 large frying pan or wok (non-stick makes life much easier)

Stoves: 1

Campfire: yes

Other equipment: bowl or spare pan for mixing, sharp knife and chopping board or plate, fork for whisking, spatula

Prep time: 20 minutes

Pack weight: about 100–150g per person, depending on use of fresh versus dry ingredients

Fuel efficiency: good

Vegetarian

This tasty dish turns out like a quiche with no base – it's good with fresh or dried ingredients, or a mixture of both.

• 6 fresh eggs or 12 heaped spoonfuls egg powder and ⅓ mugful (125ml) water • ⅓ mug (125ml) milk or 2 heaped spoonfuls milk powder and ⅓ mug (125ml) water • 1 large potato or ½ mug (75g) potato flakes made up to a stiff mash with a little water • 2 large tomatoes or 4 sundried tomatoes • 1 green pepper or a small handful dried pepper • 1 onion or a small handful dried onion • handful flour • oil • salt and pepper • optional: cheese, leftover cooked vegetables

If using fresh potato, slice it thinly and cook in boiling water for about 10 minutes or until tender. If using potato flakes, make up a thick mash with hot water. Chop the fresh vegetables finely. Soak any dehydrated vegetables in warm water for five minutes. Whisk up the eggs, milk and flour in a pan or bowl.

Heat the oil in a frying pan or camp wok and pour in half the egg mixture. After about 30 seconds, add all the vegetables, including the cooked potato and cheese if using, and season well with salt and pepper. Tip the remaining egg mixture over the top. Cook over a low heat until all the egg has solidified. Slice and serve.

Savoury Dumplings

Serves 2

Pans: 1 large

Stoves: 1

Other equipment: bowl for mixing, spoon, four pieces of kitchen muslin (roughly 20cm x 40cm), about 100cm string (undyed, natural fibre)

Prep time: 15 minutes

Pack weight: 100g per person

Fuel efficiency: moderate

Vegetarian, depending on your choice of stock and soup

Who doesn't love dumplings? This is a tasty recipe, but you can mix and match the ingredients to use up any leftovers, or to suit what's in your larder. The only essential ingredients are the flour, suet and generous seasoning – don't skimp here, or your dumplings will taste very bland.

• ⅓ mugful (80g) vegetable suet • ¾ mug (150g) flour (to vary your carb intake you can replace up to ⅓ quantity with rolled oats or oatmeal) • handful pine nuts • handful sultanas • small handful dried onion • pinch of salt • 2 chicken or vegetable stock cubes • ½ spoonful garlic powder • mixed fresh or dried herbs – parsley, sage, thyme, chives or coriander– a total of 2 heaped spoonfuls of dried, or a large handful of fresh leaves, chopped up well • salt and pepper • 2 sachets instant soup • add-ins: chopped pepperoni, a large handful chopped spinach, finely chopped ham or bacon lardons

Two-thirds fill the pan with water, add a generous pinch of salt, and put on to heat while you prepare the dumplings. Use about half a mug of hot water (it doesn't have to be boiling unless it's from a suspect source) and the stock cube to make a strong stock in a mug, and add the dried onion. Set aside for five minutes to rehydrate.

Return the pan to the stove. Mix the remaining ingredients, except the soup powder, in a bowl or spare pan, seasoning well with salt and pepper. Add the stock and onions a little at a time and use a blunt knife or spoon to mix everything into a stiff dough. Fold your muslins in half so they make squares and dollop a quarter of the mixture into the middle of each. Bring in the edges and tie them in a bunch with the string. The dumplings should be securely wrapped but not squeezed – leave them a bit of room to expand as they cook.

Drop the wrapped dumplings into the boiling salted water and boil for about 10 minutes. Fish them out rather than draining – you need the hot water for the sauce. Cut the string carefully (you can wash the muslins and use them again if you don't snag them) and tip the dumplings into your serving bowls – two each.

For the sauce, make up the soup powder using two-thirds the quantity of hot water recommended on the packet.

Note Cooking muslins are available cheaply from kitchen shops and usually big enough to cut into several useful pieces. They make the job of preparation cleaner, with no need to touch the dough with your hands, which helps if you don't have washing facilities. If you haven't got any, you can cook the dumplings directly in the boiling water. They will need to be moulded into balls first, using your hands.

Baked Fish

Serves 2

Campfire: yes

BBQ: yes

Other equipment: 1 sheet of foil per person

Prep time: 15 minutes

Pack weight: 400g-plus per person, depending on your choice of fish

Fuel efficiency: good

For each person you need:

• *1 fillet white fish, such as cod, coley, haddock or hake, or one small trout per person* • *½ small leek or about 3 spring onions (if you're making this dish for more than one person, a mixture of leek, spring onion and red onion looks and tastes even better)* • *½ lemon (or 4 spoonfuls lemon juice)* • *¼ glass white wine (optional)* • *1 spoonful butter (optional)* • *salt and pepper*

Slice the leek and/or onion finely and heap it onto the foil square(s). Place the fish on top, dot with butter if using, season with salt and pepper. Turn the foil up at the corners, add a slug of white wine if using, and a squeeze of lemon juice. If you're using fresh lemon, leave the squeezed-out skin in with the fish as you fold up and seal the package(s). Fold carefully so that it can be opened without tearing.

Cook for 10–15 minutes in hot embers. Open the foil – mind the steam – and check to see whether the fish is cooked. It should be firm, moist and flaky. If it still seems raw in the middle, reseal and give it a bit longer, but don't overdo it – overcooked fish is tragic!

Alternatives

Oily fish such as trout, salmon and mackerel work well with just lemon juice, or with fresh herbs such as thyme, coriander or basil. If you're using a whole gutted fish, stuff the herbs into the body cavity.

Note If you don't want to carry out balls of fishy foil, you could try the old trick of cooking a whole fish in wet newspaper. See *Cooking on Embers*, Chapter 7.

Fish is the ultimate convenience food! Whatever fish you choose, the fresher you can get it the better. For the simplest of all versions of this meal, simply wrap the fish in foil and bake in red-hot embers for 10 minutes – you may find you actually prefer it completely *au naturel* like this. A little seasoning and a squeeze of lemon juice before cooking will add some zing, and there are any number of variations, all of which are pretty simple. Try this one for starters, then experiment at will!

Cheese Fondue

Not only is a cheese fondue a wonderfully warming concoction, it provides entertainment as well as sustenance. It makes meals especially sociable, since everyone shares from a common pot. What's more, fondues are traditionally consumed with one or two alcoholic beverages, supposedly to prevent the molten cheese congealing in the stomach. (Based on our own completely unscientific observations, this does seem to ring true, as our teetotal friends have complained of indigestion following fondue-fests, while the drinkers were all fine – apart from the sore heads.)

Serves 4	
Pans: 1	

Stoves: 1 meths stove or 1 gas/petrol stove and 4 tea lights

Campfire: yes, but use tea lights for the gentle heat

Other equipment: 6 tea lights and a windshield, forks for dipping, sharp knife and cutting board for chopping dunkers, wooden spoon; if your cheese is not already grated, a grater is helpful but not essential

Prep time: 20 minutes

Pack weight: about 200g per person for the fondue, not including dunkers

Fuel efficiency: good

Vegetarian, depending on choice of cheese and dunkers

The idea is that the fondue sits over a gentle heat, which keeps it warm and fluid. Most gas or petrol stoves will not burn low enough, but a Trangia-style meths burner on its lowest setting is ideal – most indoor fondue sets use much the same system. Alternatively you can create a perfect set up using tea lights or candles and a few tent pegs.

Fondue
• 1 can (440ml) dry cider or ½ bottle white wine • 5 or 6 large handfuls (500g) grated hard cheese; if you can use a mixture, do so – strong cheddar, emmenthal and gruyère are a good combination, but it works with other varieties too – try experimenting • 3 spoonfuls (30g) cornflour • salt • pepper • 1 teaspoon ground nutmeg (or a whole nutmeg plus grater)

Dunkers
Any or all of·
• boiled new potatoes • French bread • apple chunks • cherry tomatoes • carrot sticks • celery • grapes • crackers • cubed ham • pepperoni chunks
and anything else you fancy – as much variety as is practical.

Boil the potatoes if using. Meanwhile, chop up your other dunkers. Set the cooked potatoes to one side. Heat the cider or wine in a large pan. When simmering, add the cheese a small handful at a time, and keep stirring until it has all melted.

Using a mug or bowl, mix the cornflour with a slurp of cider, wine or water, to a sloppy paste, then tip it into the fondue, still stirring. The fondue will thicken quickly to form a smooth gloop. Season with salt, pepper and nutmeg. If using a meths burner, use the simmer ring to reduce the heat to minimum, or transfer to a stand made of tent pegs above your tea lights. Use forks to dunk the various bits. Watch out for burning – if this happens, raise the pan higher above the heat.

Chickpea and Green Bean Casserole

This filling, hearty stew is a good option if you have vegetarians in the group. To keep the meat-eaters happy, bacon can be added to a portion of the stew at the end.

Serves 2

Pans: 1 large (2 if serving with an accompaniment)

Stoves: 1

Campfire: yes

*Other equipment: plate or board and knife for cutting additional
   ingredients (or they can all be chopped at home if you prefer)*

Prep time: 30 minutes

Pack weight: about 600g per person

Fuel efficiency: moderate

Vegetarian: use vegetarian stock and leave out the bacon

• *1 can cooked chickpeas* • *1 onion or a small handful dried onion*
• *2 cloves garlic or ½ spoonful garlic granules* • *large handful fresh
mushrooms or a small handful of dried* • *large handful green beans*
• *1 stick celery* • *1 large tomato* • *1 stock cube (vegetable or
chicken)* • *2 heaped spoonfuls (20g) cornflour, plain flour or instant
potato flakes* • *3 spoonfuls (20ml) olive or other vegetable oil or
1 golfball-sized knob (25g) butter* • *½ mug (200ml) red wine* •
*a handful fresh mixed herbs or 1 heaped spoonful dried herbs
(parsley, thyme, oregano, and marjoram are all good)* • *salt and
pepper* • *optional: 2–4 rashers chopped bacon or 100g lardons*

Finely chop the onion, tomato and celery, slice the mushrooms, top
and tail the green beans and chop and crush the garlic if using fresh.
Heat the oil or butter. Gently fry the onion until soft, then add the
garlic and all the other vegetables, except the beans. If you're making
the non-vegetarian version, add the bacon or lardons now. Fry for a
further two to three minutes.

Stir in the flour or potato flakes, then add the chickpeas, wine
and herbs, and crumble in the stock cube. Season and stir.

Cook at a light simmer for 10 minutes,
stirring occasionally. Add the beans, and
without stirring, cover the pan and let it
cook for a further five to 10 minutes. The
beans will steam without losing their colour
or crunch. Serve with rice, potatoes, bread
or bulgar wheat.

Hearty Meat Stew

Serves 2

Pans: 1 large

Stoves: 1

Campfire: yes

BBQ: yes

Other equipment: large spoon, chopping board or plate, sharp knife
 (unless all ingredients are already prepared)

Prep time: 45 minutes

Pack weight: about 500–600g per person

Fuel efficiency: low, unless you have a campfire

A full-on feast when you have a bit more time to spare. Perfect for fair-weather car camping and a great one for the campfire. The quantities are easily multiplied to serve a large group – providing you have a pot big enough to cook in. Done right, this recipe makes washing up easy, as plates are invariably licked clean.

• 2 chicken breasts and 2–4 thick rashers bacon (or a handful lardons) or 2 handfuls diced steak • 1 onion or a handful dried onion • 2 cloves garlic or ½ spoonful garlic powder • 1 large handful mushrooms • 2 large tomatoes or a tin chopped tomatoes • 1 chicken or beef stock cube • 2 spoonfuls (20g) cornflour, plain flour or instant potato flakes • 6 spoonfuls oil (40ml) or 2 golfball-sized knobs (50g) butter • ½ mug (200ml) red wine • a handful fresh mixed herbs, or 1 heaped spoonful dried herbs (parsley, thyme, oregano and marjoram are all good) • salt and pepper • optional: add any other fresh or dried vegetables – carrots, celery, green beans, courgettes or peppers; a sachet of dumpling mix

Chop the onion, tomatoes, mushrooms and any other vegetables, and chop and crush the garlic if using fresh. Slice the meat into chunks and strips. Heat half the oil or butter in a pan and lightly fry the meat until sealed and lightly browned. Set the meat to one side on a plate, leaving any juices in the pan.

Add the chopped vegetables to the pan with the rest of the oil or butter. Gently fry until the vegetables are soft. Stir in the flour or potato flakes, then add the wine and herbs, crumble in the stock cube and season with salt and pepper. Add the meat and enough water to cover everything. Cook for 10 minutes more (longer if possible), stirring occasionally.

Above: hearty chicken stew with braised cabbage; below: beef stew with dumplings

Serve with rice, bread, polenta or potatoes. Potatoes can be baked in the embers if you have a fire, or chopped into 1cm cubes and cooked as part of the stew for a one-pot stove-top wonder.

Note Be sure to wash the board and knife as soon as you have finished cutting the meat.

Sweet and Sour Chicken

This is more of a car-camping recipe as it's important that the chicken and vegetables are fresh. But the cooking itself is very easy and the more colourful vegetables you use, the more appealing it looks.

Serves 2

Pans: 1 large

Stoves: 1 or 2

Campfire: yes

Other equipment: chopping board or plate and sharp knife

Prep time: 30 minutes

Pack weight: about 700g per person

Fuel efficiency: moderate

• 2 chicken breasts • 1 onion or a small handful dried onion
• 1 small tin pineapple chunks in juice or 2 apples • juice of a lemon
• 4 spoonfuls (30ml) white wine or cider vinegar • 2 spoonfuls sugar
• 3 spoonfuls (20ml) vegetable oil • selection of crunchy fresh
vegetables – carrots, pepper and broccoli are all good • ⅔ mug
(200g) rice or 1 pack instant noodles per person

Soak the dried onion if using. Chop the chicken into bite-sized chunks. Heat half the oil in a large pan and fry the chicken pieces until they are golden brown on all sides, then set aside. Chop fresh onion if using. Fry onion gently in the remaining oil for three or four minutes.

Return the chicken to the pan and add all the other ingredients, including the juice from the pineapple tin if using, and the rice, and sizzle for a further two minutes. Add two mugfuls of water and simmer for 15 minutes or so, stirring often, until most of the water is absorbed and the rice is cooked. Add more water if and when necessary. Serve immediately.

Alternatives

For a speedier version, use instant rice and reduce the amount of water added to ¼ mugful.

If using noodles, start to cook these 5 minutes before the sweet and shour is ready.

If you have more time, marinate the chopped chicken in the juice, vinegar and sugar mixture for a couple of hours prior to cooking.

Sweet Lentil and Cashew Nut Curry

Serves 3

Pans: 1 large (2 if cooking rice separately)

Stoves: 1 (2 if cooking rice separately)

Campfire: yes

BBQ: yes

Other equipment: sharp knife and cutting board, spoon

Prep time: 30–40 minutes

Pack weight: about 450g per person

Fuel efficiency: moderate to low

Vegetarian

A tasty vegetarian curry, ideal for long warm evenings when you're not in a rush.

• ½ mug (130g) green lentils • ⅓ mug (150g) bulgar wheat • large handful cashew nuts • handful sultanas • 1 carrot • 1 onion (or dried) • 2 cloves garlic, crushed and chopped, or ¼ spoonful garlic granules • 1 green pepper • 1 stock cube • large handful desiccated coconut • tin chopped tomatoes • ½ mug (200ml) orange juice • olive oil • salt and pepper • 1–2 spoonfuls curry powder (cumin, coriander, chilli, turmeric) – depending how strong you like it • 1 mug (300g) rice

Chop the onion, carrot and pepper. Heat the oil and gently fry the vegetables for five minutes. Add the garlic and cook for another minute. Add the tomatoes, bulgar wheat, lentils, nuts, sultanas, crushed stock cube, coconut, curry powder and seasoning. Stir and cover with the orange juice.

Stir well and simmer, stirring regularly and topping up with water to stop it thickening too much, for 20 minutes or until the lentils are tender. Serve with rice (cooked on a separate stove or added to the curry for the last 15 minutes), chapattis or bread.

Thai Curry

This is great as a full-on feast with fresh ingredients, but it also works brilliantly using dried and tinned produce for real gourmet backpacking! You can buy tinned prawns in big supermarkets – look next to the tuna. If you can't find them, use tuna instead.

Serves 2	
Pans: 2 large	
Stoves: 1	
Campfire: yes	
Other equipment: knife and plate or board for chopping	
Prep time: 30 minutes	
Pack weight: about 350g per person	
Fuel efficiency: moderate	

• small pack shelled prawns (ideally raw but cooked ones are fine) or 1 tin cooked prawns in brine (200g) or 2 chicken breasts • 1 sachet (50g) coconut cream • dash of Tabasco sauce or one fresh green chilli* • 1 lime* • 1 clove garlic or ¼ spoonful garlic granules* • 4 spring onions* • 2 carrots • ⅔ mug (200g) easy-cook rice or 2 portions noodles • optional: coriander (fresh or dried)

* The asterisked ingredients can be substituted with a pot or sachet of green curry paste.

If using rice, boil 1½ mugfuls of water, add the rice, stir well, cover and set aside. Chop the spring onions and shred the carrot into something approximating matchsticks, or just thin slices. Finely chop the garlic if using, and slice the chilli (discard the seeds, and if you prefer mild dishes, only use half or a quarter of the chilli).

Heat a little oil in a pan and gently fry the chopped vegetables, garlic and chilli for a minute or two. Drain the prawns and add them to the pan. Squeeze in the lime juice, add the coconut milk (and the chopped coriander if using, and a few drops of Tabasco if you're not using fresh chilli) and stir gently.

Remove from the heat while you finish cooking the rice, or cook the noodles. Reheat the curry while you drain and serve the rice or noodles, then pour the curry over the top.

Hint: try not to touch your face or rub your eyes after chopping chillies. If you have some spare oil, rub a few drops into your hands before chopping the chilli – it will prevent the stinging juices soaking into your skin. Wash your hands afterwards.

Tinny Thai Curry

Serves 2 to bursting

Pans: 1 large

Stoves: 1

Campfire: yes

Other equipment: spoon, can opener

Prep time: 15 minutes

Pack weight: about 600g per person

Fuel efficiency: moderate

- *1 or 2 tins tuna chunks* • *1 tin sweetcorn* • *1 tin asparagus pieces*
- *1 tin or carton coconut milk* • *1 small jar or tube green curry paste*
- *2 double handfuls pasta twists or quills*

Cook the pasta and open the tins. Drain the pasta, tip in all the other ingredients and mix well over a low heat until it's all thoroughly warmed through. How easy is that?

This recipe is simplicity itself – all the ingredients are things you can keep in the larder or the boot of the car for months, even years if need be, and yet they make as tasty a camp curry as you'll ever enjoy. Traditionalists may prefer rice to pasta, but this version is true to its source – our crazy Kiwi kayaking buddy **Sue Robertson**. It's her standby meal for trips where she may end up cooking in camp, but wants the option to bail out to the nearest pub or chip shop should the weather turn foul, which in New Zealand it frequently does with little warning. With these ingredients nothing is wasted – it can all go home and be kept until next time.

Tomato Couscous with Beans and Flaked Ham

Green beans are brilliant for backpacking, because they pack close together and can withstand a fair bit of brutal treatment in transportation. What makes or breaks this dish, however, is the ham. Avoid pre-sliced 'sandwich' ham, and if possible buy from the deli counter of a decent supermarket or, better still, local ham from a farm shop or speciality grocer – you'll probably enjoy it more knowing that most of the food miles were done in your pack. Look for a thick, flaky looking ham, and if you're allowed to taste before you buy, go for one with a really salty, smoky flavour. Finally – and this is important – buy it as thickly sliced as you can – you want good hearty flakes of meat in this dish to give texture.

Serves 2

Pans: 1

Stoves: 1

Campfire: yes

Other equipment: plate, knife

Prep time: 10 minutes

Pack weight: about 180g per person

Fuel efficiency: very good

• *1 pack tomato-flavoured couscous (or half a mug plain couscous plus half a tube tomato purée)* • *a handful green beans (fine beans, runners or broad beans are all good)* • *3 or 4 thick slices of crumbly smoked ham* • *olive oil* • *small handful pine nuts* • *small handful sun-dried tomatoes* • *small handful fat sultanas* • *salt and pepper*

Put the pine nuts in a pan with a tiny drop of oil and heat for a minute until brown, then set aside for later. Fill the pan with the volume of water required to cook the couscous (use instructions from the pack, or assume 200ml per 100g dry couscous), plus about 10%. Add a little salt and set on the stove to boil.

Roughly chop the beans, and when the water boils (not before) tip them in and cook for about five minutes, or until tender enough to be forked, but not soft (overcooked beans are grey and unappetising). Turn the heat right down (or off) and add a little oil, the couscous and the sundried tomatoes (and purée if using). Stir the whole lot well, then cover with a lid and leave to soak for three or four minutes. In the meantime, tear the ham into bite-sized pieces.

Drain any excess water from the couscous and give the mixture a good stir, using a fork to fluff up any lumps. Season to taste with salt and pepper and stir in the ham, pine nuts and sultanas.

MOVEABLE FEASTS

Spicy Sausage Couscous

Serves 2

Pans: 1

Stoves: 1

Campfire: yes

Other equipment: plate, knife

Prep time: 10 minutes

Pack weight: about 200g per person

Fuel efficiency: very good

This is another recipe that can be adapted to take advantage of local produce. Buy the sausage whole or in one big chunk from the deli counter, rather than slices. It's much easier to transport like this and doesn't dry out.

• *1 pack flavoured couscous* • *a good chunk (150g) spicy cured sausage, such as pepperoni, salami or chorizo* • *4 spoonfuls (25ml) olive oil* • *large handful mangetout peas* • *small handful fresh or sundried tomatoes* • *small handful fat sultanas* • *salt and pepper* • *optional: pine nuts, few drops Tabasco sauce to taste*

Chop the mangetouts in half. Fill the pan with the amount of water required to cook the couscous (use instructions from the pack or assume 200ml per 100g dry couscous). Add a little salt and set on the stove to boil. Turn the heat right down (or off). Add a little oil, the peas, the couscous and the sundried tomatoes. Stir the whole lot well, then cover with a lid and leave to soak for three to four minutes. Meanwhile chop the sausage into small pieces.

   Drain any excess water from the couscous and give the mixture a good stir, using a fork to fluff up any lumps. Season to taste with salt and pepper and stir in the sausage and sultanas and a few drops of Tabasco, or leave each person to spice up their own.

Smoked Fish, New Potato and Bean Jumble

New-potato jumbles are among our favourite meals – never quite the same twice and easy to make really interesting. It's great to take along the basics and then seek out local speciality ingredients to add in. We cooked one on the shores of Loch Duich, the night before catching the Kyle Rhea ferry to Skye, using smoked haddock from a smokery we passed on the drive up – we still feel hungry just thinking about it!

If you're looking for something quicker, you can substitute the new potatoes with Italian gnocchi (look for them next to the fresh pasta in supermarkets, or make your own following the recipe earlier in this book), which heat in about two to three minutes. The result is tasty, but a bit stodgier than using new potatoes.

Serves 2

Pans: 1 large

Stoves: 1

Campfire: yes

Other equipment: chopping board or plate and sharp knife

Prep time: 15–20 minutes

Pack weight: about 500g per person

Fuel efficiency: moderate

• *large double handful (600g) new potatoes* • *large handful (150–200g) fresh broad or green beans* • *about 200g (2 small fillets or one large) strong smoked fish – eel, haddock, salmon – whatever you fancy* • *1 clove garlic or ¼ spoonful garlic granules* • *olive oil* • *salt and pepper*

Wash the potatoes, but leave the skins on, then cut into bite-sized pieces, or leave whole if they are very small. Add them to some cold salted water in a pan and boil for about 10–15 minutes. When they are soft enough to fork, but not quite tender, add the shelled or roughly chopped beans and cook for five more minutes (broad beans will need a little longer than green beans). Meanwhile crush and chop the garlic and cut the fish into bite-sized pieces.

Drain the potatoes and beans, add a good slurp of oil, the garlic and the fish, and season with black pepper. Give it all a good stir so everything gets coated, and serve.

Alternatives
Other jumble combinations that work well are:
• *ham and fine bean* • *cooked chicken, tomato and onion* • *sausage (cook the sausages first), broccoli and sweet chilli sauce*
• *Mediterranean (vegetarian) with olives, beans, red onion, sautéed courgette and halloumi cheese*

Stuffing Ball Jumble

Serves: 2	
Pans: 1 large	
Stoves: 1	
Campfire: yes	
Other equipment: bowl or pan for mixing, spoon	
Prep time: 20 minutes	
Pack weight: about 400g per person	
Fuel efficiency: moderate	
Vegetarian: some stuffing mixes are suitable for vegetarians	

Bring the flavours of Sunday lunch to the camp, using a good stuffing mix as the base of this easy dish, which is a great way to get a bit of meatiness into a backpacking meal without worrying about meat going off in your pack.

• *large double handful (600g) new potatoes* • *1 pack of 'interesting' stuffing mix – we like the ones that have a meaty flavour, such as Paxo Celebrations 'Sausage Meat and Thyme'* • *small handful pine nuts or sunflower seeds* • *small handful chopped apricots* • *4 spoonfuls (25ml) oil or a golfball-sized knob (25g) butter or margarine*

Accompaniment

Punnet of (about 20) cherry tomatoes, a block (250g) of halloumi cheese and a spoonful of mixed herbs

Make up the stuffing mix with water using the pack instructions as a guide, stirring in the seeds and fruit as well. Mould the mix into small balls, the size of cherry tomatoes. Heat the oil in a pan and cook the stuffing balls on a high heat for about five minutes, rolling them round the pan so they cook evenly. Set to one side.

Cook the potatoes, drain, then add the tomatoes, cubed halloumi cheese, stuffing balls, herbs, and a dash of oil for two minutes fast frying.

Spicy sausage and broccoli jumble

Cowboy Feast

A favourite with children and large groups, this is great campfire grub. You can leave a pot of it keeping warm for hours as people dip in. The quantities in this basic recipe serve two, but if you're catering for more, be a bit more imaginative with the ingredients and use a variety of the suggested extras.

Serves: as many as you like	
Pans: 1 large	
Stoves: 1	
Campfire: yes	
Other equipment: can opener, knife and board or plate for chopping, large spoon	
Prep time: 20 minutes	
Pack weight: about 450g per person	
Fuel efficiency: good	

The basic mix (serves two)

• *400g tin baked beans* • *200g tin sweetcorn (the stuff with mixed peppers adds a bit of variety)* • *4 thick rashers bacon or a pack of lardons* • *1 small onion or a small handful dried onion* • *salt and pepper* • *pinch of chilli powder* • *10 spoonfuls ketchup (about 6 sachets)* • *3 spoonfuls vegetable (20ml) oil or a golfball-sized (25g) knob butter or margarine*

Optional extras (for three or more people)

• *1 tin mixed beans* • *1 tin chickpeas* • *cooked cocktail sausages*
• *pack or tin frankfurter sausages, chopped* • *chopped celery*
• *chopped red and green peppers* • *cooked red or green lentils*
• *chopped chorizo, salami or pepperoni* • *Tabasco sauce*
• *Worcestershire sauce* • *stock cube* • *more baked beans, more chilli, more onion, more ketchup…*

Chop the onions, bacon, and other fresh ingredients if using. Heat the oil in a large pan and fry the vegetables and bacon gently for at least five minutes. Add all the other ingredients, season, stir well and heat through. Add a little water if it appears too gloopy (some beans come with more sauce than others). Serve alone, or with baked potatoes or flatbreads. For a hot lunch with a difference, the mixture keeps well in a wide-necked vacuum flask as long as you've made it fairly runny.

Cowboy feast with bannock

MOVEABLE FEASTS

Dhal

Serves: 2 as a light lunch, snack or side dish; 1 as a main meal

Pans: 1 pan with a lid that doubles as a frying pan

Stoves: 1

Campfire: yes

Other equipment: chopping board or plate, sharp knife for any fresh ingredients

Prep time: 20–25 minutes

Pack weight: about 100–250g per person (depending on fresh versus dried ingredients and side versus main meal quantities)

Fuel efficiency: moderate

Vegetarian, depending on the stock you use

• 130g or ½ mug split red lentils • 1 stock cube • 1 golfball-sized knob (25g) margarine or 4 spoonfuls (25ml) vegetable oil • 1 small onion or 1 small handful dried onion • 1 clove garlic or a large pinch garlic powder • mixed curry spices – turmeric, cumin, ground coriander, chilli powder – about 1 level spoonful in total – or use a ready-blended curry powder, or a ras-en-hanout type mix • salt and pepper • optional: any or all of the following – a small red or green pepper, a stick of celery, a handful of cauliflower or broccoli florets

Chop the onion, garlic and any other vegetables you are using. Heat the oil in the frying pan and gently fry the chopped vegetables until they soften – try not to brown or burn them. Stir in the mixed spices and seasoning and set to one side.

Put the lentils in the large pan and add 1½ mugfuls of water. Bring to the boil, crumble in the stock cube and simmer for 10–15 minutes, or until the lentils are cooked and tender. To avoid some of the lentils forming a layer stuck to the bottom of the pan, and consequent burning, stir often. Tip in the cooked vegetables, stir well and cook for a further minute or two to allow the flavours to blend.

Dhal is good served with flatbreads (chapattis, tortillas or pittas) and something fresh, such as chopped tomatoes, cucumber, spring onions, apple or pineapple chunks. If you're backpacking and want to keep the weight down, try a generous sprinkling of lightweight desiccated coconut, sultanas and salted peanuts.

Expedition kayaker **Matt Tidy** recommended this recipe – a favourite of his. On self-supporting expeditions where everything has to be transported in a kayak, Matt and his buddies find that the most basic dishes are the most popular. The food they take depends on what they can find locally at the trailhead or the last settlement they pass through, so they rely mainly on staples of rice, lentils and noodles, supplemented with curry powder, salt, sugar, milk powder and anything they can find to vary the taste.

Dhal is a staple in large parts of Asia, and it's easy to see why – red lentils are cheap, very easy to cook and extraordinarily nutritious. You can dress up this basic recipe with hundreds of variations, using whatever is available locally or just what happens to be left in your larder or pack. Be warned, though, that dhal may continue warming you and your tent in more ways than one – flatulence is pretty much guaranteed, especially if you're not a regular pulse eater. It's all part of the experience, and not a good enough reason to miss out on a camp food classic.

Green pepper dhal with chapattis and salad

Falafels

A really easy, tasty alternative to meat, falafel mixes are made of fava beans, chickpeas and seasoning. They need a little bit of advance preparation, but it's easy to open the pack and leave to soak while you pitch camp and have a brew.

Serves 2

Pans: 1

Stoves: 1

Campfire: yes

Other equipment: bowl or pan for mixing, spoon

Prep time: 10 minutes plus 60 minutes standing time

Pack weight: about 60g per person

Fuel efficiency: very good

Vegetarian

• *1 pack (150g) falafel mix* • *4 spoonfuls (25ml) oil or a golfball-sized knob (25g) butter or margarine*

When you arrive in camp for the evening, make up the falafel mix straight away with cold water as directed on the pack, stirring well. Cover and leave to stand for an hour or so. When you're ready to eat, heat the oil in a pan and dollop spoonfuls of falafel mix into the oil. Press them out so they're about 1cm thick. Cook on a high heat for about two minutes each side.

Serve in a tortilla wrap, pitta or an English muffin, with finely chopped carrot, spring onion and sweet chilli, or hoi sin sauce which you can transport in a small Nalgene screwtop jar.

Alternatives

Fry up falafels with a selection of fresh crunchy vegetables, such as carrots, peppers, red onion and tomatoes.

For a comfort-food special, serve as an alternative to burgers, with mash and baked beans.

Nut Roast

Serves 2	
Pans: 1	
Stoves: 1	
Campfire: yes	
BBQ: yes	
Other equipment: chopping board or plate, sharp knife (unless all ingredients are already prepared), foil sheets if cooking on an open fire or BBQ	
Prep time: 30 minutes	
Pack weight: about 250g per person	
Fuel efficiency: moderate	
Vegetarian: if you don't use the optional bacon	

This is another way to keep both vegetarians and meat-eaters happy, if you include bacon for the latter. Any leftovers make good sandwich fillings for the next day.

• 1 pack dry falafel mix or stuffing mix • 2 handfuls unsalted nuts (eg peanuts, cashews, chestnuts, pine nuts) • 1 handful seeds (eg sunflower, sesame, pumpkin, poppy, linseed) • ½ mug (75g) oats • small handful dried onion • ¼ spoonful garlic powder • 1 egg or 2 spoonfuls (15g) whole egg powder and 4 spoonfuls water (only needed if cooking in a pan – see below) • dash of Tabasco sauce • salt and pepper • 2 spoonfuls (15ml) oil • optional: pack of bacon lardons, ready cooked

Sauce
• 2 sachets instant soup (Mediterranean tomato and vegetable is good)

Make up the falafel mix with water, according to the pack instructions. Chop or crush the nuts and add them to the falafel mix, along with all the other ingredients, except the egg, oil and soup mix.

To cook on a campfire: use the oil to grease a sheet of foil and place the nut mixture, moulded into a flat loaf, onto the sheet. Wrap securely by bringing up the sides of the foil sheet and folding the top over – do it neatly so you can open the packet to check on cooking without tearing it. Bake in the embers for about 20 minutes.

To cook in a pan: add the egg to make the mixture a bit stickier and fry dollops in a hot pan, about three minutes on each side, or until brown and cooked all the way through. (Note that if using lardons, you need to increase the cooking time by a minute or two, to ensure that the meat is cooked through.)

Make up the instant soup using about half the recommended quantity of water and serve as a sauce with the nut loaf.

Potato Pie

This recipe is very easy, and makes good, savoury, warming stodge that will fuel you into the next day. You can adapt the fillings to take advantage of local produce, and providing you use rennet-free cheese, it's easy to make meat and vegetarian versions from the same base, so it's good for groups with mixed dietary preferences.

Serves 2

Pans: 1

Stoves: 1

Campfire: yes

Other equipment: plate or board and knife for cutting additional ingredients if necessary (they can all be pre-chopped at home if you prefer)

Prep time: 20 minutes

Pack weight: about 300–800g per person, depending on choice of fresh or dried ingredients

Fuel efficiency: good

Vegetarian, depending on your choice of optional extras

• *3–4 large potatoes or 1 mug (180g) dried potato flakes and 1½ mugfuls (600mls) water* • *1 small handful dried onion or 1 fresh onion* • *3 spoonfuls (20ml) olive or a golfball-sized knob (25g) butter or margarine* • *2 small handfuls (100g) grated cheddar or other hard cheese* • *any of the following, fresh, tinned or dried: leeks, sweetcorn, peas, carrots, tomatoes, peppers, courgettes, mushrooms, ham, bacon, tuna, olives, pine nuts, mixed herbs* • *salt and pepper*

If using dried vegetable ingredients like onion, soak them in warm water or milk for as much time as you have, or follow the rehydration instructions on the packet, but *don't* pre-soak potato flakes. Chop fresh vegetables if using them. Fry them in a little of the oil or fat (together with the onion and bacon if using) until soft, and set aside.

Wash the potatoes (no need to peel unless you're fussy), cut them into 2cm cubes and boil in a large pan for 15 minutes or until soft. Drain away the water, then mash the potato with the oil or fat, and season. Alternatively, make up the dried potato flakes according to the manufacturer's instructions. Stir all the other ingredients into the mash.

You can serve it like this, or, if you're cooking on a campfire or BBQ, or have a stove-top camp oven, you can finish it as follows. Transfer the mash to a greased or oiled camp oven or heavy lidded pan, add a little more grated cheese, cover with a lid, and bake for 10 minutes to brown it off and add a little crispiness around the edges.

Racing Snake Couscous

Serves 1

Pans: 1 water billy

Stoves: 1

Campfire: yes (though unlikely)

Other equipment: spoon

Prep time: 10 minutes

Pack weight: about 250g per person

Fuel efficiency: very good

• *1 sachet (110g) flavoured couscous* • *1 handful pine nuts*
• *1 foil pouch tuna (John West do a range with various flavourings –
take your pick)* • *optional: whatever takes your fancy among the following (we use them all!) – ¼ spoonful garlic powder, ¼ spoonful
dried chillies, heaped spoonful dried onion, heaped spoonful finely
chopped dried mushrooms, level spoonful dried parsley, level spoonful dried chives, small handful sultanas, a pinch of freshly ground
black pepper*

A great meal for multi-day mountain marathons or adventure races. Super-light, minimal washing up, much cheaper and potentially far more enjoyable than ready-mixed foil-pack versions, because you can tailor it to your own likes and dislikes.

Note Unlike most of our recipes, the quantities here serve just one person.

At home: open the couscous sachet and tip in all your other dry
ingredients. Reseal the sachet with sticky tape. Check the pack to see
how much water is required and mark off this amount plus 10% (to
allow for all the other dried ingredients) on
the pan you intend to use. You'll need a lidded pan big enough to hold 2½ times the
water volume. The one-man billies made by
Trangia (as shown) are perfect for this recipe –
using the quantities listed you'll get one brimming panful. If you have a very big appetite,
multiply up the quantities and have two
rounds.

In camp: boil the required amount of water,
remove from the heat, tip in the couscous
mix, stir well and cover. Leave to soak for five
minutes while you wring out your socks and
compare blisters with your fellow competitors, then stir again and add the tuna. It's
ready.

Lightweight Quick-cook Chilli

This lightweight, fuel-efficient recipe uses soya or textured vegetable protein (TVP) as a base. It's basically a home-made, copycat version of many of the pre-packed dehydrated chilli mixes on the market. Provided you have a reasonably well-stocked larder of camp-food ingredients at home, it can be made up extremely cheaply, and the flavours can be tailored to your own tastes. Our preferred version goes something like the following...

Serves 2

Pans: 2 (or 1)

Stoves: 1 (or 2)

Campfire: yes

Other equipment: spoon (basic recipe); can opener, sharp knife for some optional ingredients

Prep time: 10 minutes at home, 15 minutes in camp (less if using instant rice)

Pack weight: 160g per person for the basic recipe and rice; optional extras or instant rice will all add weight

Fuel efficiency: good

Vegetarian, depending on the optional ingredients

• ½ mug (50g) soya mince • ⅓ tube tomato purée • 1 stock cube (beef or vegetable) or 2 spoonfuls beef or vegetable gravy powder • ½ spoonful chilli powder (mild or hot according to your taste) • ¼ spoonful garlic powder • 1 small handful dried onion • 1 small handful dried peppers • 1 spoonful sugar • 1 spoonful vegetable suet • pinch of salt and pepper • 1 mug (200g) rice or 200g couscous, which cooks quicker, or 1–2 packs instant rice

Optional extras

• small can cooked kidney beans • fresh tomatoes and cucumber • pack-of-cards-sized block of hard cheese • 1 small pot sour cream or Greek yoghurt • 1 avocado or 1 small pot guacamole • 1 bag salted tortilla chips

Put all the dry ingredients except the rice or couscous in a bag for transportation. If you have two stoves or a campfire you can cook the rice and chilli simultaneously, but one stove will do.

Start by boiling a pan of salted water, then add the rice or couscous and cover – leave to soak while you prepare the chilli. Tip the dry ingredients into the other pan, add the purée and a mugful of water and heat, stirring often. If the mixture gets too thick, add more water a little at a time. The chilli will be ready in about 10 minutes.

Remove from the heat and cover while you finish cooking the rice. If you have accompaniments, chop or grate the cheese, chop the tomatoes, mash the avocado. Serve the whole lot heaped together on plates.

Hint: *if you're backpacking, sour cream and yoghurt are safer transported in wide-necked Nalgene bottles or ziplock bags stowed in a mug to prevent squishing – they'll usually keep OK for a day, out of direct sunlight.*

Alternatives

One-pan version: For extra speed, try this time-saving alternative. Take express or instant pre-cooked rice – it's heavier, but reheats in two minutes so you need less fuel. One pack will serve two people with small appetites, or one very hungry person! Add it to the pan when the chilli is nearly cooked, stirring in well and heating for a couple of minutes before serving.

Meaty version: If weight is no object, or you can shop nearby, or you're cooking for ravening carnivores, make a meaty version using 100g beef mince per person instead of the soya. If you use slightly fatty mince rather than completely lean, you can cook it without oil. Brown the mince over a moderate heat before adding all the dry ingredients, the purée and the water, and cook as above.

Cheating version: If you're shopping en route, or just want to simplify things still further, you can make a reasonable chilli by modifying a pre-packed soya mix such as Beanfeast or an own-brand equivalent. There tends to be a bit of snobbery regarding such products, and people are sometimes quite aghast to hear us suggesting them, and it's true that on their own they can taste very artificial and too salty. However, they're very quick and easy to reconstitute, and extremely light. With a few add-ins you can make them much more authentic and appetising.

A gourmet blow-out version of our basic chilli recipe, with all the trimmings.

Lightweight Spaghetti Bolognese

Serves 2

Pans: 1 (if lightweight backpacking) or 2 (which is easier)

Stoves: 1 or 2 (see above)

Campfire: yes

Other equipment: spoon

Prep time: 10 minutes at home, 10 minutes in camp

Pack weight: 120g per person

Fuel efficiency: excellent

Vegetarian

The concept and preparation are much the same as for Lightweight Chilli.

• *½ mug (50g) soya mince* • *½ tube tomato purée* • *¼ spoonful garlic powder* • *1 small handful dried onion* • *1 small handful dried peppers* • *1 spoonful sugar* • *1 spoonful vegetable suet* • *1 spoonful beef gravy granules* • *pinch of salt and pepper* • *2 packs instant noodles* • *optional: if you have any spare weight allowance, a couple of fresh tomatoes and some real parmesan cheese are good with this.*

Put everything but the noodles and the tomato purée in the same plastic bag for transportation. In camp, boil a pan of water then add the noodles, or pour the water over the noodles in a bowl or mug, and cover and set to one side. Tip the dry ingredients into the pan, add the purée and a mugful of water and heat, stirring often. If the mixture gets too thick, add more water gradually. The sauce will be ready in 5–10 minutes. Drain the noodles and pour the sauce over.

Lightweight Chow Mein

Serves 2

Pans: 1 large

Stoves: 1

Campfire: yes

Other equipment: spoon

Prep time: 10 minutes

Pack weight: about 120g per person

Fuel efficiency: very good

Vegetarian

Another easy-peasy lightweight recipe. Most of the ingredients – in fact everything except the noodles and potato flakes – can be bagged at home. You can expand it as you wish to take advantage of fresh, local ingredients, as seen in the picture opposite.

• *2 packs instant noodles* • *1 spoonful dried onion* • *I spoonful dried pepper* • *1 spoonful dried mushrooms* • *1 spoonful sugar* • *1 stock cube* • *pinch of salt* • *grind of pepper* • *2 spoonfuls soya mince* • *pinch of dried chilli* • *instant potato flakes (2–3 spoonfuls max)*

Put all the ingredients, except the noodles and potato flakes, into the pan with one mugful of cold water. Bring to the boil, stirring occasionally. Remove from the heat, add the noodles, and cover. Leave for three minutes, or until the noodles are tender. Add as many dried potato flakes as you need to thicken the remaining water into a sauce.

Soupy 'Smash' Hash
(Fastest Meal in the West)

This has to be one of the quickest, easiest, most fuel-efficient hot meals there is. It won't win any culinary awards, but it's hot and satisfying and packed with carbs. It's also really, really cheap! You can get similar things in ready meal packs, but they work out at about 10 times the price per serving. Soup mixes that contain bits of dried vegetables and meat work best, as they provide some texture.

Serves 2

Pans: 1

Stoves: 1

Campfire: yes

Other equipment: spoon

Prep time: 5 minutes

Pack weight: 100–120g per person

Fuel efficiency: excellent

Vegetarian, depending on your choice of stock and soup

• *1 mug (150g) instant potato flakes* • *2 sachets instant soup*
• *optional: 2 sticks spicy pepperoni*

Boil enough water to make up the mash, plus 10%. Stir in the soup powder first and give it a minute for any bits of vegetable or meat to hydrate. Add the potato flakes to the soup. Stir really well, not forgetting the bits at the bottom and in the corners. Add more water as needed, and the chopped pepperoni if using.

Note This is a good option for a hot lunch, or an end-of-day 'feed me now before I fall over' situation, as the potato has a high GI, meaning the carbs hit your bloodstream fast. You may need to eat another slower-burning meal later on.

Soupy smash hash made with chicken and sweetcorn soup and pepperami

Mushroom and Bacon Risotto

Serves 2

Pans: 2 large	
Stoves: 1	
Campfire: yes	
Other equipment: chopping board or plate, sharp knife (unless all ingredients are ready prepared)	
Prep time: 25–30 minutes	
Pack weight: 250–350g per person	
Fuel efficiency: moderate	

Risottos are one-pot wonders ideally suited to camping. This recipe is one of our favourites, but there's really no limit to the combination of flavours you can add, so start with this then try something more adventurous of your own invention. A good rule of thumb is to include a variety of colours and textures, and always use plenty of seasoning. The slower-cooking version using Arborio rice is more authentic and wonderfully gooey, but the results using instant rice can be just as tasty.

• ⅔ mug (200g) rice; short-grain Italian rice – Arborio and Carnaroli are two varieties – is perfect for risotto, but any sort will do
• 1 handful mixed dried mushrooms, or a double handful fresh ones
• 4 thick rashers smoked bacon or 2 small handfuls uncooked lardons • ¼ spoonful garlic granules or 1 fresh clove • 2 stock cubes (chicken or vegetable) • 1 small handful dried onion or 1 small fresh onion • 1 matchbox-sized block fresh parmesan or a small handful ready-grated • salt and pepper • 4 spoonfuls (25ml) olive oil, or a golfball-sized knob (25g) butter or margarine • optional: 1 carrot, 2 sticks celery, a dash of Tabasco sauce; a packet of instant mushroom soup will make the dish creamier

Soak the dried mushrooms and onions if you are using them. Chop the onion (and any other vegetables being used) as finely as you can. Using your largest pan, heat the oil or fat and add the onion and other vegetables. Allow them to cook gently for two to three minutes without browning. Meanwhile, chop the mushrooms and bacon rashers if using them. Add the mushrooms, bacon and garlic to the pan. Cook for a further two to three minutes, then remove from the heat and set aside.

Now heat about three mugfuls (1200ml) of water. As it approaches boiling, crumble in the stock cubes, add the soup powder if using, stir well and remove from the heat. Add the rice to the bacon and mushroom mixture. Stir well so that everything is coated in oil, and return to the heat. When it starts to fry again, add half the stock. Allow to simmer, *stirring often* (the rice will burn if you allow it to stick), and adding more liquid as required. Cooking time varies depending on the rice, so keep checking by sampling a

grain or two. If the stock runs out before the rice is cooked, just add more water.

When cooked, the risotto should be thick but not stodgy, so that a spoonful on your plate will spread slowly, almost holding its shape. Add the grated, shaved or finely chopped parmesan, season and serve. It's good with rustic red wine and crusty bread!

Hint: to save time and fuel, pre-soak the rice in a pan of salted water for half an hour before you start to cook – for example while you pitch camp. It will begin to swell and need less cooking time.

Alternatives

For a more backpack-friendly version, swap the bacon for a chunk of pepperoni, chorizo or other spicy cured sausage. This is bit more robust than bacon and will keep better.

Risottos are almost endlessly adaptable – if you don't have mushrooms, virtually any other vegetables will work well: green beans, carrots, courgettes, asparagus, peppers, peas… if you have it, chuck it in!

Speedy Fish and Chickpea Risotto

Serves 2 (large portions)

Pans: 1

Stoves: 1

Campfire: yes

Other equipment: spoon

Prep time: 5 minutes

Pack weight: about 600g per person (400g if using ordinary rice)

Fuel efficiency: excellent

• *2 packs pre-cooked 'express' rice or ⅔ mug (200g) regular rice*
• *1 400g tin chickpeas • 2 125g tins mackerel in tomato sauce •*
double handful fresh spinach

Boil the rice as instructed on the pack. Drain the chickpeas and add them, allowing to heat for the last minute or two. Drain the cooked rice and chickpeas and stir in the spinach, which will cook without further heating. Stir in the tinned fish and serve.

This is incredibly quick and easy, absolutely delicious, very filling and nutritionally spot-on – a winner all round. It is perfect for overnight backpacking when the weather is less than ideal! If conditions are more benign, you can save on weight and expense by using regular rice and taking a bit longer over things.

Mozzarella and Charred Vegetable Pittas/Wraps/Butties

This is either a long-winded way to make a sandwich, or a quick and easy cooked meal. It's ideal for a longer lunch break – somewhere with a good view – a fine, fresh-air alternative to the pub or teashop stop.

Serves 2–3 for lunch or a light meal

Pans: 1

Stoves: 1

Campfire: yes

Other equipment: chopping board or plate, sharp knife (unless all ingredients are pre-prepared)

Prep time: 20 minutes

Pack weight: about 400g per person

Fuel efficiency: good

Vegetarian

• *1 courgette • 1 small red onion • 1 red pepper • 1 medium-sized carrot • 1 large handful mushrooms • 1 ball of mozzarella (or any mild cheese you fancy – brie and halloumi go well) • olive oil • salt and pepper • 6 pitta bread pockets, chapattis, tortillas or bread rolls (see Snacks, Soups, Side Dishes and Starters)*

Cut the vegetables into slices and/or strips. Heat a good slurp of oil in a pan and add first the courgettes, mushrooms and onion, seasoning well with salt and pepper. Cook them until they start to brown, then add the pepper. Cook for another couple of minutes, and last of all add the carrot (you want this to retain plenty of crunchiness). Slice the cheese (if using halloumi, you can then cook it for a minute or two).

If using pittas, heat them for just a few seconds on both sides over the naked flame, open them carefully and fill with a mixture of cheese and vegetables. If using chapattis or tortillas, warm them in the same way and make wraps. If using bread rolls, slice them open and scorch them lightly in the pan so that they soak up some flavour, then pile in the cheese and vegetables to make a sandwich.

Mushroom Stroganoff

Serves 2

Pans: 2

Stoves: 1

Campfire: yes

BBQ: yes

Other equipment: chopping board or plate, sharp knife (unless all
    ingredients are ready prepared)

Prep time: 1 minute

Pack weight: about 200g per person

Fuel efficiency: good

Vegetarian

A vegetarian classic, stroganoff can be made with fresh or dried ingredients. Fresh mushrooms make a more substantial-feeling meal, but dried ones are much more intensely flavoured, so a little goes a long way, making this a really excellent option for backpacking.

• 1 large double handful fresh mushrooms or 2 small handfuls dried mushrooms • 2 sachets instant mushroom soup • 4 spoonfuls milk powder or a small pot of fresh double cream • ½ tube (40g) green pesto • salt and pepper • dash of olive oil • 4 large handfuls dried pasta or 2 servings egg noodles or ⅔ mug (200g) rice • 1 small onion or small handful dried onion

If using dried vegetables, soak them according to the pack instructions. Chop the onion if using fresh. Heat a little oil in the smaller of your pans and gently fry the onion for two minutes, then add the chopped mushrooms and cook for a further three or four minutes, stirring often to prevent sticking. Season with salt and pepper. Carefully add ¾ of a mug of water to the pan – it will hiss and spit to begin with. As soon as the water begins to boil, add the soup powder and the pesto.

   Mix up the milk powder with a small quantity of water in a mug to make a creamy mixture and add this to the mushroom sauce. Stir well and set aside. Heat a larger pan of water, and as it starts to boil add the pasta, noodles or rice and cook until tender (check the pack instructions for timings). Drain thoroughly and stir in the sauce. If need be you can return the whole lot to the heat for another minute and serve immediately.

Hint: if you can't buy pesto in a tube, buy a jar and transfer about 40–50g to a wide-necked Nalgene bottle (or similar) to carry.

Hint: if you're using standard rice, pre-soaking it for up to an hour will cut down cooking time. Instant 'express' rice heats in just two minutes.

Macaroni Cheese

There are several ways to make this 'nursery food' favourite. At home we'd use milk, wheat flour and butter to make a roux sauce, then add grated cheese, but there are some good backpacking alternatives.

Serves 2

Pans: 2

Stoves: 1

Campfire: yes

Other equipment: spoon

Prep time: 30 minutes

Pack weight: about 180g per person

Fuel efficiency: good

• *200g or 2 large double handfuls quick-cook pasta shapes*
• *6 heaped spoonfuls (45g) milk powder and 1 mug (400ml) water, or 1 mug fresh milk* • *2 heaped spoonfuls (20g) cornflour* • *1 large handful (100g) grated cheese* • *salt and pepper*

Make up the milk if using powder. Cook the pasta in the milk. When it's tender, add the cornflower and cheese little by little, stirring as you go, and the sauce will thicken. Season and serve.

Alternatives
Replace the milk, cornflour and cheese with packet cheese-sauce mix for a lightweight version. The flavour isn't as good as with real cheese, but it's perfectly acceptable.

If you can't carry real cheese, use a tube of the squirty Primula stuff. Blend the tube contents with a similar volume of warm milk before adding to the pasta.

Pasta Carbonara

Serves 2 (large portions)

Pans: 1 – the larger the better!

Stoves: 1

Campfire: yes

Other equipment: bowl or spare pan for mixing sauce, spoon for stirring; a colander and pasta servers or tongs are very helpful if you're cooking this for a large group

Prep time: 20 minutes

Pack weight: about 350g per person

Fuel efficiency: good

• 300g or 2 double handfuls pasta shapes, tagliatelle, or if using spaghetti, for each person, a bunch of the short-length type the size of a 10p coin in diameter • 1 small (150ml) pot double or single cream • 2 eggs • 4–6 rashers bacon, 1 gammon steak or 1 pack lardons • 1 large handful grated hard cheese, such as strong cheddar • ¼ spoonful garlic powder or 1 clove fresh garlic • salt and pepper • optional: ¼ mug white wine, fresh basil

Chop the bacon or gammon into small (5–10cm) strips or cubes and crush and finely chop the garlic (if using). Fry both in oil for a minute or two until just cooked, then set aside for later. Fill the pan with water and add a couple of large pinches of salt. Bring to the boil and add the pasta. Cover if you have a lid, and simmer for the time specified on the packet (usually about two or three minutes for fresh pasta, five to eight minutes for quick cook dry varieties, otherwise 10 to 12 minutes).

While the pasta is cooking, quickly crack the eggs into a bowl or pan, add the cream, wine, cooked bacon, garlic and half the cheese and mix well. Drain the pasta and return to a low heat, stirring in the creamy egg mixture. The cheese will melt, and the eggs will begin to cook and coat the hot pasta. Allow to cook for a further minute – no more – stirring gently. Serve immediately, sprinkled with the remaining cheese.

Our friend **Simon Willis** recommended this classic recipe. Si has more than 20 years' experience as an outdoor instructor and currently teaches outdoor education at the Lakes School in Windermere. He finds that carbonara is perfect for feeding hungry hordes, provided you have a big enough pot…

Once you've tasted carbonara made from fresh ingredients, you'll never want to go back to the ready-made stuff sold in pots.

Note By definition, fresh carbonara contains egg that is very lightly cooked, so is not recommended if you are pregnant.

Pasta Tonno

An extremely simple dish to prepare, but nutritionally well balanced and enjoyed by most people.

Serves 2 (large portions)

Pans: 1

Stoves: 1

Campfire: yes

Other equipment: spoon for stirring, can opener if using tinned tuna

Prep time: 15 minutes

Pack weight: about 350–400g per person

Fuel efficiency: good

• *300g or 2 double handfuls dried pasta tubes, twirls or bows, or if using spaghetti, for each person, a bunch of the short-length type the size of a 10p coin* • *1 can or 2 pouches tuna – ideally the kind in flavoured vegetable oil or tomato sauce* • *1 small (235g) can sweetcorn* • *herbs – fresh or dried* • *salt and pepper*

Boil a pan of water with a pinch of salt. Add the pasta, cover if you have a lid, and simmer for the time specified on the packet (usually about two or three minutes for fresh pasta, five to eight minutes for quick cook-dry varieties, otherwise 10 to 12 minutes). Drain, stir in all the other ingredients, heat through if needed, and serve.

Pasta Milanese

Serves 2 (large portions)

Pans: 2

Stoves: 1 or 2

Campfire: yes

*Other equipment: sharp knife and chopping board or plate, bowl or
spare pan for mixing sauce, spoon for stirring; a colander and
pasta servers or tongs are very helpful if you're cooking this for a
large group*

Prep time: 20 minutes

Pack weight: about 350g per person

Fuel efficiency: good

Another quick and easy
pasta sauce than can be
varied depending on the
availability of ingredients.

• *300g or 2 double handfuls pasta shapes, tagliatelle, or if using
spaghetti, for each person, a bunch of the short-length type the size
of a 10p coin* • *6 rashers bacon, 1 gammon steak or 1 pack lardons* •
¼ spoonful garlic powder or 1 clove fresh garlic • *1 red pepper*
• *1 courgette* • *1 tin chopped tomatoes* • *salt and pepper* • *optional:
¼ mug red wine, fresh basil, parmesan cheese for sprinkling*

Chop the bacon or gammon into small (5–10cm) strips or cubes and
crush and finely chop the garlic (if using). Fry both for a minute or
two in oil, while you chop the vegetables. Add the vegetables to the
pan and let everything fry gently for another five minutes. Add the
tinned tomatoes, crumbled stock cube, and wine if using. Cook for
10 minutes uncovered so that the sauce thickens.

Meanwhile, if you have two
stoves, boil water and cook the
pasta. If you only have one
burner, cook the sauce first and
set to one side while you boil the
pasta (usually about two or three
minutes for fresh pasta, five to
eight minutes for quick-cook dry
varieties, otherwise 10 to 12
minutes). Drain the pasta, stir in
the sauce and return to the heat
for a minute to warm through
(the sauce actually improves
with standing time).

Pasta with Smoked Salmon and Cream

A simple, heavenly classic. Absolute perfection with a glass of stream-chilled white wine and a summer sunset.

Serves 2

Pans: 1

Stoves: 1

Campfire: yes

Other equipment: spoon for stirring

Prep time: 15 minutes

Pack weight: about 280g per person

Fuel efficiency: good

• *240g or 4 large handfuls dried pasta tubes, twirls or bows, or if using spaghetti, for each person, a bunch of the short-length type the size of a 10p coin* • *1 small (150g) pack smoked salmon* • *1 small (130ml) pot double cream•* *1 lemon*

Boil a pan of water with a pinch of salt. Add the pasta, cover if you have a lid, and simmer for the time specified on the packet (usually about two or three minutes for fresh pasta, five to eight minutes for quick-cook dry varieties, otherwise 10 to 12 minutes).
    Chop the salmon into bite-sized pieces, cut the lemon in half and squeeze the juice into a mug. Drain the pasta, stir all the other ingredients into the pan, and return to a low heat for a minute or two just to heat through – but don't let it boil.

MOVEABLE FEASTS

Toad-in-the-Hole

Serves 4

Stoves: 1

Equipment: camp oven or stove-top oven (see Cookware in Chapter 3), large bowl or pan for mixing batter; a whisk is useful but not essential

Prep time: 30 minutes

Pack weight: about 175g per person

Fuel efficiency: moderate

This is one of those dishes we never expected to eat camping, but thanks to the brilliant stove-top oven, it's now a firm favourite for car camping trips.

- *500g fat pork sausages (or 2 each)* • *½ mug (100g) white flour*
- *1 egg or 2 spoonfuls (15g) egg powder* • *⅔ mug (250ml) milk or 4 spoonfuls milk powder and ⅔ mugful water* • *pinch of salt*
- *optional: knob of butter*

Place the sausages in the oven, dotted with butter if using, and cook for 10 minutes on full heat. Meanwhile, tip the flour into a large bowl or pan, and add egg or egg powder and half the milk. Beat to a smooth paste with a whisk or fork, then add the rest of the milk to make a smooth, runny batter.

Remove the oven from the heat, take out the sausages and use the remaining fat to make sure the entire oven pan is well greased. Replace the sausages – you may need to cut them to make them fit neatly – and pour the batter over the top. Return the oven to the heat and cook for about 20 minutes until the batter has risen and browned. Serve immediately – great with peas, sweetcorn and gravy, or with Cowboy Feast beans.

Alternative

You can use tinned or vacuum-packed frankfurters and omit the initial sausage baking stage. You'll need to oil the pan, though, as they're less greasy than regular bangers.

Wilf's Famous Veggie Chilli

Thanks to **Charlotte Webb** of **Wilf's Café**, in the mountain biking hotspot of Staveley in the Lake District, for this recipe. Wilf's' outdoor catering vans are a familiar and welcome sight to competitors and spectators alike at dozens of outdoor events around the country – and this is their most popular dish.

Serves 12–24

Pans: 1 – extremely large

Stoves: 1 – large

Other equipment: chopping board, sharp knife, long-handled spoon

Prep time: 2 hours

Pack weight: about 175g per person, not including accompaniments

Fuel efficiency: moderate

Vegetarian

This recipe is normally cooked in batches of 240 servings – we've cut it down to a tenth of this, but it's still a big job – recruit assistance with the chopping if you can! If you're planning a big trip, you can make up the basic chilli at home, store it in a big plastic tub and add the sauce in camp when you reheat it. This is how Wilf's manage to turn out such huge quantities from their little mobile kitchen.

• *250g celery* • *250g onion* • *100g swede* • *150g carrots* • *250g mixed peppers* • *1 spoonful dried chilli* • *1 spoonful cumin seeds* • *1 spoonful ground cumin* • *2 spoonfuls herbs* • *2 tubes tomato purée* • *¼ tube garlic purée* • *2 vegetable stock cubes* • *¼ mugful vegetable oil* • *1kg brown lentils* • *4 tins chopped tomatoes* • *2 tins red kidney beans*

Dice all the celery, onion, swede, carrots and peppers and sauté in oil. Add all the spices, the garlic purée, one tube of tomato purée and the crumbled stock cubes. Add the lentils and cover with water. Cook for about 1½ hours or until the lentils are soft. This should be quite a solid mixture, which you can keep, frozen if need be, until you are ready to use it.

When the time comes, mix in the chopped tomatoes, kidney beans and the second tube of tomato purée, and water if needed. Heat through thoroughly and serve.

Puddings, Cakes and Sweet Treats
Stove Top/No Bake

Fruit Crumble and Custard

Serves 2

Pans: 1

Stoves: 1

Campfire: yes

Other equipment: plates, spoon

Prep time: 15 minutes

Pack weight: about 180g per person

Fuel efficiency: good

This isn't a traditional crumble as there's no baking involved, and the various components only come together for a few brief moments before being demolished. But it's a great way to use locally sourced fruit, and the result is every bit as tasty as the oven-cooked version.

• 1 golfball-sized (25g) knob butter or margarine • 8 digestive biscuits • 2 handfuls porridge oats • 1 large double handful fruit, such as apples, blackberries, raspberries, rhubarb • 3 heaped spoonfuls (30g) sugar • optional: 1 teaspoon mixed spice or ground ginger, small handful chopped mixed nuts • 8 heaped spoonfuls instant custard powder

Crush the digestive biscuits in a plastic bag or on a plate with the back of a spoon. Melt the butter in a pan over a low heat. Add the crushed biscuits, oats, and nuts and spices if using, to the butter and stir well to form a crumbly mixture. When mixed, tip the crumble back into the bag and set to one side.

Chop the fruit into bite-sized pieces (removing inedible parts like pips and cores). Place in the pan, sprinkle with the sugar and add a splash of water. Heat and stir for a few minutes until the fruit is softened. Cover with the crumble mix. In another pan, boil a mugful of water and use it to make up the custard (stir carefully to avoid lumps). Pour over the crumble and serve immediately.

Squirty Fruit Crumble and Custard

Fruit purée pouches were invented as a bit of a gimmick to help parents wheedle fruit into less-than-willing children. They're often a bit too sweet on their own, but make a useful ingredient for various recipes that would normally call for heavy tins or perishable and fiddly fresh fruit. The packs are airtight so the contents keep well and they are lightweight compared to tins. Being squashy they pack a bit more easily, and once empty they crush down to next to nothing.

You could hardly wish for a faster hot pudding to round out your evening meal, filling those little corners that only something sweet can satisfy at the end of a long day.

Serves 2

Pans: 1

Stoves: 1

Campfire: yes

Other equipment: plates, spoon

Prep time: 5–10 minutes

Pack weight: about 180g per person

Fuel efficiency: good

• *1 golfball-sized (25g) knob butter or margarine* • *8 digestive biscuits* • *2 handfuls porridge oats* • *1 pouch fruit purée* • *optional: 1 teaspoon mixed spice or ground ginger, small handful chopped mixed nuts* • *8 heaped spoonfuls instant custard powder*

Crush the digestive biscuits in a plastic bag or on a plate with the back of a spoon. Melt the butter in another pan over a low heat. Add the crushed biscuits, oats, and nuts and spices if using, to the butter and stir well to form a crumbly mixture. Serve a heap of crumble onto each plate or bowl, and squirt on the fruit purée. Boil a mugful of water and use it to make up the custard (stir carefully to avoid lumps). Pour over the crumble and fruit and serve immediately.

Mars Bar Fondue

Serves: as many as you like (how many friends for life do you want?)

Pans: 1

Stoves: 1 – preferably one with a diffuse, controllable heat

Other equipment: 4 tea lights, spoon for stirring, forks for dunking,
*   spare tent pegs and windshield*

Prep time: 10 minutes

Pack weight: 200–300g per person, depending on your choice of
*   dunkers*

Fuel efficiency: good

A scrummy, decadent dessert, but if you've been out working hard all day, you deserve it. You know you do.

Hint: *the heavier the pan the better. If you're car camping, a cast-iron pan is ideal, since it helps keep the heat even and prevents burning.*

Fondue

• *1 Mars Bar per person* • *a little milk* • *optional: a dash of brandy or whisky*

Dunkers

• *fruit (bananas, strawberries and grapes are perfect)* • *marshmallows*
• *digestive biscuits*

Finely chop the Mars Bars and put them in a pan with a little milk – about three spoonfuls per Mars Bar. Heat gently and stir often to prevent sticking or burning. Once the mixture has become smooth and molten, remove from the stove, and stir in a dash of the brandy or whisky, if using.

Set the pan over the tea lights on a stand made of tent pegs – you'll probably need to set up a windshield too. Use forks to dunk pieces of fruit or marshmallows. According to fondue tradition, if you lose an item from your fork in the pan, you must pay a forfeit set by your companions…

Mars Bar fondue going down a storm on a canoe club weekend away.

Instant Fruit Fool

This has to be the easiest of hot puddings – a perfect backpacking dessert.

Serves 2

Pans: 1

Stoves: 1

Campfire: yes

Prep time: 5 minutes

Pack weight: about 100g per person

Fuel efficiency: good

• *1 pouch fruit purée (usually stocked in the supermarket near jelly and custard powder)* • *100g sachet or 8 heaped spoonfuls instant custard powder* • *optional extras: small tub thick cream, chopped fresh fruit*

Boil 1¼ mugfuls (500ml) of water in a pan and use it to make up the custard. Serve the custard in mugs or bowls, with a generous squirt of fruit purée, and topped with cream and fresh fruit if you want to push the boat out.

Alternatives
You can make a chocolate version by adding chopped chocolate buttons to the hot custard and letting them melt as you eat them.

Fruit Compote

We all know we should eat lots of fruit. Somehow it's easier to do this on a hot day, when the flavours and juices are refreshing. But fruit isn't always the most appealing snack when you're cold...unless it's in the form of a lovely warming compote like this one, which is also delicious cold with breakfast pancakes or cereal.

Serves 2

Pans: 1

Stoves: 1

Campfire: yes

Other equipment: spoon, sharp knife and chopping board or plate if using fresh fruit

Prep time: 10 minutes

Pack weight: about 400g per person with fresh fruit, 125g with dried

Fuel efficiency: good

• *800g fresh fruit or 2 big handfuls (about 250g) dried fruit (apples, mango, cranberries, raisins and apricots work quite well)* • *3 or 4 spoonfuls (30–40g) sugar (more if you're using tart fruits such as gooseberries or rhubarb)* • *optional: one level spoonful mixed ground spice*

If using dried fruit, put it in a pan of warm water and leave it to soak, preferably overnight or all day before cooking. If using fresh fruit (which really is much better), peel and chop it into bite-sized pieces.

Put the fruit in a pan, add the sugar, and spice if using, and a splash of water (about quarter of a mugful). Heat the pan until the juice bubbles, then reduce the heat and stew until the fruit is soft.

Serve with cream or custard, or on pancakes or breakfast cereal, or use to make crumble.

Rice Pudding

Serves 2

Pans: 1

Stoves: 1

Campfire: yes

Other equipment: spoon, nutmeg grater (or grate your nutmeg at home)

Prep time: 10 minutes

Pack weight: about 50g per person

Fuel efficiency: good

• 4 spoonfuls (50g) milk powder • ½ mug (75g) flaked rice or 6 heaped spoonfuls ground rice • 2 mugs (750ml) water • 2 heaped spoonfuls (20g) sugar • optional: ¼ teaspoon grated nutmeg, sultanas, jam, chocolate chips

This recipe uses flaked rice, which cooks three or four times as quickly as regular grains. You can also use ground rice, which cooks even quicker, but is more likely to burn, and gives you a texture closer to like semolina. Milky puddings seem to be one of those things that people either love or hate. If you're a fan, this could make your day from the outset – we sometimes have it for breakfast as an alternative to porridge. It's just as good as a dessert, although if you're eating it on top of a main course, you might want to reduce the quantities by about a quarter.

Make up the milk powder in a pan using the water, and add the rice. Bring to the boil, then simmer for five or six minutes, until the rice flakes are tender and the pudding is thickening. Stir in the sugar and transfer to bowls or mugs if you have them, or serve in the pan. Sprinkle with nutmeg if using, and set aside for another five minutes to cool and thicken further before eating. This will prevent you burning your mouth – and we think the pudding tastes better warm rather than hot.

For variety, add dried fruit along with the sugar, or bring along a single serving of jam for each person.

Cheesecakes and Banoffee Pie

Serves 4

Pans: 1 regular and 1 shallow (an 18cm non-stick Trangia frying pan is perfect)

Stoves: 1

Campfire: yes

Other equipment: spoon and chopping board or strong plastic bag for crushing biscuits

Prep time: about 15 minutes plus 1 hour cooling

Pack weight: approx 1kg depending on toppings used

Fuel efficiency: excellent

Vegetarian

Base (same for all flavours)
• *10 digestive biscuits (150g) – or a mixture of digestives and ginger nuts is even better* • *3 golfball-sized knobs (75g) butter or margarine, or a syrup made from 6 spoonfuls vegetable oil (not olive), 3 spoonfuls water and 6 spoonfuls sugar* • *optional: small handful finely chopped mixed nuts*

Crush the biscuits using the back of a spoon – aim for crumbs, but a few bigger bits won't hurt. Melt the butter over a high heat (if using the oils-sugar-and-water mix, heat it gently until the sugar is dissolved). Add the crushed biscuit, and nuts if using, and mix well so that the fat is evenly distributed.

Tip the mixture into the frying pan (if you don't have non-stick, grease it first), and press down firmly in an even layer using the back of a spoon. Set aside to chill. You can do this either in a shallow stream, with the pan safely sealed inside two large ziplock bags, or on an ice block in a cool bag, or just putting it in a shady spot is fine if that's all you have. Make up the topping (see below) and spread onto the base. Chill the whole thing as best you can until it's time to eat.

Toppings

Lemon and Lime
• *1 large tub cream cheese* • *½ tube condensed milk* • *1 lemon and 1 lime*

Mix the cheese, condensed milk and juice from the lemon and lime. Spread onto the base and decorate with slivers of zest.

Strawberry
• *1 large tub cream cheese* • *½ tube condensed milk* • *1 pack strawberry Angel Delight* • *optional: strawberries to decorate*

Mix the cheese, condensed milk and Angel Delight, and spread onto the base. Decorate with sliced strawberries.

Banoffee Pie
• *1 large tub cream cheese* • *½ pack toffee-flavour Angel Delight*
• *½ tube condensed milk or 6 spoonfuls toffee spread (using both is a bit too sickly sweet)* • *3 bananas*

Mix the cheese, Angel Delight, and condensed milk if using. If using toffee spread, smear it onto the biscuit base. Slice the bananas, lay them onto the base and cover with the cheese mixture.

Rocky Road No-bake Cake

We make this at home and in camp using slightly different ingredients. The camp version substitutes potentially messy golden syrup with condensed milk and either a Mars Bar, Double Decker, Curly Wurly, or other chocolate-and-toffee bar.

Serves 4

Pans: 1 regular and 1 shallow (an 18cm non-stick Trangia frying pan is perfect)

Stoves: 1

Campfire: yes

Other equipment: spoon, knife and cutting board or plate, shallow pan or tub

Prep time: 10 minutes plus 1 hour cooling

Pack weight: about 180g per person

Fuel efficiency: excellent

• 12 sweet biscuits: Rich Tea give the best crunch, but others work just fine; Bourbons add extra chocolatey-ness; Hobnobs give a more wholemeal character – use a mixture if you like • 5 golfball-sized knobs (125g) butter • 5 spoonfuls golden syrup or 3 spoonfuls condensed milk with a Mars Bar or 2 Curly Wurlys • 100g bar dark chocolate • 1 handful mini-marshmallows, or ordinary marshmallows cut into quarters • optional: if you want to pretend this is healthy food, you can add a small handful of mixed dried fruit or chopped nuts

Line the shallow pan with foil. Lightly crush the biscuits on a board using the back of a spoon – leave plenty of chunks, you don't want to pulverise them completely. Chop the marshmallows and the nuts if needed. Over a low heat, melt the butter and *either* the syrup *or* the condensed milk/Mars Bar/Curly Wurly combination, together with the broken-up chocolate. Keep stirring until the chocolate is melted. Remove from the heat and add the marshmallows, crushed biscuit, fruit and nuts. Mix well, then tip the mixture into the pan. Leave to set in a cool spot – ideally for a couple of hours – or refrigerate if making at home.

The home-made version will slice into neat bars. The camp version is usually crumblier, and makes a good dessert eaten from a bowl with custard.

Peanut Butter Scoffables

Makes about 10 balls

Pans: 1 (or a bowl)

Other equipment: spoon, plastic bag to pack the balls in

Prep time: 5 minutes

Pack weight: about 100g total

Fuel efficiency: as good as it gets – no cooking required

These are superb power snacks, best suited to winter outings (they will go very soft on a hot summer day). You can make them at home or in camp if need be, and the recipe is easily adapted to suit your personal preference, or what you have in the larder.

• 1 golfball-sized knob (25g) crunchy peanut butter • 1 golfball-sized knob (30g) set honey or 2 spoonfuls runny honey • 2 spoonfuls (10g) condensed milk or a heaped spoonful milk powder • 2 small handfuls of oat bran or wheatgerm or ground rice or wholemeal flour, or a mixture of any of these • 2 spoonfuls (20g) cornflour • 2 spoonfuls (20g) icing sugar • optional: ½ spoonful mixed spice or ground ginger, small handful finely chopped nuts or dried fruit

Put everything except the cornflour and icing sugar in a bowl and mix well to form a stiff paste. (Note that you may need to add more of the dry ingredients if you are using runny honey and condensed milk.) Form spoonfuls of the mixture into balls and roll them in a mixture of cornflour and icing sugar. Pack the balls in a tub or plastic bag, along with the remaining cornflour and sugar to prevent sticking.

Pears in Chocolate Sauce

This is a very posh-sounding pudding, but it's incredibly easy to make. Save it for when you want to impress someone!

Serves 2

Pans: 2

Stoves: 1

Campfire: yes

Other equipment: spoon for mixing

Prep time: 10 minutes

Pack weight: about 250g per person

Fuel efficiency: good

Vegetarian

• 8 squares or one small bar really dark chocolate • 4 spoonfuls (25ml) condensed milk • 1 golfball-sized knob (25g) butter • 1 tin pear halves in syrup

Boil half a pan of water. Open the tin of pears and pour the equivalent of about 8 spoonfuls of the syrup into a separate pan. Put the pear halves into the hot water, cover and set aside.

To the syrup pan add the chocolate (broken into small pieces), butter and condensed milk, and melt everything together over a *low* heat, stirring continually to prevent anything sticking and burning. Drain the heated pears thoroughly, put them into bowls and pour the chocolate sauce over them.

Lala Goo

Serves 2

Pans: 1

Stove: Yes

Campfire: Yes

Pack weight: About 300g per person

Preparation and cooking time: 10 minutes

Fuel efficiency: Good

This recipe owes its name to our niece Izzy, who used to call bananas lalas when she was learning to talk. It's great for using up over ripe bananas or bread that's gone a bit stale or become too squashed for sandwiches.

• *Two bananas* • *4 slices bread or 2 bread rolls* • *1 bag chocolate buttons or a small bar chocolate, broken into small pieces* • *one mugful milk or six spoonfuls (45g) of powdered milk made up with water* • *four spoonfuls (30g) sugar* • *half spoonful ground mixed spice*

Put the milk in a pan and heat gently. Chop or break the banana into small pieces and add to the milk. Allow to simmer for two or three minutes, then stir in the sugar and spice. Tear up the bread and add that, and the chocolate. Cover with a lid and leave to soak for a minute until the bread disintegrates into a mush and the chocolate begins to melt. Serve alone or as a topping for pancakes.

Alternative

Most people have cooked bananas in their skins on a camp fire or barbecue, but you can do it on a camp stove just as easily. Bring a pan of water to the boil and add the banana still in its skin (if using a small pan you'll have to cut banana in half first). Boil for about five minutes, until the skin is black or brown and the flesh soft. To eat, slit the skin lengthways and scoop out the flesh with a spoon. Banana cooked this way is fantastic on its own, for desert or breakfast, but for a special treat sprinkle with chocolate chips or chocolate buttons and allow to melt before serving.

Baked Sweets: Make at Home or Camp Oven

Sponge Cake/Pudding

This may seem like a lot of trouble, but really it's very easy – five minutes of mixing, another five setting up the wet oven, and the rest is just a waiting game. If you set it up just before you start your evening meal it'll be ready in perfect time for dessert.

Serves 3–4

Pans: 2 lidded pans or billies – one must fit easily inside the other, check before leaving home – or a camp oven

Stoves: 1

Campfire: yes

Other equipment: a sturdy spoon for mixing, 2m undyed, natural fibre string, sharp knife and chopping board or plate for any optional ingredients that need chopping (if using a proper camp oven you won't need the string but you will need an additional large pan or bowl for mixing)

Prep time: 30–40 minutes

Pack weight: about 150—200g per person

Fuel efficiency: moderate

Vegetarian

- ½ mugful (150g) flour (it should be self-raising – if you use plain you need to add a ½ spoonful of baking powder) • ½ mugful sugar • 4 golfball-sized knobs (100g) butter or margarine • 2 eggs or 4 spoonfuls (30g) whole egg powder made up with 8 spoonfuls water • ¼ spoonful baking powder

Flavourings
Choose from:
- apple – our favourite! Add either 1 large cooking apple, such as a Bramley, 2 Braeburns or 3 small Coxes, peeled and chopped into small chunks, plus a ½ spoonful of mixed ground spice • lemon: either the zest of a lemon, removed with a peeler or sharp knife and chopped as finely as you can (pieces should be no more than 1mm thick), or, if that sounds too fiddly (it usually is), a few drops of lemon flavouring does nicely • banana: 2 ripe bananas, chopped • spotted dick: a large handful of sultanas • ginger: a level spoonful of ground ginger • chocolate: replace about a fifth of the flour with cocoa powder and a handful of dark chocolate chips • coffee: 2 spoonfuls of instant coffee, dissolved in a very little warm water

Use a smear of butter to grease the camp oven pan or the smaller of your two billies. Put all the dry ingredients in a bowl or the larger of your two pans, add the rest of the butter and crack in both eggs (or add the reconstituted egg powder if using). Beat the whole lot together using a sturdy spoon. This will take five minutes, and keep you warm even on a cold day. Keep going until you have a smooth but light, creamy looking mix (or your arms are ready to drop off). Prepare your additional ingredients and stir them into the mix. Tip it all into the small pan, put the lid on, then go and wash up the big pan. Bring it back about a quarter full of water, put the lid on and set it on the heat to boil.

Meanwhile, use the string to tie up the pudding pan like a parcel, making a loop in the top so that you can lift it out safely when it's really hot. When the water boils, lower the sponge pan into the water, which should come about halfway up the sides – no more. Put the big lid back on and adjust the heat so the water maintains a gentle boil – check the water level every now and then to ensure that it doesn't boil dry.

After 25 minutes, remove the oven from the stove and use the string loop to lift the small pan out. Untie it quickly and take a peek inside. If it's still *really* gooey, seal it again as fast as you can and give it another few minutes. If it looks cooked, give it a poke with a knife blade – if the blade comes out more or less clean, it's ready. You can serve it from the pan with a big spoon, or tip it out onto a plate and cut with a knife. Serve with instant custard or jam.

If you have a purpose-built camp oven you can cook the sponge directly in that – don't forget to grease the pan.

Hint: *if you make more than you need, keep half for tomorrow's snack – it will slice well once cold.*

Hint: *mix up the dry ingredients before you leave home and you can then transport them in one bag.*

Hint: *halve the ingredients for a two-person version (a mini Trangia pan is the ideal size) – cooking time will be reduced to 15–20 minutes.*

Top right: Apple sponge pudding cooked in a wet oven is fantastically gooey; above: Sponge cakes cook beautifully in the Optimus oven, often faster then they would at home.

Flapjacks

Makes about 16

Pans: 1

Stoves: home oven heated to 180°C/gas mark 5 (or camp oven over moderate heat)

Other equipment: 20 x 20cm square baking tin, sheet of greaseproof paper

Prep time: about 40 minutes

Vegetarian

This is probably best made at home to eat on the go, although you can use a camp oven to make flapjacks outdoors. Flapjack recipes usually only include oats, butter, sugar and syrup, so the extra flour, fruit and seeds in this one give it a bit more nutritional clout.

• 1¼ mugfuls (200g) oats • ⅓ mug (100g) self-raising flour • 5 dollopy spoonfuls (100g) golden syrup • 6 golfball-sized knobs (150g) butter • ⅓ mug (100g) soft brown sugar • 3 handfuls (100g) mixed dried fruit • 2 small handfuls (50g) sunflower and sesame seeds

If cooking at home, heat the oven to 180°C/gas mark 5. Melt the butter, sugar and syrup together in a pan over a low heat, then add all the dry ingredients and mix well. Tip into a greased baking tray, lined with greaseproof paper. Bake for about 30 minutes. Remove from the oven and cool for five minutes, before turning out upside down onto a wire cooling rack and allowing to cool completely. Use a sharp knife to cut into slices, wrap in greaseproof paper, and pack in a tub, foil or plastic bags for carrying.

Brownies

Makes about 16

Pans: 1 (plus baking tray or shallow pan if cooking in camp oven)

*Stoves: home oven heated to 180°C/gas mark 5, or camp oven over
moderate heat*

*Other equipment: 2 large bowls (1 glass), 20 x 20cm square baking
tin, sheet of greaseproof paper*

Prep time: about 40 minutes

Vegetarian

• *1 large bar (120g) dark chocolate* • *4 spoonfuls (50g) cocoa
powder* • *5 golfball-sized knobs (125g) butter* • *2 eggs* • *¾ mugful
(200g) granulated sugar* • *6 spoonfuls (60g) plain flour*
• *½ spoonful baking powder* • *pinch of salt*

If cooking at home, heat the oven to 180°C/gas mark 5. Grease and
line the tin with greaseproof paper. Heat a pan a quarter full with
water and place a glass bowl over the top. Break up the chocolate
and melt it in the bowl. Add the cocoa and butter, stirring until it's all
smooth.

Put the other ingredients in another bowl and pour in the melted
mixture. Mix thoroughly and pour into the lined tin. Bake for 30 minutes. Remove from the oven and cool for five minutes, before turning
out upside down onto a wire rack and allowing to cool completely.
Use a sharp knife to cut into slices. Wrap in greaseproof paper and
pack in plastic bags for carrying.

Another one best made at
home, although there's no
reason you can't make
them in a camp oven if
you like. The brownies
are dark and gooey, great
for a civilised evening
around the camp fire or a
snack-stop when walking,
but probably a bit too
rich for eating on the run.

Fruit Slice

Makes about 16

Pans: 1 (plus baking tray or shallow pan if cooking in camp oven)

Stoves: home oven heated to 180°C/gas mark 5

Other equipment: deep baking tin 20 x 20cm, sheet of greaseproof paper

Prep time: about 35 minutes

Vegetarian

A moist and gooey treat, packed with a mixture of fast- and slow-burn carbs, this is great as a snack on the hoof or as an evening treat in camp. As with all the baked recipes in this book, fruit slice can be made successfully using a camp oven or stovetop oven over *moderate heat*.

- *1 mugful (200g) oats* • *1 mugful (200g) self-raising flour* • *1½ mugfuls (200g) dates and/or other dried fruit, such as prunes, apricots, sultanas, cranberries* • *8 golfball-sized knobs (200g) butter or margarine* • *½ mugful (125g) soft brown sugar* • *large pinch of salt* • *½ teaspoonful baking powder* • *4 generous spoonfuls golden syrup* • *pinch of salt*

Heat the oven to 180°C/gas mark 5. Grease a deep baking tin and line it with greaseproof paper. Heat the dates in a pan with half a mugful (200ml) of water. As they soften up, use a wooden spoon to beat them to a jammy consistency and set aside. In a large bowl, beat the butter and sugar together until soft and creamy, then chuck in the flour, oats and salt. Mix well.

Warm the syrup (30 seconds in the microwave, or stand the tin in a bowl of hot water until the syrup is runny) and stir it well into the mixture. Spread half the mixture into the tin, then spread the date mixture on top. Top off with the rest of the oat mixture and bake for 20–30 minutes, until firm and browning on the top. When cooked, remove from the tin and cool on a wire rack. Slice into squares. Keeps well in an airtight container for at least three days.

Bread Pudding

Makes about 16 slices

Stoves: home oven heated to 170°C/gas mark 4

*Other equipment: deep 20 x 20cm baking tray, sheet of greaseproof
   paper, or camp oven over moderate heat*

Prep time: about 90 minutes including soaking time

Vegetarian

• *5 slices (225g) stale bread* • *½ mugful (110g) dried fruit (use a
mixture)* • *4 spoonfuls (50g) soft brown sugar* • *2 spoonfuls (25g)
vegetable suet* • *2 golfball-sized knobs (50g) butter or margarine*
• *½ spoonful mixed ground spice* • *1 egg* • *1 mugful milk*

If cooking at home, heat the oven to 170°C/gas mark 4. Grease and
line the baking tin. Tear or chop the bread into small pieces and soak
it in the milk for 30 minutes. Squish out most of the excess moisture
and place the soggy bread in another bowl. Add the other dry ingredients, then the egg – it should form a sloppy mixture.

   Transfer this to the baking tin and bake for 45 minutes or until
just firm to the touch. Allow to cool for 10 minutes before turning it
out onto a cooling rack. Slice when completely cold and wrap in
greaseproof paper for carrying.

One of Roy's childhood
favourites, and this recipe
is almost as good as his
mum's! Bread pudding is
very moist, which makes
it easy to eat when you're
working hard. It contains
a mixture of carbs, and
also extra fat in the form
of suet – a good way of
boosting calorie intake on
long days out. It's heavy
compared to other
snacks, but worth it!

DRINKS

Camp Coffee

Serves as many as you like

Pans: 1

Stoves: 1

Campfire: yes

Other equipment: spoon

Prep time: 5 minutes

Pack weight: 15g per person per brew

Fuel efficiency: good

Who needs a posh coffee machine or a fancy filter? With a little care you can have the pleasure of real coffee with minimal kit.

• *2 heaped spoonfuls fresh ground coffee per person* • *milk and sugar to taste*

In the pan, boil a mug of water per person. Take the pan off the stove and stir in the coffee grounds. Let it brew for a couple of minutes then tap the side of the pan with a spoon (or similar) to encourage the grounds to settle. Pour slowly and carefully.

Hot Toddy

Serves 4 (one serving contains about 2 units of alcohol)

Pans: 1

Stoves: 1

Campfire: yes

Other equipment: sharp knife, spoon

Prep time: 10 minutes

Pack weight: about 50g per person

Fuel efficiency: good

- *½ mug (about 150ml) port* • *½ lemon* • *1 small handful cloves*
- *water* • *optional: sugar*

Heat 1½ mugfuls of water. Cut two thick slices of lemon, halve them and stick a few cloves into the flesh of each half slice. Put two fingers of port and a lemon slice into each mug and top up to halfway with hot water. People with a sweet tooth may want to add a little sugar, but it's usually delicious without.

For a whisky toddy, make as for port – but most people will want to add a little sugar.

A perfect night cap… for the grownups anyway. This one uses port, but you can use whisky instead.

Mulled Wine

Serves as many (or as few!) as you like. These quantities represent about 10 units of alcohol

Pans: 1 – large

Stoves: 1

Campfire: yes

Other equipment: sharp knife, spoon

Prep time: 10 minutes

Pack weight: about 1kg per brew, assuming you decant the wine from the heavy glass bottle to a lightweight plastic one

Fuel efficiency: good

- *1 bottle cheap red wine (use a plastic bottle for carrying)*
- *¼ mug (100ml) cheap brandy (other spirits will do)* • *½ mug (200ml) orange juice* • *1 mug (400ml) water* • *½ spoonful mixed ground spice* • *4 spoonfuls sugar* • *1 orange* • *optional: whole cloves and cinnamon sticks are really nice if you want to make a proper festive brew!*

Chop up the orange, and put everything in a pan together. Heat to a simmer (but don't allow to boil), stirring occasionally, and serve.

Normally associated with Christmas, mulled wine makes a nice treat year round in camp, warming your cockles and adding to a convivial atmosphere…

Real Hot Choc

Serves as many as you like

Pans: 1

Stoves: 1

Campfire: yes

Other equipment: sharp knife, spoon

Prep time: 10 minutes

Pack weight: about 50g per person, using powdered milk

Fuel efficiency: good

Per person: • about 30g dark chocolate • ¾ mugful (300ml) milk or 3 spoons milk powder and ¾ mugful water • 1 spoonful sugar • optional: dash of brandy or whisky, thick cream, chopped marshmallows

If using powdered milk, make it up with water. Heat gently in a large pan (don't boil). Shave or finely chop the chocolate. Add the chocolate flakes to the hot milk and stir until it melts. Add sugar to taste and serve.

Lightweight Hot Choc

Per person: • 1 or 2 spoonfuls cocoa powder • 2 spoonfuls (20g) milk powder • 1 or 2 spoonfuls sugar • 3/4 mugful water

Heat the water. Put the cocoa and milk powder in a mug and just add a dribble of water first. Mix to a smooth consistency, making sure you get rid of any lumps, then add the rest of the water and stir well. Add sugar to taste.

Hot Fruit Punch (non-alcoholic)

Serves 4

Pans: 1

Stoves: 1

Campfire: yes

Other equipment: sharp knife

Prep time: 5–10 minutes

Pack weight: about 250g per person

Fuel efficiency: good

- 4 individual-sized (200–300ml) cartons mixed fruit juice (2 orange, 1 apple and 1 cranberry is a good mix) • 1 lemon • about 6 cloves • 2.5cm piece fresh ginger • 2 mugs water • sugar or honey to taste

Tip all the juice and the water into a large pan and heat gently. Slice the lemon and the ginger finely, and add them to the pan with about six cloves. Heat until the drink is steaming and the spices have infused. Sweeten to taste.

Alternatives
If you want to travel light, you can make a nice hot punch with powdered fruit drinks. There's usually no need to sweeten these.

If you like the sound of this, but fancy a more grown-up version, you can always add a slug or two of vodka or brandy. (We won't tell.)

Fruit Tea Refresher

Fills two 500ml drink bottles

Pans: 1 large

Stoves: yes

Prep time: 10 minutes plus cooling time

Pack weight: negligible (500g per person when made up)

Fuel efficiency: good

- 3 fruit teabags • sugar or honey • 1 litre water

Boil the water. Take off the heat, add the teabags and the sweetener and allow to brew for five minutes. Remove the teabags and cool the tea before transferring to your drink bottle.

Fruit teas are always easy in camp because they don't need milk. But slightly sweetened and allowed to cool they also make a very refreshing change from water and can be drunk from a bottle during the day.

Hydration Drinks

Fills two 500ml drinks bottles

Pans: 1 large

Prep time: 2 minutes

Pack weight: 500g per person

- 1 500ml bottle fruit juice • 500ml water • 1 heaped spoonful sugar • pinch of salt

Blend all the ingredients in the bottles.

This is the perfect drink for someone suffering the effects of heat or a stomach bug – it's also an excellent budget alternative to proprietary energy drinks while you're on the move.

FURTHER INFORMATION

BOOKS
Campcraft
Drake, PG (2006) *Campcraft and Wilderness Skills*, Southwater

Hostetter, K (2003) *Don't Forget the Duct Tape: Tips and Tricks for Repairing Outdoor Gear*, The Mountaineers Books

Mears, R (2002) *Bushcraft: An Inspirational Guide to Surviving the Wilderness*, Hodder & Stoughton

Townsend, C (1997) *The Backpacker's Handbook*, Ragged Mountain Press

Cooking and Recipes
Coustick, D (1996) *The Backpacker's Cookbook, A Practical Guide to Dining Out*, Neil Wilson

Kesselheim, AS (2002) *Camp Cook's Companion: A Pocket Guide*, Ragged Mountain Press

Miller, DS (1998) *Backcountry Cooking: From Pack to Plate in 10 Minutes*, The Mountaineers Books

Pearson, C (1997) *NOLS Cookery*, Stackpole Books

Philpott, D and Philpott P (2005) *The Campfire Cookbook: A Handbook for Hungry Campers and Hikers*, Collins & Brown

Pilkington, M (1997) *The New Zealand Outdoor Cookbook: The Tramper's Guide to Appetizing Lightweight Food*, The Printing Press

Saint, D (ed) *Recipes and Planning for Camp Cooking*, Printforce Books

First Aid
Duff, J and Gormly, P (2007) *Pocket First Aid and Wilderness Medicine*, Cicerone

General Interest
Winser, S (ed) (2004) *Royal Geographic Society Expedition Handbook*, Profile Books

Nutrition, Physiology and Performance
Heaton, K (1999) *Understanding Your Bowels*, Family Doctor Publications

Clark, N (1997) *Sports Nutrition Guidebook*, Human Kinetics

Stroud, M (1999) *Survival of the Fittest: Understanding Health and Peak Physical Performance*, Vintage

McLatchie, G (2000) *Understanding Sports and Exercise Medicine*, Family Doctor Publications

Wilson-Howarth, J (1999) *Bugs, Bites and Bowels*, Cadogan Guides

Rowell, S (2002) *Off-road Running*, Crowood Press

Wild Foods
Culpeper, N (1826; 1981) *Culpeper's Complete Herbal and English Physician*, Harvey Sales

Pringle, L (1978) *Wild Foods: A Beginner's Guide to Identifying, Harvesting and Cooking Safe and Tasty Plants from the Outdoors*, Four Winds Press

USEFUL WEBSITES
Kit Manufacturers and Suppliers
Backpacker's Pantry (suppliers of outback ovens) www.backpackerspantry.com

Basecamp (suppliers of Optimus camp oven) www.base-camp.co.uk

Camelbak www.camelbak.com

Expedition Foods www.expeditionfoods.com

Filtastraw www.filtastraw.org.uk

Jetboil www.jetboil.com

Light My Fire www.lightmyfire.com

Lyon Outdoor (UK suppliers of Ortlieb and Jetboil) www.lyon.co.uk

Miox Corporation www.miox.com

MSR www.msrgear.com

Platypus www.platypushydration.com

Primus www.primus.se (click 'choose English')

Rosker (UK suppliers of Primus, Steripen and Travellunch) www.rosker.co.uk

Steripen www.steripen.com

Trangia www.trangia.se/english/

Other Useful Organisations
Adventure First Aid www.adventurefirstaid.co.uk

Calorielab calorie calculator www.calorielab.com

Duke of Edinburgh's Award Scheme www.theaward.com

Fell Runners Association www.fellrunner.org.uk

Marine Stewardship Council www.fishonline.org

Open Adventure (UK adventure race organisers) www.openadventure.com

Original Mountain Marathon www.theomm.com

St John's Ambulance www.sja.org.uk

Sleepmonsters Adventure Racing www.sleepmonsters.com

The Countryside Code www.countrysideaccess.gov.uk

INDEX

If you're looking for a particular recipe by name, or a recipe to meet particular requirements, check the Index of Recipes *on pages 184–5.*

LISTING OF CICERONE GUIDES

For full and up-to-date information on
our ever-expanding list of guides,
please check our website:
www.cicerone.co.uk.

Cicerone's mission is to inform and inspire by providing the best guides to exploring the world

Since its foundation over 30 years ago, Cicerone has specialised in publishing guidebooks and has built a reputation for quality and reliability. It now publishes nearly 300 guides to the major destinations for outdoor enthusiasts, including Europe, UK and the rest of the world.

Written by leading and committed specialists, Cicerone guides are recognised as the most authoritative. They are full of information, maps and illustrations so that the user can plan and complete a successful and safe trip or expedition – be it a long face climb, a walk over Lakeland fells, an alpine traverse, a Himalayan trek or a ramble in the countryside.

With a thorough introduction to assist planning, clear diagrams, maps and colour photographs to illustrate the terrain and route, and accurate and detailed text, Cicerone guides are designed for ease of use and access to the information.

If the facts on the ground change, or there is any aspect of a guide that you think we can improve, we are always delighted to hear from you.

Cicerone Press
2 Police Square Milnthorpe Cumbria LA7 7PY
Tel: 01539 562 069 Fax: 01539 563 417
info@cicerone.co.uk www.cicerone.co.uk